CHURCHILL AND APPEASEMENT

Also by R. A. C. Parker

A Short History of the Second World War

Chamberlain and Appeasement:
British Policy and the Coming of the Second World War

R. A. C. Parker

CHURCHILL AND
APPEASEMENT

MACMILLAN

First published 2000 by Macmillan
an imprint of Macmillan Publishers Ltd
25 Eccleston Place, London SW1W 9NF
Basingstoke and Oxford
Associated companies throughout the world
www.macmillan.co.uk

ISBN 0 333 67583 5

Copyright © R. A. C. Parker 2000

1 3 5 7 9 8 6 4 2

A CIP catalogue record for this book is available from
the British Library.

Typeset by SetSystems Ltd, Saffron Walden, Essex
Printed and bound in Great Britain by
Mackays of Chatham plc, Chatham, Kent

Contents

Acknowledgements

IN THIS BOOK I have tried to form my own views from the evidence. There are several printed collections of evidence: easily the most important are the books of Sir Martin Gilbert. For the 1930s the Companion Volumes 2 and 3 to the Volume 5 of his life provides over 3,000 pages bound, not surprisingly in volumes which are not suitable for train or aeroplane journeys, let alone bed-time reading. The larger volume weighs in at over 2 kg/ 6 lbs. Volume 5 of his *Life* presents much evidence. Gilbert's work inspires respectful awe. Editing is superb; the amount of information provided is incredible. Anyone who wants to know Winston Churchill has to consult Martin Gilbert.

Then there is the compilation of Churchill's complete speeches gathered, in the interests of scholarship, by Sir Robert Rhodes James. He has not survived to receive my grateful thanks. He assembled 8 volumes containing about 600 pages on the 1930s.

Lady Soames, DBE, as Sir Winston's daughter, obviously possesses special personal knowledge. Mary Soames inherited her father's talent as a historian, demonstrated in the biography of her mother, Clementine. More recently, she presented *Speaking for Themselves*, a collection of letters between her father and mother, superbly edited. Together with David Coombs, she has illuminated Churchill's painting.

The *Official Report*, Fifth Series, on Parliamentary Debates in the House of Commons is very important. Parliament was far more effectively reported in the press in the 1930s than at the end of the century. Churchill made dramatic speeches, carefully worked out in advance, and obviously intended to give his thought-out views on topics as they arose. They are generally highly readable, though sometimes portentous.

Since I have tried to rely on sources I have not appended a bibliography of the numerous books on Churchill. There is an admirable and up-to-date one in Graham Stewart, *Burying Caesar, Churchill, Chamberlain, and the Battle for the Tory Party* (London 1999). My book is on the whole sympathetic to Churchill. For a different view, excellently presented, John Charmley's books *Chamberlain and the Lost Peace* and *Churchill the End of Glory* may be read.

I am grateful to Birmingham University Library for access to the Chamberlain papers and the Cambridge University Library, especially for the Baldwin papers. Churchill College, Cambridge, has the Churchill papers and an agreeable and helpful staff led by Piers Brendon. Another pleasant place for research is the Bodleian Library, Oxford, especially room 132 in the New Bodleian. The Queen's College library with its pleasant and patient staff has been invaluable. The London Library has proved indispensable.

My thanks are due to Michael Gautrey for information about the RAF, to Nick Owen on the Empire, to Lord Blake, who knew the 'Prof' and told me about him, to Maria Misra, Keble College, on India and to Veronika Vernier, who translated Russian documents. Tanya Stobbs, Georgina Morley and Stefanie Bierwerth, at Macmillan, have been especially kind and helpful. Peter James copy-edited the material with care and made many corrections. Derek Johns, my literary agent from A. P. Watt, gave great encouragement.

Without Janette Swaine, the Fellows' Secretary at Queen's College, this book could not have been written.

Introduction

To BEGIN THIS book, its author will expose his prejudices. He thinks that Churchill could have prevented the Second World War. If Churchill had controlled British foreign policy, he would have made a 'Grand Alliance', to group other European countries round a firm Anglo-French alliance. The Alliance would have pledged defence against any German armed attacks. It might have stopped Hitler, or caused moderate Germans to stop him. Churchill might even have managed to make Britain and France seem to Stalin to be safer collaborators than Nazi Germany. Perhaps he could have contrived, therefore, to win Soviet acceptance of the independence of Rumania, Poland and the Baltic States. We shall never know how far Hitler's conduct might have changed if a Grand Alliance had existed, and, so far, we are denied evidence on Stalin's thoughts. It is, however, hard to imagine that any conceivable alternative chain of events could have been worse than what happened in 1939–45.

The author wrote these sentences before starting to compose this book. Historians, however, must explain what happened and not dream about what might have happened. So this book aims to find out what Churchill tried to do in the 1930s, to work out how it differed from the 'appeasement' policy of British governments, and how and why they rejected Churchill's ideas and kept him out of office. Before settling down to these political problems the first chapter sketches the extent of Churchill's preoccupations outside politics. He was, in the words used by one of his closest associates in the 1930s, supremely egocentric and, it seems, thought he could dominate politics without their taking up too much of his time.

Naturally, Churchill would be out of office during the purely Labour government of Ramsay MacDonald. Two events in those years, in retrospect, determined Churchill's future in the 1930s. One was his adoption of right-wing attitudes on foreign affairs and, at home, 'anti-socialist' principles, though he never demanded the grinding of the faces of the poor. He objected to 'disarmament'. He wanted British rule in India to be sacrosanct. So Churchill effectively challenged Baldwin's less combative leadership of the Conservative Party, especially when he withdrew from the shadow cabinet. Then there came the 'National' government which Baldwin and his Conservative party dominated, though MacDonald remained the nominal Prime Minister. The government favoured a search for 'disarmament'. Churchill responded to the growth of the Nazis by demands for increases in British armed strength. The arguments he put forward for British military power changed during the 1930s. At first it was to ensure British independence and isolation from Europe whose disputes should be controlled by France, whose power must not be reduced by 'disarmament', following the foolish doctrines of enthusiasts for the League of Nations. Then Britain should support France in Europe. Finally, an Anglo-French alliance should be reinforced by European co-operation to restrain the Nazis. The League could justify this 'Grand Alliance'. Churchill began to praise the League and no longer to sneer contemptuously.

Churchill's support for the League had emphatic limits. He showed indifference to the League cause in the Far East over Manchuria and China. He disliked intervention against Mussolini's conquest of Ethiopia. So he detached himself from League supporters in Britain. In other ways he alienated the sort of people who backed the League. He supported King Edward VIII; he took an unpopular view of the Spanish Civil War. Disquiet at his exclusion from government expressed itself when he was given no cabinet role in defence preparations. But serious anxiety began in 1938 and grew in 1939 corresponding to the advance in German aggressiveness. It followed the German invasion of Austria in March 1938. Then the Munich 'settlement' reinforced it and after the German seizure of Prague in March 1939 it became almost overwhelming. Neville Chamberlain, a skilled politician, knew that he must appear to take up Churchillian policies, while evading them in practice. That complicated Churchill's ambition for office. Should he support the leaders of the Conservative Party or challenge them? Until the India Bill got through parliament in 1935, he chose to challenge. After that, sometimes he gave support, especially because of Chamberlain's evasions.

This book offers an extended examination of these propositions.

CHAPTER ONE

Friendships, Pleasures and Profits

THIS BOOK CONCERNS politics in the years before the Second World War. Yet Churchill, its hero, was as far from a full-time politician as a future Prime Minister could possibly be. The sweep and range of his interests and concerns still astonish. He was writing extensively, both to earn money and for his own pleasure, and those earnings he devoted in great part to maintaining his house and land at Chartwell, agreeably situated in Kent not far from London. Churchill himself worked on the estate, especially building and bricklaying; but his favourite pastime was painting. Long ago, and few people now alive will have read it when it first appeared, he set out his credo in an article in the *Strand Magazine* in 1922, 'Painting as a Pastime'. Today anyone who reads it is likely to feel urgently impelled to spread out some canvas and lunge at it with brushes laden with oilpaints. Their success may not rival Churchill's. He painted pictures of serious quality, as enjoyable to look at as they seem to have been enjoyable to do.

He had, it is true, aid, advice and collaboration from sound, impressive, professional artists. First of all came Sir John and Lady Lavery. Characteristically Churchill proclaimed his new interest in two well-paid articles. Lady Lavery supplied the decisive moment, and Sir John Lavery remarked in his memoirs that Churchill had been called a pupil of his, adding that 'had he chosen painting instead of statesmanship I believe he would have been a great master with the brush'. In 1915, when it all started, Churchill and Lavery made portraits of each other. They painted together. A few years later another friend, Charles Montag, organized an exhibition in a reputable Paris art gallery in which some pictures of Churchill's appeared under a pseudonym; some, it seems, were sold but it is not certain to whom or under what circumstances. Montag remained a friend for life. Several other friendships came with painting, an activity in which, as a post-war director of the Tate, Sir John Rothenstein, once noticed, Churchill combined 'extremes of humbleness and confidence'. Perhaps painters found friendship with Churchill easier than those who had less to offer. The same artist, while noting Churchill's extraordinary and unvarying consideration and courtesy, felt a sense of detached remoteness, and observed of him that 'he seemed at first apathetic and dry' until 'his interest was aroused and he became cheerful and animated'.[1] Churchill seems to have been one of those alarming conversational companions, at first openly bored and unresponsive, and then, if his attention was attracted, sparkling and presenting brilliant, unforgettable, enchanting monologues. Humility was imperative in his conversational partners; with artists less was required.

Three artists ranked as friends in the 1930s. All of them were serious and respected and all are still attractive to collectors: Walter Sickert, William Nicholson and Paul Maze. None was an abstract artist. All believed in representational art. Paul Maze shared Churchill's partiality to colour. Sickert and still more Nicholson were comparatively restrained. All helped and guided Churchill. Indeed, his style often reflected that of his companions of the moment. Churchill's daughter Mary Soames, who inherited her father's talent as a historian, is the best guide to his pictures, helped by and helping his cataloguer, David

Coombs. She distinguishes between the artist friends. Sickert and Nicholson were approved by Churchill's wife, Clementine; Paul Maze, though, she disliked as something of a bounder or buccaneer. So, though Churchill and he associated closely, especially when Churchill wrote an eloquent introduction to Maze's wartime memoirs, his visits to Churchill's home at Chartwell became infrequent. Sickert was modest, but while witty and discursive, radiated common sense and imparted valuable instruction. He encouraged Churchill to use photographs, sometimes projected on to canvas by that now out-of-date piece of technical equipment the 'magic lantern'. Here was valuable support for an artist who had never received formal lessons and whose draughtsmanship could be correspondingly erratic.

In the 1930s, however, Churchill's closest friend among artists, to all of whom he showed flowing gratitude, was Sir William Nicholson. He commended himself to Churchill's family. Clementine clearly approved of his painterly restraint. As a critic who knew him well wrote after his death, he showed 'a sensitivity to the possibilities of pure, pale colour, which could achieve anything except richness or exuberance', and he detested 'Bohemianism'. Neither Churchill nor his family objected to the hint of 1890s dandyism he showed with his 'delicately spotted shirts, canary-yellow waistcoats and pale gloves'. Churchill said that Nicholson 'taught me most about painting'.[2]

Apart from when Montag intervened in Paris, Churchill's pictures appeared in public before the war, it seems, on only one occasion. In 1929 he exhibited a painting anonymously at an amateur art competition; the painting was acclaimed by the eminent judges. His activity as a painter became known just the same. In January 1939 he replied to an American lawyer from Montana who had asked to buy a picture. Painting was for pleasure, not for money-making. The opportunity, however, was

3

not missed. 'I hardly ever sell a picture and have never sold any below the price of £50. I should be glad to sell you one that I like if that is agreeable to you.'[3] That price today would correspond to at least two thousand pounds.

One of Churchill's two closest friends in the 1930s, Sir Edward Marsh, formed a link between Churchill's various lives. As a civil servant until 1939 he probably had more effect on public policy in that decade than the other close friend, Professor Frederick Lindemann, though 'the Prof' was certainly better known in the outside political world. When Churchill became a junior minister in the Liberal government in December 1905, Marsh was appointed his private secretary. Whenever Churchill was in government thereafter, Marsh was with him. From 1929 he worked with Jimmy Thomas in the Labour government and in the MacDonald coalition, and then with Malcolm MacDonald in 1935–7. Yet he remained close to Churchill. Eddie Marsh had met Sickert when Marsh was a Cambridge undergraduate working for his double First in Classics. Soon he became a private collector, and encouraged Mark Gertler, John and Paul Nash and Stanley Spencer. Marsh, though more adventurous in art than Churchill, showed his liking for representational pictures rather than abstracts. Even so, he served for several years on the committee of the Contemporary Art Society and was its chairman for sixteen years. He was also a trustee of the Tate Gallery. At the same time, he helped to publish poetry, especially the so-called 'Georgian' poets, and was a member of the council of the Royal Society of Literature. For his own part in the 1930s he brought out a translation of some of the fables of La Fontaine. According to his biographer 'he was eminently sociable' and 'always anxious to please in social intercourse'. His official connection with Churchill ended in 1929, but their friendship remained.

Another of Churchill's friends of the 1930s, Desmond Morton, later complained that his friendship went only to those who were useful to him. It is fair to reply that Churchill did so much in the 1930s that he could hardly have spared time for those who were not useful. Certainly, he balanced generous hospitality to Eddie Marsh by constantly seeking his help and advice. Thus, not long after inviting him to stay at Chartwell to recover from pneumonia, he asked his help in retelling 'great stories – summarising celebrated literary classics' – and there was a generous fee for each story. When Sotheby's, London, put on an exhibition of Churchill's paintings early in 1998, it was arranged for the sale room mainly by David Coombs, the leading authority. Coombs reprinted two reviews in the *Daily Mail* of Royal Academy Summer Exhibitions in 1932 and 1934 under the title 'Churchill as Art Critic', and seemed surprised to discover that the reviews were for the most part written by Eddie Marsh.[4] It is the main difficulty in assessing Churchill's work in the 1930s that it is uncertain what proportion was actually done by him. He was certainly the head, the managing director and chairman of Churchill Enterprises.

By his own standards his income was exceedingly small, in contrast, say, to those of Neville Chamberlain or Stanley Baldwin, the descendants of successful middle-class entrepreneurs. Churchill lived on a grand scale, hospitably and sociably. After the First World War he acquired Chartwell as his base outside London. Its rebuilding, its parkland, the gardens, the heated swimming pool, its extension, its comfort and its upkeep required money. It had to house adequate servants, chauffeurs, domestics and nannies. There had to be space for children. There had to be comfortable rooms for half a dozen overnight guests and provision for daily callers. There had to be everything that might be expected of a country house; a London flat, also essential, was more easily administered. A country house had to have large ponds or small lakes, to be lived in by glamorous fish and populated by enjoyable waterfowl. Churchill himself administered and supervised these works. Indeed, he joined in. He

5

showed himself to be a skilled bricklayer; constructing brick walls became one of his diversions from gloomier business. It was all part of Winston Churchill's 'Chartwell dream'. It cost a lot and provoked the money troubles 'which were a nagging cause of worry', especially to Clementine.

Churchill's solution was hard work, to make ends meet by intense literary activity. Late in 1931 he sailed to the United States to lecture, a remunerative thing to do. On 13 December he was knocked down by a car in Fifth Avenue, New York City. He behaved with courage – and in January sold a well-paid article 'Run down by a Motor' and restarted his energetic lecture tour. When he came back to London in March 1932 he received a present, a luxurious Daimler car. It was arranged for him largely by two friends, Archibald Sinclair, the Liberal leader and the most loyal and devoted of his political supporters, and Brendan Bracken, who assembled a dazzling collection of sub-scribers. Bracken, a financial journalist, did not win Clementine Churchill's full trust; she thought him an adventurer and was not amused by the silly gossip that he was Winston's illegitimate son. Yet it seems Bracken rescued Chartwell from disaster. In 1937 the Churchills discussed selling it; early in 1938 it was actually offered for sale. Bracken arranged for a rich contact to intervene: Sir Henry Strakosch took over several shaky invest-ments Churchill had made and covered his losses. (In today's terms, something like half a million pounds was involved.)[5] Chartwell gave relaxation and enjoyment, but it mattered in Churchill's public life. Discussions took place there, plans might be made. Visitors brought information. One of the most familiar was Desmond Morton, who lived not far away. He was a favourite at Chartwell, yet he seemed resentful after the war and declared that he had been exploited and that Churchill had been courteous and kind only for his own advantage. Possibly this emotion derived from envy of the importance he gave in his wartime government to the Prof, soon to be Lord Cherwell.

More probably it came from the impossibility for Churchill of maintaining all his social amiabilities through and after the war.

Chartwell sustained Churchill's painting, that most enviable achievement of his relaxation in the 1930s. There were studios and landscapes. But colour and sunshine appealed most. So the South of France drew Churchill for his holidays. Mrs Churchill disliked the vulgar luxury of English visitors there: that worried Churchill not at all. Then on the coast there loomed the alarming attraction of casinos, which would dangerously distract him from his more domestic games of bezique, mah-jong and backgammon. Churchill stayed with Lord Rothermere and Maxine Elliott, among others, and did so, as his daughter puts it, 'on his own terms: he would usually come accompanied by his valet and a secretary'. All depended on the secretary, who would stay up late, very late, to take dictation, check proofs and anything else required to meet the next deadline. Everything hinged on writing. In the 1930s, on average, Churchill's income from writing year by year amounted to what would today be nearly half a million pounds.[6]

His literary output varied between the trivial 'potboilers' at one end and scholarly, portentous contributions to serious history at the other. In January 1939 a reviewer in the *English Historical Review* wrote these words on Winston Churchill's *Life of Marlborough*: 'After nearly ten years' toil Mr Churchill may lay down his pen secure in the knowledge that his history of his mighty ancestor will rank among the greatest biographies in the English tongue.' This came from a respected military scholar, A. H. Burne, published in what remains one of the periodicals which historians still regard as a journal whose approval they relish. (The fact that Burne had come to lunch at Chartwell and had an illustration reprinted in Churchill's book does not perhaps diminish the impact of his praise.) Churchill wrote books even when he was a Cabinet minister in the 1920s, not least his study of the Great War, *The World Crisis*. He abandoned writing for a time in the Second World War. This helps to explain his ready dependence on Eddie Marsh, his private secretary, for all kinds of help and support. It is odd, none the less, that Churchill felt free to complain directly to Marsh about the conduct of his civil service masters.[7]

Some of Churchill's books were recycled newspaper articles or speeches, thus providing double benefit – for example, *Thoughts and Adventures* (1932) and *Great Contemporaries* (1937) or, on foreign policy, *Arms and the Covenant* (1938), a collection of Commons speeches, and *Step by Step* (1939), a reprint of articles written for the press. In 1930 Churchill produced what remains an enjoyable autobiographical essay, *My Early Life*. Before publication the *News Chronicle* serialized it: that newspaper, now defunct, printed several essays over Churchill's signature. The *News of the World* also contributed to Churchill's earnings. Among other productions it gave its readers 'The World's Great Stories Re-told by the Rt Hon Winston S. Churchill'. Eddie Marsh helped, as we have seen, sometimes writing the entire 5,000 words allotted to great stories such as *A Tale of Two Cities* or *The Count of Monte Cristo*. The *News of the World* also printed autobiographical sketches from Churchill's career. Here someone called Marshall Diston, not a close friend like Eddie Marsh, gave decisive help, extracting drafts from books already published by Churchill. Churchill's articles also appeared in the *Daily Mail*, and the *Strand Magazine* printed much from him. However, for foreign policy, as the threat from Hitler grew, the *Evening Standard* and then the *Daily Telegraph* had Churchill's most important journalism. To Churchill's annoyance the *Evening Standard*, owned and controlled by Lord Beaverbrook, stopped publishing his thoughts because his hostility to appeasement diverged from the line taken by the paper. Lord Camrose, the proprietor of the *Daily Telegraph*, however, agreed with Churchill. All these, like most of Churchill's writings, appeared in other parts of the UK and in many foreign papers; the income from them increased after Emery Reeves took over the agency for publication in foreign languages. In the United States *Collier's Magazine* and the *Chicago Tribune* provided means of literary expression.[8]

At the end of the 1930s work began on *A History of the English-Speaking Peoples*. For this Churchill found a first-class assistant – Alan Bullock, later the author of an outstanding study of Hitler and the effective founder of St Catherine's as a fully developed Oxford college. But *Marlborough: His Life and Times* dominates Churchill's writings in the 1930s. When Churchill told his wife in the summer of 1937 that he was 'overwhelmed with work', he added that it was 'always Marlborough'. More than 2,000 pages of text appeared in four volumes (the United States edition has six), published in London in 1933, 1934, 1936 and 1938. The achievement is awesome for a highly active politician, even one out of office. Certainly, all the research and much of the work on early drafts were sub-contracted. Churchill's active supervision, however, is evident above all in the readability of these bulky volumes and the emphasis and force in the interpretations. The most important of the paid subordinates were Maurice Ashley, a respectable historian of the seventeenth century, and William Deakin, a young Oxford academic. Deakin especially became a friend.

Ashley wrote a revealing book on Churchill as a historian. Churchill dictated to a secretary, often late at night. He relied on researches undertaken by his assistants, and did none for himself in unprinted sources, though he might read printed books, assembled for him. A critical part of the process was the repeated amendment of the original texts in typescript and then in an extensive series of proofs. Churchill had, Ashley explains, an 'editorial staff which checked and rechecked his facts and his fancies'. He reports that Churchill treated him 'with the utmost kindness – almost as an equal ... He was the soul of

9

consideration, courtesy and charm.' Ashley writes with retro-spective pleasure of his visits to Chartwell and of the excitement of dining with Churchill before hard work began.

Churchill told his wife early in 1937 after Deakin had been at Chartwell four days, 'he shows more quality and serviceable-ness than any of the others'.[9] There were many 'others'. Martin Gilbert notes that in 1933 alone Churchill received 420 letters and wrote 308. Sixty-two letters came from Maurice Ashley, supported by two distinguished historians, Keith Feiling in Oxford (sixteen letters) and G. M. Trevelyan in Cambridge (fifteen letters). Then on military matters there were in that year thirty letters from Colonel Pakenham-Walsh; and, as Churchill noted in his preface, he was helped on naval matters by Commander J. H. Owen. Deakin became important in the war, especially in encouraging co-operation with Tito rather than Mihailović, and helped in Churchill's writing after the war. He, too, became head of an Oxford college, the cosmopolitan St Antony's. Churchill called in anyone who might help with research into Marlborough. For instance, he wrote to Joachim von Ribbentrop, then German ambassador to Britain, to tell him that Deakin was about to inspect archives in Hanover, and suggesting that Ribbentrop might in some way help him.[10]

The book is beautifully produced, by Harrap's, on good paper, sumptuously bound. It is lavishly illustrated. Volume III, for example, has twenty-one plates reproducing pictures of people involved (though because of their wigs the men are sometimes mutually indistinguishable) and more than sixty maps and plans, which usually, though not always, make it easy to work out battles and campaigns. Churchill's personality is evi-dent; his combativeness and his eloquence make most of this mighty book highly readable. Boredom rarely interrupts, but there are too many contemporary letters to struggle through – some, tiresomely, in ye original spelling. His emancipation from academic constraints helps readability, if not reliability. Quotations are carefully footnoted, but there are long passages where no references are supplied, even for controversial assertions. And there are others where we are told what the hero must have been thinking: usually to the credit of his honesty and intelligence. Occasionally there are lapses from literary decorum. One demonstrates Churchill's obstinacy, which according to Ashley sometimes moved him to anger. Volume I, which described Marlborough's career before Queen Anne came to the throne, contains a defence of Churchill's hero, especially against Macaulay. Proofs went to Duff Cooper, one of the most literate politicians of the day, who complained of Churchill's wish that Macaulay should attach 'the label "Liar" to his genteel coat tails': 'you reduce yourself,' Duff Cooper declared, 'to the level of a mischievous schoolboy cocking a snook at the master behind his back'. It went in none the less.[11]

Two reservations about Churchill's interpretations may be offered. The first is that, looked at from more than sixty years later they are old fashioned and out of date. Marlborough founded and assured the greatness of Britain and Empire; in the 1930s Churchill believed it remained. When Anne succeeded to the throne 'the power and the glory of England were soon to rise gleaming among the nations'. The House of Commons in 1707 enables us 'to feel the beating of those resolute English hearts which . . . built up the greatness of our island'. In 1708 'England had now been raised by Marlborough's victories to the summit of the world'. Marlborough was 'the chief architect of Britain's Imperial power'. Social and economic analysis is absent. There is no hint of the critical fact that Parliaments, effectively representing the tax-paying classes, had met every year since 1689 and guaranteed national borrowings so that British interest rates were kept low and investment stimulated, and the first industrial revolution made more likely.[12] Secondly, one may take issue with Churchill's belief that the 'party system' from then on controlled British politics. 'Henceforward the party cleavage and party system became rigid, formal, and – down to our own days – permanent'; the 'party system was entering into its long supremacy'. This will not do. Party divisions certainly were clearer under William III and Anne than they subsequently became. But, as Churchill's own volumes show, royal favour counted immensely. Then, though more so later in the eighteenth century, those ambitious for power or profit attended Parliament more regularly than the country gentlemen, who disliked London and found it expensive. Certainly, those country MPs were more likely to be there when politics were fraught and serious, as they were under William and Anne. Marlborough himself showed more perceptiveness of this when he attributed opposition to the war he was fighting to 'country gentlemen' aiming 'at living like their ancestors when England took no part in external affairs . . . they are weary of the taxes'. On some landowners, indeed, direct taxation in Marlborough's time was at its highest until the twentieth century.[13]

Understandably, scholarly reviewers took Churchill's book seriously. Sir Richard Lodge, on the first volume, commented that Churchill's 'incessant denunciations of Macaulay may have gratified himself, but they are apt to become rather irritating to his readers'. Still, that 'experienced reviewer may state with confidence that few academic historians, dealing with a period of fifty years, have made so few blunders in matters of fact, though many readers may differ from him in matters of opinion'. On the next volume, that reviewer gave qualified praise. He explained that 'It is excellent in its estimate of Marlborough's personal character and conduct in those years' (1701–5) and 'equally excellent in its narrative of military movements'. Moreover 'it is good in its account of domestic politics', but then 'only moderately good in its sketch of contemporary events in Europe. But it is all eminently readable.' For a sample of readability, the chapters on Ramillies, the clearest victory, may be recommended – that is, chapters six and seven of Volume III.

The journal *History* included Churchill's book in a survey of recent writings on Anne's reign beside those of established professionals like Trevelyan and G. N. Clark. Again, the reviewer pointed to defects in Churchill's understanding of continental Europe. However, the book gave 'an authoritative account of Marlborough's life and supersedes earlier works, though . . . books of reference should be consulted on points of general history'. The reviewer for the *American Historical Review* noticed one way the book contributed to the growing belief in the 1930s, especially towards the end of that decade, that Churchill should be in the government, to encourage standing up to Hitler. She wrote, 'To the civilian mind an ominous exhilaration over wars flames in Mr Churchill's text,' and, on the final volume of the US edition, 'Mr Churchill constantly prefers the larger, simple conclusions of the battlefield.'[14] Another of the book's influences on Churchill's standing as a politician came from Marlborough's need to organize a coalition of diverse nations in the 'Grand Alliance'. This may have helped Churchill to espouse the League of Nations, which certainly enlarged his political appeal in the late 1930s.

Unlike Neville Chamberlain, Churchill had no serious interest in music, but how rich his life was! Few, if any, serious politicians, and politics mattered most to him, combined such skill in painting and literature. He cared for his family. All this combined with far-ranging sociability and, on innumerable occasions, superb skill as a conversationalist – or, perhaps more accurately, as a talker.

CHAPTER TWO

1931: No Government Place for Churchill

IN 1929 THERE was no great war to prevent. Peace seemed assured. Churchill, on a visit to Canada, told an audience in Montreal that 'the outlook for peace has never beem better for fifty years'.[1] Looking back, however, 1929 counted. It was the year when Churchill lost Cabinet office, to return only after the Second World War had begun. In 1929, when the Conservatives narrowly lost the general election, his eventual return to office seemed certain. Two years later that changed and, when hopes for peace dimmed in the 1930s, Churchill remained out of office. Why?

Before the 1929 election, Churchill, as Chancellor of the Exchequer, held high station and seemed politically strong. He fought the election with his usual spirit. His campaign was violently, virulently 'anti-Socialist', denouncing fears and perils heightened by his imaginative rhetoric. As usual, he spoke with a verbal hostility which fitted his belief that vigorous denunciation of individuals did not imply personal enmity towards his opponents: this opinion was not always shared by victims of his rhetoric.

The 1929 election made British politics unstable. No party had a majority. Labour had the most seats in the Commons, but the defeated Conservatives were not far behind. The Liberals, a quarrelsome, disparate group, who for the moment accepted the leadership of Lloyd George, held the balance: they decided who governed, and put Labour in. The Liberals had fought the election on a programme of cutting unemployment, calling for government spending on public works. The spending of those given work would bring still more jobs, because yet more demand would follow their spending and so on. Conservatives denounced it as an extravagant, wasteful sham. Reducing unemployment, of course, was Labour policy too. Unemployment grew worse, not better, after Ramsay MacDonald formed the Labour government. The Treasury and the Labour Chancellor, Philip Snowden, favoured reduction of government spending and keeping taxation down. Maintaining the value of the pound sterling, set at a high level when Churchill was Chancellor of the Exchequer, became a mounting embarrassment. 'Confidence' in sterling required, nearly everyone agreed, balanced budgets and prudent economy. As the Great Depression deepened after 1929, Labour grew more divided and restless. The Liberals, of course, had to back one side or the other to gain influence, to win 'electoral reform' that might give them the chance of office. But it was hard to force a government to legislate to make elections more rewarding to Liberals, without seeming to put party before country too blatantly to make any electoral success possible. For Conservatives another election had to be secured as soon as possible to restore them to power.

Who would lead the party to renewed victory? As usual, an electoral defeat weakened the prestige of the existing Conservative leader, Stanley Baldwin. Where did Churchill stand? In the last months of Baldwin's Conservative government, Churchill's prestige in the Cabinet declined. His great 'achievement' as Chancellor, the restoration of sterling's interchangeability with gold at a fixed price, fixed at a high level, though it meant rising standards for those in work, weakened exports and did not encourage employment, investment or industrial innovation.

Moreover, Churchill had failed to follow the fashion for disarmament. Instead of thinking of disarmament negotiations as the great climax in the search for peace, he thought them a cause of quarrelsome nationalistic self-assertion. In the closing months of Baldwin's government he proved his own argument by his insistence that any naval negotiations should embody what he thought the essence of British naval ascendancy – more cruisers for the Royal Navy than for any other, including the United States Navy.

In 1927 the US President had invited Britain and Japan to a conference to discuss limitation of naval armaments. Calvin Coolidge wanted two things: to limit spending on cruisers and smaller warships while avoiding open American acceptance of British naval supremacy. Churchill believed that the Royal Navy should have more cruisers than any other to enable it to defend British merchant ships in every part of the world. He favoured no conference and no discussion; that way, quarrels with the Americans which might encourage American shipbuilding could be avoided. Baldwin felt that successful disarmament conferences won votes and that quarrels with the USA would not follow; his speciality was conciliation not conflict. Churchill's combativeness already seems, before the end of the Conservative government in 1929, to have made Baldwin feel that Churchill should somehow be given a less important office than that of Chancellor of the Exchequer if he formed another government. Ramsay MacDonald, once he formed his second Labour government in 1929, conciliated American admirals and the new President, Herbert Hoover, more successfully and smoothly than the Baldwin government had done, and in 1930 a conference assembled in London.[2]

In February 1930, Churchill addressed the Navy League, supporters of a strong Royal Navy, in London. 'We all wish the Conference to reach an agreement,' he declared, but added, 'British naval requirements ought to be fixed by ourselves alone, because our life depends on the sea.' So agreement should mean only that the naval powers should announce their intended scale of warship building. But 'we seem to be the only great nation which does not speak up for itself ... There is a feeling that England under the Socialists is down and out.' Still, 'our hope is that ... the British nation will still have the sanity and resolution to sustain that ancient naval power which across four centuries has so often defended good causes and has never defended good causes in vain'.[3] By this time, with Ramsay MacDonald as Prime Minister, kept in by Liberal votes, and Stanley Baldwin continuing in his sometimes precariously held position as leader of the Conservative Opposition, Churchill was opposing both of them. Stanley Baldwin was the model of a 'one nation' Conservative. Treat the Labour government sympathetically and tolerantly: Liberal and even Labour votes might then be won over to the Tories. Churchill's line was totally different: denounce socialism as an un-British set of alien doctrines, and Ramsay MacDonald as a weak-kneed betrayer of the national interests.

Then there was Egypt. The British proconsul, the High Commissioner Lord Lloyd, had begun to cause alarm to many in the Foreign Office and to the Conservative Foreign Secretary, Austen Chamberlain, by his hesitation over allowing Egyptian independence any more reality by limiting British interference. The new Labour Foreign Secretary turned him out. His enforced resignation came up in Parliament in July 1929. Churchill intervened energetically after Baldwin had spoken as leader of the Conservative Opposition. Neville Chamberlain thought he was trying to take the lead away from Baldwin. More likely, Churchill could not fail to give that impression because his speeches were energetic and emphatic in contrast to Baldwin's mild and conciliatory manner. Ramsay MacDonald considered that 'no possible exception could be taken' to Baldwin's speech, but he attacked Churchill's, 'the mischievous character of which it is impossible to exaggerate'. Churchill claimed that

Lloyd's enforced resignation would 'cause difficulties all over the British Empire'. For it was an example 'of the fate which overtakes, under the present Government, public officials and public servants if they stand up with some firmness and stiffness for British rights and interests, and refuse to lend themselves to sloppy surrender and retreat'.[4]

Behind everything loomed the future of India. Should the British Raj bring more non-British into government? Would this weaken or strengthen British control of defence and foreign policy? Would further 'Indianization', which from the beginning had been characteristic of the Raj, make it easier or harder to keep order without more British men and money? Order made it possible to collect taxes to finance the Indian army, which multiplied British regular battalions into a substantial force of infantry, valuable especially for the defence of imperial interests in Asia.

In January 1931 Churchill finally declared himself a political force separate from the associates and collaborators of Stanley Baldwin. He withdrew from the Conservative Parliamentary 'business committee' – the shadow Cabinet – and gave up his place on the Opposition front bench. To make a mark as a back-bencher an MP must either be assiduously sociable and persisently present in the House, or create sensations. As a part-time politician, Churchill could not be a conscientious back-bencher; but creating a sensation suited him admirably. The position he had adopted was that of the great defender and preserver of the British Empire against self-interested sedition and weak-kneed conciliators. This had its advantages. He believed in it; Churchill was not like subtle politicians, skilled at hypocrisy and humbug. Concern for the Empire appealed to Conservatives, especially the right of the party. Churchill naturally became the most articulate by far in expressing the views of these 'diehards'. As always, emphasis, not academic argument, characterized his utterances.

The Commons debate on 26 January 1931 marked the break – the next day Churchill abandoned the Conservative shadow Cabinet. He objected to attempts to reach understanding with those who demanded independence for India: 'the Indian Congress and other extremists'. British control of India had been weakened, he claimed, by the Viceroy's declaration that India could look forward eventually to being a self-governing Dominion like Australia or New Zealand. The round-table conference of Indians in London was discussing 'a federal constitution for all India, embodying the principle of a responsible Indian Ministry at the summit and centre of Indian affairs'. Indians would think Britain was preparing to depart; they would look to the unhealthy self-seeking nationalist agitators as their future rulers. In the end, the British people, when they realized what was happening, would not 'consent to be edged, pushed, talked and cozened out of India'. Baldwin, as Conservative leader, intervened in the debate, though 'I never like disagreeing with a colleague.' He did not believe 'that you are going to get any permanent solution of the question of Indian government until you get a complete co-operation and understanding and goodwill between Indians and ourselves'. And that needed 'unanimity among the political parties' in Britain. As so often, Baldwin did not wish the Opposition he led to oppose; Churchill did. A few weeks later Churchill spoke up in his Essex constituency:

> We ought to dissociate ourselves in the most public and formal manner from any complicity in the weak, wrong-headed and most unfortunate administration of India by the Socialists . . . It is alarming and also nauseating to see Mr Gandhi, a seditious Middle Temple lawyer, now posing as a fakir of a type well known in the East, striding half-naked up the steps of the Vice-Regal palace . . . to parley on equal terms with the representative of the King–Emperor.[5]

Appealing to the right wing of the Conservative Party meant appealing to the most active constituency workers, especially in those seats which returned Conservative MPs even when the party nationally was defeated. In those days, these constituency parties contained a substantial number of retired army officers and colonial and Indian civil servants. Appealing to the right is a good way of winning support in the Conservative Party, especially when the party is out of power. Still, Churchill had his deficiencies as a possible Conservative leader. He had quite recently been an active Liberal social reformer, he remained attached to free trade when Conservatives were increasingly persuaded of the need for protection, including 'food taxes'. Moreover, he had been a Cabinet member when the government put through the last set of Indian reforms. Worse still, for diehards, he had been closely involved in the treaty which set up the Irish Free State, and had shaken hands with an IRA terrorist, Michael Collins, soon to be murdered in his turn. To all this had to be added his limited tolerance of bores. There were some moments in 1929–31 when Baldwin's continued leadership was uncertain. Whoever might succeed (and, especially after Churchill's withdrawal from the front bench, Neville Chamberlain seemed most likely), it would have been difficult and dangerous to keep Churchill out of a Conservative Cabinet after new elections.

Baldwin stuck to his conciliatory policy towards the Labour government's attempts to increase support among Indians for British government in India. Moderate nationalists there would be encouraged by offers of constitutional progress, with more pledged to come after an uncertain number of years. It was not a question, as Churchill suggested, of arranging that Britain should give up control of India. Baldwin proposed subtler means of perpetuating that control. He justified his leadership in these months by standing up to the newspaper magnates, Rothermere and Beaverbrook, who agreed with Churchill over India but not over tariffs, and by standing up to Churchill himself. No two politicians could be more unlike than Baldwin and Churchill.

Baldwin pretended to be stupid and simple-minded, so claiming to be an ordinary but especially trustworthy expression of that English rusticity which so appealed to suburban populations. Churchill advertised rather than disguised his intellectual and oratorical talents. He proclaimed his greatness and gloried in it.

On Thursday 12 March 1931 Baldwin showed his skill when the Commons debated policy towards India. He presented his usual tribute to the Viceroy, Edward Irwin (now better known as Lord Halifax). He had 'enlarged the area of goodwill and co-operation . . . I would quote a few words on that subject, written with more lucidity of thought and felicity of style than I could ever hope to attain, being a man of plain speech.' Baldwin then quoted large parts of Churchill's speech in July 1920, when the Amritsar massacre was debated at Westminster. He claimed to be generous in quoting them, 'because they will make the rest of my speech sound like a Sunday school textbook'. In 1920 Churchill had insisted that:

> our reign in India or anywhere else has never stood on the basis of physical force alone, and it would be fatal to the British Empire if we were to try to base ourselves only upon it. The British way of doing things . . . has always meant and implied close and effective co-operation with people of the country . . . in no part have we arrived at such success as in India, whose princes spent their treasure in our cause, whose brave soldiers fought side by side with our own men, whose intelligent and gifted people are co-operating at the present moment with us in every sphere of government and of industry.

Baldwin said he had agreed 'with every word of that when it was spoken in 1920, and I agree with every word of it today'. He defied his rivals for the Conservative leadership over India. 'If there are those in our party who approach the subject in a niggling, grudging spirit, who would have to have forced out of their reluctant hands one concession after another, if they be a majority, in God's name let them choose a man to lead them.' He had just demonstrated that Churchill's past opinions made him a recent convert to diehard views on India. Churchill, though as ambitious for power as any politician, never calculated. He said what he thought with grandiose rhetorical emphasis and assumed that he would be able to convince. When many people shared his views, his influence was unsurpassable: often most people did not. If what he thought diverged from the conclusions that Baldwin's subtler perceptions detected among potential supporters, he believed it was others who were wrong. Baldwin's speech weakened Churchill's contribution when he spoke a little later that afternoon. His attacks on Gandhi, who 'has become the symbol and the almost god-like champion of all those forces which are now working for our exclusion from India', fell flat. The next speaker, Colonel Wedgwood, observed that 'the House was against him when he started, and has remained against him to the close of his speech. Never before has a Rt Hon Gentleman spoken to a House so hostile.'[6]

In the middle of March 1931 more immediate, more domestic, problems had descended on Britain. Demand for British exports was falling, more and more people were out of work. The gold exchange parity of the pound sterling could be defended only by loss of gold reserves and foreign currency. During most of the twentieth century skilled observers, led by the Treasury, imagined that they knew the solution: curtail government spending, balance the budget, reduce spending on social welfare, push down wages and so restore 'confidence'. In February the Labour government, with the agreement of the Conservatives and the Liberals, had set up a committee under Sir George May to examine those remedies. At the end of July the May Committee recommended elimination of the budget deficit. Its majority thought taxes already hit producers too hard. Government spending should be cut, with the largest saving coming from a reduction in unemployment benefit. Snowden, the Labour Chancellor of the Exchequer, promised action; Liberals and Conservatives would be consulted. Together with short-term credits from Paris and New York to curb speculation against the pound, all seemed arranged and everyone went off for their holidays; Churchill to Biarritz, Baldwin, as usual, to Aix-les-Bains, Ramsay MacDonald home to Lossiemouth, Neville Chamberlain also to Scotland, to the Highlands near Loch Tummel. Soon they all came back. The promise of stern economies to come in the autumn did not restore 'confidence' in the foreign exchange markets. Sterling needed more and more support for its parity, by way of Bank of England purchases of sterling paid for by British reserves of gold and foreign currency.[7]

Ramsay MacDonald and Philip Snowden, the Chancellor of the Exchequer, knew that a purely Labour government itself aroused the suspicion of financiers. Moreover some Labour MPs and Cabinet ministers would reject the economies sought by the May Committee majority report. If Labour ministers were to carry them through they would need Conservative and Liberal support. This would show that Labour could meet a financial crisis. Alternatively, they could give way to a Conservative government backed, for this purpose, by the Liberals. Another solution was an all-party 'national' government to surmount the crisis. King George V favoured this, Ramsay MacDonald had already thought of it. Baldwin preferred to leave the Labour government responsible for economic severities. That would help the Conservatives to win the election, which could not long be delayed. On the other hand, he showed sympathy towards Labour.

In the end, what explained the failure of the Labour government to survive was the refusal of many Cabinet ministers to accept the cuts in unemployment benefit put before them on 23 August 1931. The Labour Prime Minister, Ramsay MacDonald, and the Chancellor of the Exchequer, Snowden, thought greater cuts in unemployment benefit were needed to satisfy the markets than the Cabinet would tolerate. At this stage, Baldwin and the Liberals agreed to a national government. It was a less portentous decision than it seemed later; everyone thought of it as a temporary, provisional expedient, above all to secure some Labour acceptance of 'equality of sacrifice', a euphemism for disproportionate losses inflicted on the poorer sections of society.

Churchill, in his brief return to London, explained, as usual, that he opposed any contact with the Labour Party or any help for it; Conservatives should expose 'socialists'. Co-operation of some kind with Lloyd George he always welcomed: something utterly distasteful to Baldwin and to that rising Conservative star Neville Chamberlain. Ramsay MacDonald had faced relentless hostility from Churchill and, as 'the boneless wonder', had been the victim of his oratory. By the time Churchill returned from the South of France he had been left out of the new national government. Baldwin allowed MacDonald to remain Prime Minister and was joined by only three Conservatives in the new Cabinet. Churchill's omission is no surprise. At that moment, however, it seemed temporary: the national government would get through the financial reforms and then the parties could separately fight an election. No one imagined that the national government would last until the war. Churchill, it seems, assumed he might be called to office in a future Conservative government.

Churchill spoke – as a back-bencher – soon after his return from France on 8 September. The next speaker was Jimmy Maxton, the amusing and popular Independent Labour Party Clydesider. Having recognized that 'the House is always willing to listen' to Churchill 'whenever he has a contribution to make to our debates', he remarked that his speech showed 'that he is not throwing himself whole-heartedly behind the new national government'. Churchill had contributed a growl about India: 'This government ... is not in a position to make any large departure in Indian policy.'[8] Two weeks later, the attempt to maintain the gold standard at the fixed parity of sterling ceased. The Bank of England and the new national government concurred. Loss of gold and foreign currency had continued – 'confidence' had not been restored. Politicians disputed whether or not a general election should come at once. The Bank and the City advised a rapid end to uncertainty. Early in October the Conservatives agreed that the national government should fight the election rather than the individual parties comprising it. Ramsay MacDonald should continue to be Prime Minister. For Baldwin and the Conservatives 'patriotism' combined with the search for party advantage. A national government seemed more likely than party conflict to restore the confidence of the markets, while it enabled the Conservative Party, as Baldwin always wished, to appeal to moderates, to what later in the twentieth century came to be called 'Middle England', to the spirit of compromise and fair play rather than smiting party enemies hip and thigh. Churchill, who had taken up a position on the right of the party, did not fit. Here was a political conjuncture which no one could have predicted a few months before when he had renounced the Conservative front bench.

The election was quickly over – voting for or against the 'doctor's mandate' sought by the healing national government took place on 27 October. Even during the election campaign Churchill attacked 'the doubting incoherent policy of the socialists in India', which 'has not only brought discord and suffering upon that large proportion of the human race who dwell in India, but has impaired our own position in the eyes of the world'.[9] In the event, the national government had continued that 'incoherent policy of the socialists'. October 1931 transformed British politics. The emergency expedient of a national government was perpetuated. For working with Ramsay MacDonald, for winning over Liberal MPs and Liberal voters, Baldwin made far more sense than Churchill. Churchill couldn't very well abruptly mutate his views on India into Baldwin's and so give up his challenge to his party leader. In any case, though Churchill certainly took it for granted that he ought to hold office, he may not have been unconditionally eager for it. Office would mean a fall in income. He had already held every important office except those of Foreign Secretary and Prime Minister. The Baldwin–MacDonald partnership could certainly not tolerate a manager of foreign policy with Churchill's belief in the folly of discussions about disarmament. (How the 1930s would have changed if Churchill had been there instead of Simon, Hoare, Eden and Halifax!) As for the Prime Minister's post, MacDonald and Baldwin blocked any chances, perhaps small in any case in the early 1930s.

The election surprised the prophets. The national government won most votes, with the Conservatives dominant. Five hundred and fifty-four MPs were returned to support the government, of whom 470 were Conservatives.[10] This reduced the proportion of Conservatives from safe seats, who were able to be more independent and were often more to the right of the party than those from more marginal seats. Baldwin offered calm and caution; to such a leader Churchill's presence in government would be an inconvenient anomaly.

CHAPTER THREE

The Rise of Hitler

AFTER THE 1931 election, Churchill explained what he thought the national government should do. It should 'pronounce without hesitation upon the fiscal problem, the currency problem, the Indian problem and the Imperial problem'. For the economy he now advocated tariffs and, sensibly enough, an increase in spending based on increased credit. India, of course, required a strengthened Raj and, with respect to the Empire, Churchill was uneasy about the definition of Dominion status in the Statute of Westminster, enacted that year, especially in its possible effects on the treaty of 1922 which had set up the Irish Free State. Churchill did not mention the European problem, or the German problem. Yet Hitler and the Nazis were now to be taken seriously. In the German election of 1930 the Nazis had won six million votes and become the second largest party in the Reichstag. President Hindenburg and the Chancellor, Heinrich Brüning, had to rely on Social Democratic 'toleration' of their conservative government. In 1932 enlarged voting strength for the Nazis further weakened Brüning's hold on power. In March eleven million voted for Hitler as a candidate for the German presidency; in April he won more than thirteen million votes. In the Far East, Japan unleashed aggression in Manchuria. Supporters of the League of Nations worried, at this time, more about Japan and China than about Hitler; Churchill did not worry about Japan and began to register alarm about Hitler and the Nazis. On 13 May 1932 he expounded yet again his theme that disarmament conferences brought about increases in armaments rather than reductions and caused trouble and dissension rather than tranquillity. They concentrated attention on armed strength and on hypothetical wars 'which certainly will never take place'. They had unduly weakened the Royal Navy.[1]

Now Churchill took up the burgeoning problem of German demands. The German government called for 'equality of status' – that is, for the size of the German army to be allowed to become equal to that of the French. Churchill categorically opposed this demand:

> those who speak of that as though it were right or even a mere question of fair dealing, altogether underrate the gravity of the European situation. I would say to those who would like to see Germany and France on equal footing in armaments 'do you wish for war?' For my part, I earnestly hope that no such accommodation will take place during my lifetime or that of my children.

Less ambitiously and more cautiously he wanted to keep the present foundation of European peace – French strength – until some other foundation of peace had been set up 'through the patient and skilful removal of the political causes of antagonism which a wise foreign policy should eventually achieve'.[2] Appeasement as a prelude to disarmament: Chamberlain sought the same in 1938 in Munich. Meanwhile, to Churchill, French power would preserve peace. There he critically differed from other appeasers and from Chamberlain later on at Munich. For the latter, France and French strength stood out as the obstacle to appeasement. In the early 1930s German demands for equality with France in military strength appeared as the most immediate German grievance. Moreover, supporters of the League of Nations believed a disarmament treaty to be an indispensable condition of a secure peace: they were in Churchill's words 'the poor good people of the League of Nations Union'. When Churchill again set out his thoughts on the decay of German democracy in November 1932, Hitler had refused to support the new Chancellor, Franz von Papen, and Papen's subsequent attempt to run a conservative government against the left without the Nazis had failed; Papen's successor, General von Schleicher, who attempted and failed to split the Nazis, had not yet been chosen. All was ominous confusion. Democracy was departing from Germany.

Churchill again rejected French disarmament and German rearmament to bring about equality of status. 'All those bands of sturdy Teutonic youths, marching through the streets and roads of Germany, with the light of desire in their eyes to suffer for their Fatherland, are not looking for status. They are looking for weapons, and when they have the weapons, believe me they will then ask for the return of lost territories and lost colonies.' What was Britain to do about these alarming young people? The answer, it turned out, was to leave it to the French. French military superiority, which the British should not challenge or oppose, would keep Europe in peace. The British could, and should, keep well clear: 'we ought not to take any further or closer engagements in Europe beyond those which the United States may be found willing to take' – that meant isolation. Britain had to be militarily powerful to make sure of being safe in isolation. Its government should, within 'restricted limits', try to prevent war and make sure that 'if war should break out among other powers, our country and the King's Dominions can be effectively defended', and so preserve 'that strong and unassailable neutrality from which we must never be drawn except by the heart and conscience of the nation'. No one should be pressed to disarm; grievances arising from the post-1918 settlement should first be cured: 'the removal of just

29

disagreed

grievances of the vanquished ought to precede the disarmament of the victors'. To urge appeasement would be safer than demanding disarmament. Pressing for disarmament would mean offering, in return, promises of support and so drag 'us deeper and deeper into the European situation'. Urging redress of grievances, on the other hand, would mean that Britain, if no one heeded, could withdraw 'from our present close entanglement in European affairs' – an obscure remark which must have meant giving up the Locarno promise to help Belgium and France against German aggression or Germany against French and Belgian aggression.

allowing Germany to do what wanted

That was Churchill's posture as Hitler advanced to power. Two months later Hindenburg reluctantly made him Chancellor, persuaded by Papen that he, as Vice-Chancellor, could control Hitler, helped by a gaggle of conservative associates. (Hitler's Nazi associates, though, won control of 'law and order' through Hitler's insistence on Wilhelm Frick as Minister of the Interior for Germany with Hermann Göring as Minister of the Interior for Prussia, easily the most important of the German provinces.) The thirtieth of January 1933, when Hitler became German Chancellor, is a date more fraught with horror to us than to those who lived then. It was months, even years, before Hitler turned himself into the menacing dictatorial Führer of the Third Reich and discarded the ambiguities and opaqueness of his early years. Even so, his advent was recognized as a disquieting novelty.

Strangely, as it now seems, disarmament remained British policy. A 'preparatory commission' for the Disarmament Conference was set up by the League of Nations, and Germany, the Soviet Union and the United States were invited to join. This was in 1925; the Disarmament Conference itself began only in February 1932. There were two dominant motives in British minds. An 'arms race', thought to be the alternative to 'disarmament', many believed to be a cause of war. Secondly, the

break
peace

disarmament of Germany had been established in the treaty of Versailles in 1919 as a preliminary to general arms limitation; it came to be thought of as one of those German grievances that threatened the pacification of Europe. German governments demanded equality. In July 1932 Germany withdrew from the Conference and refused to return until it adopted that principle. Later in 1932 this was done; by the time the Conference reassembled Hitler had become German Chancellor. In October 1933 Hitler withdrew again and at the same time renounced membership of the League of Nations; 'equality', Germany alleged, should be applied immediately and not delayed or be supervised by prying inspectors. Indeed, not only did British foreign policy continue to struggle for 'disarmament', it did so more urgently and insistently after Hitler's rise to power. Cajolery or bullying to induce the French to accept 'disarmament', which for France, given the German demand for equality, meant German rearmament, seemed even more necessary now that French intransigence over revision of the treaties had, as many believed, signally contributed to the growing ferocity of German nationalism.

Churchill's foreign policy, too, stayed the same. A few weeks after Hitler's appointment he told some of his Essex constituents: 'There is no likelihood of a war in which Great Britain would be involved. Even if foreign countries go to war with one another, I know of no reason why a wise and honourable foreign policy should not enable us to stand aside . . . the government has very rightly refused to extend our obligations in Europe or elsewhere.' The League of Nations could not force Britain into war 'against our better judgement of what is right and wrong'. France should be encouraged to keep a strong army. The British should keep out of Far Eastern quarrels 'and not wantonly throw away our old and valued friendship with Japan'. A month later he commented on Hitler's Germany in the House of Commons: 'We watch with surprise and distress the tumultuous insurgence of ferocity and war spirit, the pitiless ill-treatment of minorities, the denial of the normal protections of civilised societies to large numbers of individuals solely on the ground of race.' Provisionally Churchill decreased his emphasis on appeasement as a preliminary to disarmament. Ramsay MacDonald, to whom he in this speech attributed 'the gift of compressing the largest number of words into the smallest amount of thought', had just visited Rome. There Mussolini persuaded the Prime Minister to agree to the idea of a four-power pact: Britain, France, Germany and Italy would discuss frontier revision in Europe and then arms limitation. (Nothing came of this rehearsal of Munich, which was vetoed by France's allies.) Churchill now thought that 'the situation has deteriorated to such a point in the last year that such a plan is not nearly so hopeful now as it would have been some years ago or as it might be perhaps at no distant date in the future'. Meanwhile France should remain strong: 'As I have been saying for several years "Thank God for the French army".' Attempts to weaken France would entangle Britain in European quarrels. Of course, Britain should be powerful: 'I am strongly of the opinion that we require to strengthen our armaments by air and upon the seas to make sure that we are still judges of our own fortunes, our own destinies and our own actions.'[4]

The reactions of horror and fear in British opinion towards Hitler and Nazi Germany were profound – perhaps even more clearly then, when Hitler's dictatorship began, than later on. In mid-April 1933 Attlee, for Labour, noted in the Commons that 'no one can fail to observe the spontaneous outburst from all parties in this House'. Austen Chamberlain, Neville's half-brother, denounced what he attributed to the new Germany 'the all-Prussian imperialism, with an added savagery, a racial pride, an exclusiveness which cannot allow to any fellow-subject not of "pure Nordic birth" equality of rights and citizenship within the nation to which he belongs'. Eleanor Rathbone found that, since she had been an MP, 'I have seldom been in a debate in which feeling seemed to be so unanimous,' faced with 'an evil spirit which bodes very ill for the peace and freedom of the world'. Victor Cazalet believed 'there can be no question in any quarter of the House as to the opinion of the people of this country on recent events in Germany'.[5]

It may seem strange that British government policy continued to seek agreement on arms limitation with this new Germany and even showed added urgency. Here arose the dilemma facing the British government in the 1930s. Should Hitler be conciliated, odious though he was, or confronted? Churchill favoured confrontation, though he would leave it to the French and their allies. Britain should be powerful enough to be safe in isolation. There were snags. Everyone's object had to be to prevent another great war. But it was usual to suppose that the war of 1914–18 had been caused by rival alliances and the arms race that went with those alliances. Now the League of Nations and 'collective security' should supersede alliances and bring about disarmament with internationally agreed limitations on weapons and soldiers. Only so could trade revive and prosperity return. Competition in armaments would reduce civilian living standards. A war breaking out in Europe might well involve Britain as it had done in 1914. Moreover, Churchill's insistence that British naval and aerial rearmament should have the highest priority threatened British budgets and so, it was widely believed, recovery from the great slump.

Parliament met at Westminster in November 1933 after a long recess; this meeting, by coincidence, took place soon after Hitler's withdrawal from the Disarmament Conference and from the League of Nations. It offered a good opportunity to consider what to do about Nazi Germany. In the first two weeks discussion on disarmament took up about fifteen hours. The second debate was on a Labour proposal for the next far-reaching steps the government should take at the Disarmament Conference.

The motion was defeated by 409 to 54, a characteristic expression of the overwhelming strength of the national government. That did not prevent disagreement among government supporters; rather it encouraged it. Churchill's stance had not changed. Indeed in one way it reverted to an attitude that made more sense before Hitler. 'The great dominant fact is that Germany is rearming ... We see that a philosophy of blood lust is being inculcated into their youth to which no parallel can be found since the days of barbarism.' He welcomed assurances that Britain had no binding commitments in Europe. 'Now we have our freedom, our freedom to decide, let us be very careful that we do not compromise it or do not whittle it away.' We should work with the League 'not in taking a leading part but in coming in our proper place, with all the neutral States and the smaller States of Europe'. Then the League would re-create the Concert of Europe 'not for the purpose of fiercely quarrelling and haggling about the details of disarmament but in an attempt to address Germany collectively, so that there may be some redress of the grievances of the German nation'. More armaments were needed 'to maintain our neutrality effectually'.

All this, though suitably right-wing in its contempt for disarmament, was unreal romancing: the notion that France could safely make concessions to Germany without abandoning its eastern allies and, as would follow from the refusal of firm British support, the proposal to yield to Hitler the mastery of eastern Europe showed less sensitivity towards the reality of Hitler than was shown by Churchill's close associate over India, that caricature of a right-wing conservative Brigadier Sir Henry Page Croft. The Brigadier actually urged his hearers to read Hitler's *Mein Kampf* in the original – 'either translated or have it translated for them'. He quoted an important passage where Hitler explained that the 'settling of accounts with France' was only for 'covering our rear for an expansion of territory in Europe'. Like Churchill, Page Croft of course wished Britain

34

strong, but at that stage he was less isolationist than Churchill: Britain should be 'free to intervene if we have to do so'. He did not mention this episode in his memoirs – perhaps India seemed more important then as probably it was for Churchill too – though he did discuss 1938, when he supported Chamberlain and Munich against Churchill.[6]

Leo Amery, another out-of-office, ambitious Conservative, shared Churchill's views of 'disarmament'. More definitely than Churchill, he put the Empire first; Europe was best ignored. However, he opposed Churchill on India, unlike Page Croft. Those who preached what now seems the most realistic and sensible foreign policy were two very different people. One was an eccentric and unpredictable Labour MP, Colonel Josiah Wedgwood, one of the celebrated family of potters, who represented, appropriately, a town in the Potteries. Shrewdly he pointed out that the Nazis could 'only retain power by perpetuating the idea of a grievance among the German people . . . I do not care what revision you make of the Versailles Peace Treaty, you will not stop the rearmament of Germany, or the threat that the rearmed Germany will hold over the whole of civilisation . . . No international control, no inspection and no threats of the League of Nations will stop Germany rearming now.' He wanted the government to make plain at what point it would fight to stop Germany and explain it to the French and Italian governments. From the Conservatives came the support of General Spears, who became, once Churchill agreed with him, one of Churchill's closest associates and friends. As for Italy, Spears argued that it would also follow a strong British lead. The lead he asked for, 'the premium' to be paid for peace, 'is to undertake to stand by any nation that is attacked'. He spoke, it is clear, of Europe.

George Lansbury (the party's leader), Clement Attlee and Stafford Cripps expounded Labour policy; the first confusedly, Attlee with sober clarity and Cripps with provocative fervour. It was to 'support the collective peace system'. What this meant was universal disarmament with remaining weapons in the hands of an international police force at the disposal of the League. The League's decisions should be carried out – so Britain had betrayed the League by not imposing economic sanctions against Japan over the Manchurian crisis. This alleged betrayal of the collective peace system and of the League of Nations meant that disarmament was less likely to come about since it required confidence in collective peace-keeping. Attlee stressed that even Nazi Germany should somehow be brought in: 'I do not believe that it is very much use in this House to indulge in strong language against the Nazi regime. I do not believe that you will do very much by outlawing the Nazi regime ... We have to live in the same world as Germany under its present rulers.' For Cripps, dilatoriness in disarmament meant that the British government had contributed 'very largely' to the rise of Hitler by refusing equality to Germany. At this stage, Cripps and Attlee expounded similar attitudes, something by no means true throughout the 1930s. Sir Herbert Samuel, leader of the independent Liberals, took the same line as Labour; the government had not tried hard enough to make a reality of disarmament. Now to bring about a disarmament agreement 'the nations should make an offer to Germany which Germany could reasonably be expected to accept'. Himself Jewish, as he pointed out, he felt 'bitter resentment and indignation' towards the Nazis, yet the pursuit of peace had to come before justified moralizing.[7]

In the second disarmament debate in November 1933 John Wilmot gave his maiden speech. He had been returned in the East Fulham by-election a few weeks earlier. Some months later Churchill accused 'pacifists' of venting 'unscrupulous vitupera-tion' uttered 'in the squalid election at Fulham'. Whatever the reservations of later historians, Wilmot had no doubt about why he turned a Conservative majority of 13,500 in 1931 into a

Labour majority of nearly 5,000 in 1933. It was, he asserted, 'a passionate and insistent desire for peace' and 'a demand that that desire should be translated into some practical disarmament accomplishment'. The by-election reinforced Conservative sympathy for disarmament, especially among that substantial number with marginal seats.[8]

Four ministerial speeches in November 1933 promised significant efforts towards international disarmament: the Foreign Secretary, Sir John Simon, twice, and the Prime Minister Ramsay MacDonald and Anthony Eden, then Under-Secretary for Foreign Affairs. Simon, as usual, pleaded his case with ordered lucidity: 'We have with consistency and courage pursued the course we will continue to pursue: that is to leave no stone unturned to secure for the world the enormous benefit which international disarmament accomplished by world agreement would bestow upon us and our children.' Eden was sorry that Germany had left the Disarmament Conference, 'because we wish to work in cooperation with Germany, as with all other nations, in friendship'. He certainly meant what he said. Three months later, in February 1934, he visited Hitler in Berlin, and thought him to be 'sincere in desiring a disarmament convention, as he wished to be able to push on with the long programme of internal reconstruction'. Hitler thus showed his political skill.[9] He could persuade interlocutors that he really did not believe some of the things he was obliged to say in public but was able to explain his real concerns in private; it was well that Churchill never met Hitler! Politicians from democratic countries were vulnerable because they were accustomed to the need for partial pretence.

In his speech to the House of Commons in November 1933 Eden noticed one 'refreshing aspect' of the debates on disarmament: 'that a policy of isolation has scarcely any friends'. One friend to isolation, at that time, was Churchill. Together with his views on India, it aligned him with the right wing of the

Conservative Party, persons like Page Croft and Colonel Gret-
ton. Earlier in 1933 Josiah Wedgwood had jested to the Commons about Churchill's evolution from radical progressive to
diehard reactionary. 'I used to think we were singularly lucky in
this country in having Sir Oswald Mosley to lead the Nazi
movement – otherwise it might have been Churchill! And in
that case the fate of this country might have been very different,
but we need no longer worry.' Churchill 'has shown that he is
completely happy, and so felicitous in this House that he will
never lead the Fascist Movement'. Churchill's praise in the
Sheldonian Theatre in Oxford for Parliamentary institutions
'precious to us almost beyond compare' which 'stand as an
effective buffer against every form of revolutionary and reactionary violence' does not make him seem a likely candidate for
Mosley's role.[10]

Nineteen-thirty-four had cheerful economic news for
Britain, especially southern England. The economy continued
to recover, mainly because of the fall in the pound after the
departure from the gold standard, balanced by the world fall in
commodity prices. But gloom in foreign policy deepened. The
Third Reich continued its violent disregard of law and morality.
For Churchill in that year the campaign to stop Indian self-
government reached its unhappy, embarrassing climax. To the
German menace he replied with eloquent, passionate demands
for a great British air force. Now it should no longer be merely
the equal of any air force in striking distance, it should be
made stronger than the German air force. In the first week
of February 1934 a Commons debate on 'disarmament' on the
Tuesday led on to a discussion of 'defence' on the Wednesday.
The government claimed to be all in favour of disarmament and
ready to struggle with difficulties to win agreement. Once again,
Simon and Eden claimed that the government was striving for
an international agreement to disarm. The Labour and Liberal
oppositions argued that the government should try harder.

From the Labour side, though, one MP emphatically dissented. Frederick Cocks, a former member of the National Council for the Prevention of War, denounced Hitler, who he said, intended to make Germany 'the strongest military power in Europe to enforce her will on her neighbours, whether they be little unarmed Denmark or Austria, to tear up the Treaty of Versailles . . . and to enlarge her territories'. The British government's policy meant 'taking off its hat to Hitler and edging away from our ancient ally France, instead of standing by her as we ought to do'. Germany was already rearming. Cocks objected to the refusal of European responsibilities. He wanted Britain 'to enter into a collective system deliberately and boldly for the purpose of preserving peace', since in any case Britain would be dragged into a European war.

Next day, Churchill praised his speech. In Germany 'tremendous covert armaments' were proceeding, as Frederick Cocks had pointed out 'in a most interesting speech yesterday'. Churchill demanded 'an Air Force at least as strong as that of any Power that can get at us'. He spoke of the 'ten-year rule' which, as Chancellor of the Exchequer, he had made into a constant restraint on the armed forces by turning it into a rule that Britain's financial management would be based on the assumption that there would be no great war within ten years, the rule being automatically extended day by day. The rule had been abolished two years before, but Churchill remained understandably defensive about it. He described, vividly, the presentation of ultimatums by Germany in 1914. Britain needed a strong air force in addition to a great navy if it was not to fear their revival. At this stage, however, he relied on Cocks's figures on German arming, figures which 'may or may not be strictly accurate, but which now bear a very close relation to the grave underlying facts'. Unlike Cocks, Churchill did not suggest how this powerful air force should be used and insisted only that Britain could not be safe without it. Baldwin followed Churchill:

re-armament

'I am very glad that my Right Hon Friend has been able to come down today' – perhaps a polite suggestion that Churchill's presence could not be counted on, except perhaps over Indian matters. Churchill, Baldwin said, 'had given a characteristic and very powerful speech bringing to our attention a great many things that we ought to attend to'. As usual, Baldwin employed emolient if sometimes vague phrases. He had enjoyed the debate and always felt such debates 'serve a useful purpose'. He concluded, 'fundamentally there is agreement about it in every way' and left it uncertain what this 'agreement' covered.[11]

In 1934 Churchill gave about a dozen major public speeches on armaments and foreign policy – the same number as he delivered on India. These two topics dominated his oratorical output. His concern to block Sunday trading and his support for betting and national lotteries found much less expression in his speeches. In early March the air estimates came before the House of Commons. Once again Churchill called for immediate parity in the air with the strongest European air force. Once again it was to preserve British freedom to choose what to do 'in any contingency or in any emergency which may arise upon the continent of Europe'. Now he expressed doubts about Stanley Baldwin's famous remark that the bomber would always get through: 'It ought to be possible by making good arrangements both on the ground and in the air, to secure very real advantages for the force of aeroplanes which is defending its own air and which can rise lightly laden from its own soil.' He ended with a direct appeal to Baldwin, who 'possesses the control of overwhelming majorities of determined men [Conservaties] in both Houses of the Legislature'. Baldwin need not worry about public opinion thanks to the confidence in the 'sobriety of his judgements and in his peaceful intentions'. Baldwin responded at once, speaking 'on behalf of the whole Government', and accepted 'parity'. However, acceptance was more guarded and hesitant than was subsequently alleged. He would continue to seek international agreements on arms limitation and, failing that, agreement on limitations on bombing. Baldwin concluded, 'so I am not prepared to admit here today that the situation is hopeless'. He did not believe he would have to say soon that everything had failed and that 'we must immediately spend vast sums of money'. Only 'if all our efforts fail, and if it is not possible to obtain this equality' by negotiation, the government 'will see to it that in air strength and in air power this country shall no longer be in a position inferior to any country within striking distance of our shores'.[12]

Now it was nearly dinner-time, about 7 p.m., and Churchill and Baldwin left the House. Josiah Wedgwood from the Labour benches spoke next with a cataclysmic exaggeration of the power of air forces which could decide wars in a few hours. Next there rose a serious expert on air force matters, Colonel J. T. A. Moore-Brabazon. He complained about Churchill 'coming down at 6 o'clock, scooping the cream of this Debate and getting a reply' from Baldwin, 'whereupon they both retire from the House of Commons and leave us to continue . . . if they want to talk about foreign policy and disarmament let them use another debate' and leave others to talk about 'air matters'. No Cabinet minister at all remained in the Chamber. Moore-Brabazon grumbled again about the discourtesy that Churchill 'should come along and throw off one of his disarmament speeches', that Baldwin should at once reply and that they should depart without waiting to find out what other MPs thought about what they had said. Stafford Cripps grumbled too. 'Cabinet Ministers rush in to hear some particular speech, and immediately the speech is made out they go. The Right Hon Gentleman the Member for Epping (Mr Churchill) appears here and at once there is a flood of people who rush in.'

Baldwin was forced to come back just after 9 p.m. to vote against an immediate adjournment. One hour later Vyvyan Adams spoke and apologized that Baldwin should be 'more or less compelled to be here to listen to me . . . Earlier this evening we had a remarkable speech' from Mr Churchill 'but it would be incredible for him to wait to hear a speech from me'. Later on, Adams became a devoted supporter of Churchill. Now he disagreed with him, expressing the regular League of Nations view and opposing rearmament. At the beginning of the debate Attlee, leading for Labour, gave a standard verdict on Churchill as 'one of those brilliant and erratic geniuses who, when he sees clearly, sees very, very clearly'. All this confirms, and there is repeated evidence elsewhere, that Churchill stood out as the great political star, a position which evoked, among his political contemporaries, a mixture, in divergent doses, of admiration, envy and resentment.

Moore-Brabazon stayed in the house, and after 11 p.m. he and three other Conservatives annoyed Baldwin by trying to find out when his pledge about 'parity' would be put into effect; ministers often, of course, resent demands to explain what their remarks actually mean. Baldwin had 'nothing to add', because 'I have always been under the impression that when I try to make a clear statement to this House it can be understood by every Member of the House'. Admiral Taylor criticized Churchill for contributing to Baldwin's opacity about the timing of 'parity' by supporting the idea of a convention to restrict bombing of civilian targets. Taylor said, 'I totally disagree' with Churchill. 'The whole nation joins in war, every man and woman does war work, and it is certain that our industrial areas, our ports, our docks and this city of London, the most important centre for this country in time of war, will be subjected to bombing from the air.' The war proved him right. In general, though, the Admiral agreed with Churchill's arguments for getting on with the great air force. Those Conservatives (and Josiah Wedgwood from Labour) show that the notion that Churchill was alone in a 'wilderness', a solitary voice pleading for what is now thought to be right and reason, is not correct.

He always attracted attention and nearly always some support, though not enough to impose himself on governments with huge majorities or to dictate to them.[13]

In July 1934 Churchill spoke to his constituents at Wanstead. When was 'parity' to be attempted? Why 'is Mr Baldwin's promise not fulfilled?' He continued with a sentence the Liberal leader later described 'as the language of a Malay running amok': 'We ought to have had a large vote of credit to double our Air Force – we ought to have it now, and a larger vote of credit as soon as possible to redouble the Air Force.' Then he went on, 'We ought to concert plans for mutual protection with the French and with the peace-loving powers which are in danger from what is happening and might happen in Germany.' There had just occurred a sensational episode of Nazi brutality: most of the high command of the SA, paramilitary Nazi thugs, had been murdered. Moreover, Hitler's predecessor as Chancellor, General von Schleicher, and his wife, had been shot down. It may have been in consequence of these threatening events that Churchill, for the moment, seemed to be calling for a full-scale Anglo-French alliance. If so, he soon renounced it and most of his 1934 utterances continued to urge strength in order to defend isolation. At the end of July, at Westminster, Churchill insisted on the need 'for freedom to place our own interpretation upon our Continental obligations, which it seems to me, is absolutely vital to the sound conduct of our affairs'. He went on, though, to say, 'if however, owing to the long delays to which we have agreed in the hope of arriving at some arrangement at Geneva [to disarm] we have fallen behind and are not able to put ourselves in a secure position, it seems to me that we must harmonise our policy with that of France and of the other powerful countries who are associated with France'. So an anti-Nazi alliance based on Anglo-French co-operation remained the second-best solution. The stronger Britain became, the less France could rely on British support.

Curiously, at the same time, Neville Chamberlain was taking up exactly the same position within the government. He was advocating the creation of a bomber force to deter Germany from war without the necessity of Britain's having to collaborate with France. There was another respect in which Churchill's thoughts coincided with those of Neville Chamberlain: in the same Westminster speech Churchill confirmed his distaste for those supporters of the League of Nations who denounced Britain's lack of action to curb Japan. He referred to Baldwin's famous statement that the British frontier was on the Rhine: 'If the socialist opposition have their way, I gather that we should now have added the cold, unforgetting, unforgiving hostility of Japan to all those other serious preoccupations' and Attlee 'would be reminding us that our frontiers were the Yangtze'.[14]

Baldwin clouded another of his celebrated utterances of the 1930s. In November 1932 he told the world that the 'bomber will always get through', that 'the only defence is in offence, which means that you have to kill more women and children more quickly than the enemy if you want to save yourselves', and that, when the next war came, European civilization would be wiped out. Now Baldwin claimed that he had made his formidable statement 'to try to attract attention', and he made a concession – it was worth while to try to intercept enemy bombers attacking Britain. Stafford Cripps, of course, agreed with Baldwin's earlier view: national armaments served only to weaken international co-operation and the necessary advance towards a world government. The cautious, small-scale expansion of the air force Baldwin had promised caused Cripps to 'feel that he, as well as the more pacifist elements – I should say more sensible elements' in the government, 'has had his hands forced by the wild men like the Right Hon Gentleman the Member for Epping . . . it comes down to this, there is a vague fear that Germany may attack us . . . We do not believe in relying on anyone else,' so collective security which would make increased armaments unncessary was rejected. For Cripps, then, as for most commentators on foreign affairs at that time, Churchill advocated an 'arms race' which would make war almost certain. Cripps thought armaments for 'collective security' might be justified: national armaments, however, were yet another poisonous product of capitalism. Baldwin, as usual, appealed to moderation: a little cautious rearming would not destroy hopes of limitation of armaments; it would strengthen Britain's independent influence or might be useful in support of the League and collective security. So Baldwin and Simon would hope to maintain broad-based support and make Churchill seem a 'wild' extremist.[15]

At the end of November 1934 Churchill exceeded in dramatic force even his own earlier pronouncements on the need to arm. This high moment he advertised beforehand. He moved an amendment to the vote of thanks for the speech of George V at the opening of the new session of Parliament. It appeared on the order paper well in advance: Churchill handed it in to the Speaker on 20 November and moved it in the House eight days later. Earlier Baldwin had received a copy of the points he intended to make. (Churchill also sent a copy to Lloyd George.) The motion insisted 'that the strength of our national defences, and especially of our air defences, is no longer adequate'. A special meeting of the Cabinet was called to work out how to deal with this motion, and the subject dominated two other full Cabinets. A special Cabinet committee considered the issue. The views of the Committee of Imperial Defence and its subcommittees were taken into account. The Foreign Office put up a paper, asking what should be done if Germany engaged in 'open defiance', after which events might 'rapidly develop in the direction of an Anglo-French alliance coupled with special arrangements for the defence of Holland and Belgium'. Knowing as we do Hitler's subsequent defiance, this seems the rational policy. The Foreign Office thought Hitler would then be 'ready to compromise', and so a 'Disarmament Convention' might emerge. The government recalled the British ambassador in Berlin, Sir Eric Phipps, for consultations. The Foreign Secretary informed the French, Italian, Belgian and United States governments of this move, explaining that Churchill's motion compelled a more urgent exposition of British policy towards German rearmament than the British government would have wished, in what the Foreign Secretary called a most important debate. British representatives in Berlin set out their worries about German rearmament to the Foreign Minister, Baron Konstantin von Neurath, and to Hitler himself, who spoke more irritably than the Foreign Minister, but said the same things: that German rearmament was exaggerated and that it was defensive in purpose.

Churchill had set off a big fuss. Samuel Hoare, the Secretary of State for India and formerly for Air, of course, interpreted it unfavourably. Churchill, in 'doing his utmost to get a bigger following, staged with great care and ingenuity the debate that took place on Wednesday on air defence ... Fortunately, we knew all about his machinations.' The Foreign Secretary, John Simon, thought as Hoare did that the armaments debate might have an impact on discussions about India's future constitution. 'Important members of the extreme right would support Churchill's thesis,' and the opposition would seize the chance to attack the government. There would be a danger that the Cabinet might be discredited in the eyes of the public before India was debated. Churchill, it seems probable, believed in what he was trying to do on air strength as much as Hoare and Simon believed in their own purposes.[16]

On 28 November the much heralded speech began after questions in the Commons. It lasted about fifty minutes, as did Baldwin's reply (the Cabinet had agreed that Baldwin should speak immediately after Churchill). Churchill deployed some of the more dire, catastrophic predictions of the effects of German bombing. Within a week or ten days London would suffer 30,000 or 40,000 casualties. Then 'at least three million or four million people would be driven out into the open country around the Metropolis'. They would be there without shelter or food. The whole of the army would be absorbed in controlling and caring for this disordered multitude. Defence against bombers should be studied by a strong governmental committee and experiments encouraged. Churchill said he had 'heard many suggestions'. Here is evidence of the influence of one of his closest friends, Frederick Lindemann, Physics Professor at Oxford. Already, in August, the Prof had written to *The Times*, which gave prominence to his letter, urging that it was 'profoundly improbable' that 'no method can be devised' by all the 'resources of science and invention' to find some defence against bombing attacks. But, Churchill went on, 'Pending some new discovery, the only direct measure of defence upon a great scale is the certainty of being able to inflict simultaneously upon the enemy as great damage as he can inflict upon ourselves.' Churchill made comparisons between the strength of the German air force and the British. So far the British were ahead, but on present assumptions the German air force would, after one year, be at least as strong. Two years ahead the German air force would be much stronger.[17]

Baldwin's much meditated-upon reply proved evasive. He had to try to reassure three very divergent groups of critics. Churchill's supporters needed rapid rearmament; the League of Nations supporters wanted agreement to limit armament; and Hitler, Baldwin was advised, should not be provoked into competitive rearmament. Baldwin announced an acceleration in the building of aircraft announced in July 1934 to add forty-one new squadrons to the RAF in 1934–9, so that by the end of 1936 twenty-nine of these would have been completed. However, Baldwin had 'not given up hope either for the limitation or for the restriction of some kind of arms'. From Berlin on 27

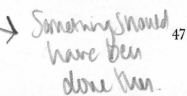 Something should have been done then.

November the British air attaché urged 'most strongly that an exaggerated figure for German aircraft should be most carefully avoided by the Government in the House of Commons tomorrow'. In Cabinet a week before the debate it was reported of Germany that 'there was reason to believe that in a year's time she would have as large an air force as the United Kingdom'. In his speech Baldwin denied this: the RAF would by then be one and a half times stronger than the Luftwaffe. As he had promised the Cabinet that morning, he 'avoided the mention of any precise figure' for German strength: it might be between 600 and 1,000 military aircraft. Sir John Simon, closing the debate as Foreign Secretary, stated yet again that the government was still seeking disarmament, though he spoke less confidently than in the past: 'If we can get it, we should like agreed disarmament at a very low level ... if there is no possibility of that, and we cannot get the unattainable ideal, we must seek to secure agreement at the lowest level at which it can be got.'[18]

Solution?

In these two years, the first years of Hitler's rule, Churchill showed unfailing consistency in demanding an air force capable of defeating the German air force. What he thought should be done with that revived British strength was less clear. His main message fitted the right-wing position he had adopted. Britain had to be strong enough to defend isolation from European quarrels. In November 1934, however, Churchill showed his growing uncertainty about his hopes for isolation from Europe:

There are those who say 'let us ignore the continent of Europe. Let us leave it with its hatreds and its armaments to stew in its own juice, to fight out its own quarrels, and cause its own doom' ... there would be much to be said for this plan, if only we could unfasten the British islands from their rock foundations, and could tow them 3,000 miles across the Atlantic Ocean ... for my part I have come to the conclusion – reluctantly I admit – that we cannot get away.[19]

48

The idea that German grievances had to be remedied got less emphasis as time passed, while French eagerness to maintain the post-war settlement got increasing applause. The League of Nations earned more sympathetic references than before, but support for the League did not amount to a pledge of any definite action in any confrontations that might arise.

CHAPTER FOUR

India

CHURCHILL HAD A full life – over-full by any normal human standard. Apart from painting and conversation and travel, his distractions earned money to finance a family and the 'life of a gentleman'. Three public distractions from the dominant political worry of the 1930s, which can adequately be summarized in two syllables – Hitler – stood out in 1933, 1934 and the first half of 1935. One represented support for state interference, the second objection to state interference, India, which provided the third and greatest distraction, concern for imperial power and grandeur.

Churchill acted as president of the Early Closing Association. This respectable body, backed by eminent ecclesiastics and a royal duke, vigilantly supervised the granting of weekly half-holidays for shopkeepers and shop assistants, opposed Sunday trading and took an interest in the provision of lavatories for employees. Here is a sample of his presidential advocacy:

> I have always urged the closing of shops in accordance with the hours agreed upon. My opponents said there is no need to close the shops if the hours of the assistants are regulated. That is a wholly fallacious view and a dangerous view. To see whether shops are open or shut is pretty easy, but to ascertain whether assistants are being employed over their

time or not would involve very great expenditure and multiplication of officials. When people complain to me that they cannot buy chocolates or cigarettes after a certain time, I always reply that if they cannot get their goods within the ample hours shops are open they had better practise self-denial on themselves.[1]

The enactment of the Betting and Lotteries Bill in 1934 followed the lengthy deliberations of a Royal Commission. In November the full House of Commons took the committee stage to discuss the proposals in details. The bill had two main purposes. It sought to regulate greyhound racing and the associated gambling, though it was the latter which mattered most, except perhaps for some of the dog-owners. The racing would be limited to 104 days a year in any one area, not Sundays, Good Friday or Christmas Day. Churchill intervened frequently in the debate. He concerned himself with the law on lotteries. Some were now to be legalized, but only small, restricted, private lotteries as, for instance, at church fêtes. Churchill wanted 'three or four large national sweeps a year' and complained that the government refused a free vote on it since it thought to be undesirable lotteries either to help the Exchequer or to subsidize good causes. Churchill proclaimed that the statute would allow working men to ruin themselves and their families at dog-racing 'casinos' while forbidding them well-organized, more decorous forms of gambling. The rich, he argued, could gamble undisturbed, while anyone hawking tickets for the popular 'Irish sweep' was to be pursued by the police and punished by the courts.

Sir John Gilmour, the Home Secretary, who pushed the bill through the Commons, complimented his most energetic opponent and spoke of 'the usual pleasure with which we listen to the speeches that he delivers'. He spoke after Churchill, just before midnight on 6 November 1934. Close associates, of course, knew well that midnight and after found Churchill in high oratorical form. Over the lotteries he intervened on about twenty separate occasions. Some of the speeches are still highly amusing today. Obviously Churchill had completely recovered his command of the House of Commons, if indeed he had ever lost it. His setbacks, such as the humiliating rejection of his complaint of breach of privilege over India (see below), affected him heavily but only for a moment. Soon he returned, when he had time enough, to dazzle and intimidate and dramatize. His action over the Betting and Lotteries Bill demonstrated his intermittent talent for championing popular causes, on this occasion appealing to Conservative emotions against Baldwin's habit of conciliating Labour and Liberals. Samuel Hoare, Churchill's main target over Indian disputes, thought he was trying 'to accumulate merit with the discontented members of our party'. Even Hoare, at this stage the most unfriendly observer of Churchill's activities, credited him with 'a good many small successes in the House' over the Betting Bill.[2]

Until the middle of 1935, India, first and above all, distracted Churchill from the problems and threats presented by Hitler's Germany. India raised two issues. The first was how to maintain British control over India to prop up British power and prosperity. The second was to determine the Conservative Party's policy and its leadership. Churchill wanted energetic and sustained hostility to what he chose to denounce as 'socialist' aspirations. Baldwin preferred a softer, gentler, vaguer, more conciliatory approach to persuade some 'progressives' that they could safely vote Conservative. Churchill put the party-political aspect of his campaign over India to a meeting of the 'anti-socialist union' in London early in 1933. The Tory Party had to be truly Conservative. For Churchill that did not mean grinding the faces of the poor. On the contrary, 'anti-socialists' should 'revive the strong, warm sense of regard for the weak and the poor'. Truckling to socialists weakened the national spirit. He remarked, as he often did for years to come, applying the bludgeon of incomprehen-

sion to the vote of the Oxford Union when it refused to fight for
'King and country': 'We have all seen with a sense of nausea
the abject, squalid, shameless avowal made in the Oxford Union
. . . a very disquieting and disgusting symptom'. (Addicted to
old-fashioned symbols, Churchill did not grasp that voting would
have been quite different if it had been a question of fighting for
the League of Nations and 'collective security'.) 'These callow
ill-tutored youths' had been 'set a bad example by people much
older and higher up.' (Evidently here he meant Baldwin and his
associates rather than incompetent Oxford tutors.)

At the election of 1931 the people of Britain had voted 'for
its flag, its power, its fame'. But, unbelievably, the Tory Party
'has swallowed lock, stock and barrel the policies of the last
Socialist Government about the Indian Constitution . . . yet
three-quarters of the Conservative Party in every constituency
throughout the country are opposed to the Socialist policy upon
India'. What was needed was 'one deep-throated growl from the
National Union of Conservative Associations'. Churchill planned
to lead the growling.[3] The dispute was simple. Everyone, or
nearly everyone, in politics – apart from a few dedicated left-
wingers such as G. D. H. Cole, Leonard Barnes and sometimes
Stafford Cripps – took it for granted that Britain should remain
dominant in India into the remote future. How should this be
contrived? As Viceroy of India, Irwin (later Lord Halifax),
supported by Ramsay MacDonald and Baldwin, thought it was
best to win support among Indians by giving them more
influence in India and by suggesting that British rule might not
be eternal. Churchill insisted that the British should make it
plain that they were there to stay – only so would Indians obey
their rulers. 'Once it is believed that British authority is about to
be replaced by something new, that the Great Power which has
hitherto ruled with irresistible force all over India and kept it
quiet and safe from harm is about to wind up its affairs and
depart, naturally, even its most loyal adherents must address

themselves to a new situation, must prepare themselves for a new system.' This resulted not from 'a change of facts in the problem of India'. The cause was the apparent lack of will-power and self-confidence exhibited by the representatives of Great Britain.

Some of Churchill's predictions on the future of India and its peoples, if British feebleness led to abdication, justify Josiah Wedgwood's comment after one of Churchill's speeches on the subject. He described Churchill as 'the brilliant, witty, irrespon-sible enfant terrible of this House'. But his audience 'was against him when he started and has remained against him ... I think that is really because he does not believe in his own arguments.' Churchill protested and Wedgwood substituted, 'I cannot believe that he believes in his own arguments.' Pathan tribes-men, insisted Churchill, were 'molesting and insulting' the city of Peshawar 'only because they had been led to believe that Lord Irwin's government was clearing out of India and that rich spoils lay open to their raids'. 'If the destinies and fortunes of the Indian people are handed over to the politically minded, highly educated Hindus' – he had in mind Nehru, for instance – 'once they obtained power and control of India they would reduce that country to the deepest depths of Oriental tyranny and despotism.' Usually Churchill stressed British obligations to the peoples of India, especially the 'Untouchables' and the Moslems, but British interests were also involved: 'Sever that partnership, destroy that union, let the relations of Great Britain and India sink to the level of those between Great Britain and China ... and you will see in this island another million unemployed' – presumably through loss of British exports, particularly of textiles. Since the Hindus, as it was then sup-posed, were not 'fighting races', once they had got the British out, 'an army of white janissaries, officered if necessary from Germany, will be hired to secure the armed ascendancy of the Hindu'.[4]

Duty to the inhabitants of India gave Churchill his main justification for opposing the government of India by Indians. (What are now known as 'Pakistanis' then came under the 'Indian' label as a minority within the population of the Indian sub-continent.) One reason he never mentioned – it may not even have been consciously in his mind as a justification for British imperial rule – was the provision of 'respectable' occupations for the sort of people who still dominated the active membership of the Conservative Party. 'Gentlemen' and members of the middle classes who aspired to that status still looked down on 'trade', the making and selling of goods as a source of income, except perhaps for the older-established brewers.

'Respectable' careers could be found in the armed services, within which the Indian army provided opportunities for those who found it difficult, on limited pay, to keep up the standards of living expected of officers in the better-class British regiments, the law, banking, the Church of England, the diplomatic service, the home civil service, the colonial service and, commanding high respect, the Indian civil service. In the nineteenth century the so-called 'public schools', boarding schools, expanded in number and in number of pupils, in part to meet the mounting demands of Empire. Administrators, as distinct from scientists and technologists, overwhelmingly came from Oxford and Cambridge colleges, which were still largely restricted to 'superior social categories', with a seasoning of those undergraduates chosen for intellectual ability. In defence of Churchill's view, however, there can be quoted the words of a devoted enemy of Empire: 'The modern official . . . sees himself not as an Empire-builder, but as a builder and decorator of native societies. His strength lies in his courage, his endurance, his capacity for hard work in exacting conditions, and his loyalty in honouring his bond by disinterested service in return for the remuneration he has accepted.'

Duty called: early in the campaign, before the coming of the national government transformed politics, Churchill predicted that the political division in Great Britain would 'be drawn between those who are willing to abandon India if the Indian political classes so demand and those who believe that we have an abiding responsibility to the masses of the Indian people and that we should discharge our mission with inexorable determination'. Indian self-government was bad for Indians. The Montagu–Chelmsford reforms, presided over by a government of which Churchill was a member, had failed. 'Every service which has been handed over to Indian administration has deteriorated; in particular, Indian agriculture, the sole prop of the life of hundreds of millions, has not advanced in accordance with the ever-growing science and organisation of the modern world.' The Montagu–Chelmsford reforms had encouraged partial Indianization of provincial governments in British India (as distinct from the 'princely states'). Now the London government planned more, but 'every extension of Western electioneering systems in India will be accompanied by worse deterioration in the honesty and efficiency of Indian government'.

The threat against which Churchill struggled for five years was that of a partially elected federal government of India, albeit with limited powers. He made one concession: provincial government could be developed but 'no federal union, no airy United States of India should be attempted until provincial units ... have proved themselves capable of showing loyalty to the Crown and giving decent administration to the Indian masses'. Disconcertingly he sometimes pointed out that free elections had disappeared in many European states, which apparently justified their denial to Indians: 'You offer this bouquet of faded flowers of Victorian liberalism which, however admirable in themselves, have nothing to do with Asia and are being universally derided and discarded throughout the continent of Europe.' This was another example of the widespread British conviction that only white members of the English-speaking peoples could be trusted with representative electoral systems. He went on in the same speech to insist that 'the police and judiciary must not be handed over to Indian control now nor in any period that we can foresee. Certainly not until the hideous strife of races and religions in India has definitely ended.' It could perhaps be argued that some of Churchill's fears relating to the withdrawal of British power in India were justified at the time of partition in 1947.[5]

Churchill's awful prophecies appealed most effectively, as he was aware, to the prejudices of senior Conservative militants. The further removed they were from prudent Parliamentary party managers, the freer their reactions. Indeed the only emphatic national vote against the government's plans was at the Women's Executive of the National Union of Conservative Associations, encouraged by the Duchess of Atholl, an MP who had an impressive capacity for lending moral acceptability to the various causes she espoused. For Churchill and his diehard associates, among whom Brigadier Sir Henry Page Croft stood out, discouragement and encouragement alternated. In October 1932, at the Conservative Party conference, Samuel Hoare, the Secretary of State for India, managed a strong majority for the government, but at a meeting of the Central Council of the National Union he barely defeated Churchill and Page Croft, with 181 votes to 165 and, alarmingly or encouragingly, 151 abstentions. In April 1933, on the composition of the select committee of both Houses of Parliament, set up to consider the Indian constitution, the government got its way but with no fewer than seventy-nine Conservative MPs voting against. When he opened the debate, Samuel Hoare conceded that there were Conservatives – 'it may be a large group' – who have either not made up their minds or at any rate have not yet declared their minds'. In March 1934 at the Conservative Party Central Council the opponents of Indian reform mustered 314 votes against 419 on the government side.

Soon afterwards, what probably proved the decisive event in the government's favour took place at Claridge's Hotel, a suitably comfortable place for undecided but influential Conservatives regularly to meet for lunch. Hoare had talked at length to Austen Chamberlain, who then won over the group at Claridge's. Even so, at the Conservative Party conference that October the opposition was only narrowly defeated by the government, by 543 to 520 votes. The government had relaxed: their spokesmen were from the second rank. On the other side, Churchill chose to cruise in the Mediterranean rather than attend the conference, but Page Croft, the direct, straightforward diehard, led the opposition. It was, however, a near-defeat for the government only on tactics. Baldwin had tried to get the conference to postpone discussion of the issues until the Select Committee reported. For the government all came right again at the Central Council early in December. Government and opposition arrayed their full forces, Baldwin and Austen Chamberlain led in support of the government's proposals, and Churchill, for the diehards, attacked the 'sapping the foundations of our forefathers' structures'. Nearly all those present voted on an amendment to the government's plans rejecting change to the central government of India. The committee rejected the amendment by 1,102 votes to 390.[6]

In 1934 Churchill had suffered a serious defeat; for someone less resilient it might have generated a long period of humiliated silence. On 16 April, in the House of Commons, he charged Lord Derby and Sir Samuel Hoare with breach of privilege. They had persuaded the Manchester Chamber of Commerce, so he claimed, to change its evidence to the Joint Select Committee examining the Indian constitution. Recent scholarship suggests he was right. The Committee of Privileges, however, rejected his claim.[7] This seemed, of course, to be a direct attack by Churchill on Sir Samuel Hoare, Secretary of State for India, and Leo Amery, a former cabinet colleague of Churchill, prepared a devastating joke at Churchill's expense. He described it with relish in his diary and added that his speech 'was much the most successful one I have ever made from a purely parliamentary point of view, and I have been overwhelmed with congratulations ever since'. He attributed to Churchill the motto 'Fiat justitia ruat caelum'. In the Commons it would be normal for a member to demand a translation. But Amery's plan reached a level of high comedy when 'Winston turned round and asked me to translate. I had scarcely dared to hope that the fish would swallow my fly so greedily.' Amery's 'translation' was not literal: 'If I can trip up Sam, the Government's bust.' Noted Amery, 'the House was convulsed'. Churchill had given Amery a ducking in the pool at Harrow in 1889: now Leo Amery reckoned he had replied and 'given Winston the best ducking he has had'.

Amery correctly went on, however: 'but he remains unsinkable'. And during what was left of the discussion of the report of the Privileges Committee, Churchill made nine combative interventions.[8] Soon came his brilliant debating speeches on betting and lotteries. Since he and the diehards got most of their support from party activists, their defeat at the National Union of Conservative Associations, where many were present in December, made it almost certain that Samuel Hoare would get the India Bill through the Commons in the first half of 1935. Churchill fought to the end just the same, speaking at length on the second and third readings and rising repeatedly during the intervening committee stage. Churchill's hopes revived from time to time. Early in 1935, during the committee stage, he told his wife, who was then cruising in the South Pacific, 'I am in the House all day two or three days a week, speaking three or four times a day ... always without notes ... I seem to be able to hold my own and indeed knock the Government about to almost any extent. The Government supporters are cowed, resentful and sullen. They keep 250 waiting about in the libraries and smoking rooms to vote us down on every amendment.' He was encouraged by the increasing emphasis of the heads of the Indian states in opposing federation. Sam Hoare, though alarmed from time to time, stuck it out and relied on endless detailed discussion to avoid sensational episodes. A contemporary supporter commented on Hoare's handling of the India Bill:

> No-one who listened to his exposition could doubt that he was dealing with a matter of infinite difficulty demanding indefatigable industry. As his thin voice set out line upon line ... there was rooted a well-informed objection to much of what he said, but Hoare was able to wear down antagonisms of some of his audience by the simple and time-honoured expedient of boring them.[9]

In the second-reading debate Herbert Samuel, the Liberal leader, spoke of 'the mighty conflict which has been waged' between Churchill and Hoare; at the end of the debate eighty Conservatives defied the Whips and voted for Churchill against Hoare, but with just over 400 votes for the government Churchill had led a rebellion which, however impressive, did not shake the government or block the bill. During the five-year struggle, that familiar compound of awed admiration and fearful hostility attended Churchill's steps. Samuel, a steady supporter of the India Bill, having praised Hoare's patience, courtesy and knowledge, went on to claim that everyone should admire 'the persistence, the resource and the brilliance' shown by Churchill, and he continued, 'every subject which comes before this House is an opportunity for his wit and humour and irony ... the greatest of our Parliamentary orators of the present day has had a happy time in the Debates on this Bill'. Moreover, when Churchill spoke in any debate 'the House always crowds in to hear him. It listens and admires. It laughs when he would have it laugh, and it trembles when he would have it tremble – which is very often in these days' – this was in June 1935. Then came the acid: the House of Commons 'remains unconvinced, and in the end it votes against him'.

A Conservative, Richard Law, who later became, over appeasement, a supporter of Churchill, remarked that he 'has made many most brilliant speeches on India . . . and I, like the rest of the House, have been attracted and almost mesmerised by those speeches'. But, he went on, a speaker supporting Hoare 'wiped out' the effects of this oratory. Another Conservative, Edward Campbell, was more venomous: 'I admit him to be the most brilliant speaker in the House and the most attractive, but hardly the most sincere, consistent or reliable . . . do not let us allow mere oratory, based on personal animosity and ambition, to turn us from our duty to India.' The Duchess of Atholl, who spoke next, rightly defended Churchill's sincerity. There can be no doubt at all that Churchill firmly believed that Indians and other inhabitants of what later came to be called the 'third world' were best governed and policed by the British. As for ambition, any first-rank politician must be 'ambitious'. That is to say, they must believe it to be beneficial for their society that they themselves should have power: without that conviction the effort required to reach the first rank would be intolerably tedious. In the debate on the setting up of the Select Committee, Lord Winterton, Conservative MP for Horsham and Worthing, had complained of Churchill's claiming to speak in the Commons 'only as a humble private Member'. 'Here,' said Winterton,

> you have one of the most powerful figures in politics in this or any other country . . . with immense power and ability to sway masses outside, as certainly, in my 30 years' experience, I have seen them swayed. Here is the man who gets a longer report in any newspaper than any other living man. He has a great position outside, and he is leading a group within the Conservative party against its accredited leaders.[10]

The strangest result of the immense efforts over more than five years in legislating for Indian constitutional reforms is that it made very little difference in India. The federal scheme came to nothing as Indian princes became less and less inclined to support the creation of a central legislature with any actual influence. From the start of the Second World War, into which India was brought with no attempt to consult Indians, British rule became more powerful than ever and much more costly. The heated controversy and conflict in Britain over the India Bill took place within the Conservative Party; it did not much worry the general public. In the 1930s it continued to be assumed that the British Empire remained a permanent, and prominent, part of the arrangement of the world. Nearly every-one took it for granted that India was run by the British and would continue to be run by the British. The detailed and complicated mechanisms which this required aroused little interest outside the small section of society which dominated the Conservative Party in those days. As Parliament plunged into protracted discussion of the minutiae of Indian government early in 1935, one influential journal commented, 'The India Bill ... is of little interest to the man in the street, and the fact that interminable sittings will have to be devoted to it in the next few months means that public interest in the work of Parliament will be in abeyance.' By contrast, the same periodical observed that the 'various issues raised in Parliament this week in the course of the defence estimates are by long odds the most important by which the people of this country are faced'.[11]

In June 1935 when the India Bill at last reached its third reading in the House of Commons, Churchill noted, in effect, how it had distracted attention 'at a time ... when the continent of Europe is drifting steadily nearer to the brink of catastrophe, when we have before us for so many months to come that awful hiatus in our air strength and in the vital defences of Great Britain'. He blamed the government, of course: 'What has astounded me is that the Government should have pressed forward so obstinately with this Indian policy, which causes so much distress to so many important elements in the Conservative party.'[12] Those who felt distress sometimes supported Churchill's later opposition to Chamberlainite appeasement; many did not. Conservatives like Alan Lennox-Boyd, Henry Raikes and Churchill's partner in opposition to the India Bill, Henry Page Croft, supported Munich. Brendan Bracken always went with Churchill, and Lord Wolmer and the Duchess of Atholl agreed in opposing appeasement. But later supporters of Churchill, Vyvyan Adams, Richard Law and Churchill's friends Bob Boothby and Louis Spears, voted with the government on India. The large numbers of Conservatives voting against their Whips proved only temporary Churchillians, though it was indeed serious revolt. Only Hoare's diligence and Baldwin's unobtrusive shrewdness prevented the government's overthrow, since many party members felt uneasy about any suggestion of a weakening of Empire.

Chamberlain's counter-attack against Churchill's opposition to appeasement employed different tactics from those of Baldwin and Hoare. Chamberlain, reluctantly, made concessions to keep safe his majority in the House of Commons – though it is true that his majority was smaller after 1935 than that at the disposal of the national government during the fight over India. On India Churchill had more support than over his distaste for the moves of the Irish Free State towards republican detachment and for his opposition to the explicit liberation of the Dominions in the Statute of Westminster. What the struggles of these years overwhelmingly demonstrated was Churchill's stature as the greatest orator of the twentieth century. When his emotions and beliefs corresponded with those of most of the British people, as in 1940 (and not in 1945), he possessed unequalled, indomitable power and influence.

CHAPTER FIVE

Defence and the 'Rhineland Crisis'

NEW POLITICAL EMBARRASSMENTS beset Churchll early in 1935. This time they came from his son. Churchill stands out as a devoted parent, but parental devotion does not guarantee regular and orderly children and, with one exception in his youngest daughter, his children endured troubled and difficult lives. In January, Randolph Churchill, twenty-three years old, declared himself a candidate at the by-election in the Wavertree division of Liverpool. Though he was angry and made it clear that he had had nothing to do with his son's decision, Winston Churchill felt compelled to support Randolph. The consequence was that a safe Conservative seat went to Labour, since Randolph Churchill, by opposing the government's India policy and the official Conservative candidate, split the Conservative vote. In February, to his father's anger and dismay, Randolph encouraged another candidate to stand as a dissident Conservative at another by-election, though this time the official Conservative succeeded.[1]

Though sometimes angered by the clumsiness of his son, Churchill showed no sign in public of any distress. Nor did the great distraction of India weaken his expression of concern over the threatening struggle for mastery in Europe, though India enabled him to make a display of genuine liberalism when he complained about the lack of 'humanity and commonsense' after twenty-seven people were shot dead in Karachi in March 1935, the week Churchill spoke, by British troops in suppressing a riot. In March he denounced once more the government's failure to maintain 'parity' with the German air force. Once again, he set out in advance to Baldwin what he intended to say: 'I propose to renew our discussion of last November and to analyse as far as I can your figures of British and German air strength for home defence.' He would argue that the promise of 'parity' was not being fulfilled. Once again the idea, now usual, of Churchill's being stranded in a solitary 'wilderness' as a 'failure' is exposed as misleading. In an ambiguous, uncertain way he remained, if not a part-time member of the government, at least an outside adviser. Against Churchill's attack and denunciations, Baldwin did not hit back, whatever he felt privately – his style was always emollient. So Churchill never felt himself separated from him by unbridgeable hostility; with MacDonald such hostility is more plausible. Comparisons of strength, Churchill pointed out in this speech, were 'a very complicated subject' on which he was afraid that his remarks were 'going to be extremely dry', a modest disclaimer perhaps not entirely applicable to this closing paragraph: 'From being the least vulnerable of all nations we have, through developments in the air, become the most vulnerable and yet, even now, we are not taking the measures which would be in true proportion to our needs.'[2] In the end Baldwin found it best to involve Churchill in limited participation in the mechanism of government.

After Professor Lindemann's letters to *The Times* of August 1934 in which he argued for scientific enquiry into means of foiling enemy bombers, Churchill and Lindemann followed up with a visit to Baldwin during his holiday at Aix-les-Bains. The close friendship of Lindemann and Churchill meant that Churchill relied entirely on the Prof for scientific information and advice. For others it meant that working with Churchill meant working with Lindemann. Already a committee had been set up attached to the Air Ministry under Air Chief Marshal Brooke-Popham, Commander of the Air Defence of Great Britain. Brooke-Popham and his committee, which began to meet in October 1934, considered current weaponry, especially searchlights and anti-aircraft guns. Though Lindemann attended one meeting, this was not what he wanted. He wanted consideration by scientists of new devices in a committee which had access to the highest political levels and so would be able to encourage experiments and their financing. Lindemann set out these thoughts to Baldwin and Lord Londonderry, then Secretary for Air and, as was not unusual among the British aristocracy, an acquaintance of the Prof's, in whom snobbery softened the combativeness he showed towards his social equals, especially towards potential scientific competitors. Londonderry told Lindemann that he had set up another committee within the Air Ministry to consider how science and technology might strengthen defence against enemy aircraft. This was the Committee for the Scientific Study of Air Defence. It was to be presided over by Henry Tizard, who still thought himself a friend of Lindemann's, with P. M. S. Blackett and A. V. Hill as academic scientists. Tizard had been in the government department of scientific and industrial research and then became Rector of Imperial College, London. Hill was a physiologist, attached to University College London, and Blackett was then Professor of Physics at Birkbeck College, London. Londonderry urged Lindemann to get in touch with Tizard and present his thoughts to this new committee.[3]

For the Prof this was not good enough. At the beginning of 1935 he asked the advice of Austen Chamberlain, the other great political person excluded from the national government, although his brother Neville was there as Chancellor of the Exchequer. Austen was far less a critic and opponent of the government than Churchill – indeed over India his support for the government was crucial. However, he took up the issue of defence against bombers. In mid-February 1935 he joined Churchill and the Prof in putting the case for more research to Ramsay MacDonald, still Prime Minister. Four days later Lindemann addressed the 1922 Committee of Conservative MPs, an unusual and highly privileged political demonstration. 'There is no group of men I would sooner address,' he told them. 'For if I can only persuade you that my views are right you are in a position to see that the necessary action is taken.' Enemy bombers could be stopped. Lindemann knew how to do it: barrage balloons, but, above all, 'something in the nature of an aerial minefield was required'.

Sir Austen followed up this speech with two questions in Parliament. At last, in the middle of March, the Prime Minister gave way and announced the Air Defence Research Sub-Committee of the Committee of Imperial Defence, one of the most important of Cabinet committees. A Cabinet minister, Philip Cunliffe-Lister, soon to be Air Minister and, a little later, to become Lord Swinton, was made chairman of the new body. Baldwin and MacDonald thought it wise to invite Sir Austen Chamberlain to join the committee; he declined owing to his preoccupation with the dispute over India. When India faded from constant debate another approach was made to Sir Austen; again he refused, but proposed that Churchill should be invited. For the government, a combined attack from Winston Churchill and Austen Chamberlain might be serious and it had to avoid offending them both. Churchill was therefore invited. At this stage, Austen Chamberlain urged Lindemann to accept the invitation to the Air Ministry's departmental scentific committee, presided over by Henry Tizard. Evidently, Chamberlain's activities were decisive. Six months before, he had advised Lindemann not to accept until the politically influential CID committee was agreed. Now, therefore, Churchill joined the Swinton Committee and Lindemann the Tizard Committee.[4]

All was prepared for a mighty quarrel as Lindemann continued to use every means and every sort of pressure to get what he wanted.

Before and during the Second World War, Lindemann (who in 1941 became Lord Cherwell, named after the tributary of the Thames flowing past the meadows which lay under the windows of his Oxford college home) was the closest of Churchill's friends and the one who had the greatest influence on him. He had inherited wealth sufficient to enable him to be relaxed in the company of rich men and women. He was an excellent tennis player, which fitted well into inter-war society. The aristocratic and rich acquaintances he thus acquired found him pleasant and amusing company. His eccentricities, his vegetarianism, whose later-twentieth-century association with 'political correctness' might have led him to renounce it, and his total abstinence from alcohol ought to have seemed especially curious to F. E. Smith, Lord Birkenhead, the eminent lawyer and close friend of Winston Churchill before his early death in 1930. With Birkenhead, Lindemann's connection derived from lawn tennis; association with Birkenhead necessarily brought acquaintance with Churchill.

Those connected with Lindemann's early scientific career had the highest possible reputations, and his own ability and clarity of mind stood out. Above all, he had a capacity, which understandably appealed to Churchill, for clarifying complicated scientific arguments for the benefit of non-scientists. Yet with all these talents and advantages the Prof often aroused extreme dislike and resentment. What scholars produce is intangible. It is the effect of their discoveries and interpretations on the minds of other scholars. Academics therefore often feel unsure of their success. Without the reassurance of strong self-confidence they may be suspicious of other academics, especially those who think themselves important and deserving of high status. Anyone Lindemann thought to be an independent competitor, particularly a competitor among physicists, aroused contemptuous rudeness. To those whose youth exempted them, and indeed to those he could help, he was gentle and charming. Always he wished to be thought 'important' and as a result he sought power and influence, often with valuable results. In Oxford he created a university physics laboratory of the highest quality which, for instance, led the world in low-temperature physics. He contributed to saving science from some of the disasters of Hitler's rule by encouraging scientists to escape Nazi persecution and endeavouring to find opportunities for them to continue their work – several in Oxford. His own scientific research after his arrival in Oxford generated fewer results than his earlier career had made to seem likely. Perhaps that made him touchy and combative. He wanted, and used every means, to have his own way.

The aspect of preparation for war in which he became involved in 1935, that of defeating enemy bombers, meant making sure of resources to press forward the lines of experiment he favoured. RDF, later known as radar, presented little difficulty. Lindemann attributed its success to an individual. Robert Watson-Watt, who, the Prof claimed, owed his triumphs to evading the inhibitions imposed by departmental committees. Barrage balloons were uncontroversial. Lindemann wanted to develop infra-red detectors to show the position of enemy bombers at short range at night. Most important, for him, were 'aerial mines'. Destructive wires or small explosive charges might be dropped ahead of enemy bombers, suspended from small parachutes. Experiments into these means of detecting and foiling air raids needed the highest priority and adequate finance. Neither device turned out to be much use against bombers in the air war against Hitler.

If other scientists disagreed, they had to be bullied or out-manoeuvred. Winston Churchill had to be called in – he could be counted on to support his friend the Prof – and all his powerful political influence among his contacts deployed. Before the fourth meeting of the Swinton Committee, the first which Churchill attended, he submitted a paper, 'with much diffidence' as he implausibly claimed. It outlined the strategy of the next war, concentrating on the need to defeat any attempt at a 'knock-out blow' by the German air force, especially one directed at London. Several paragraphs of the paper advocated aerial mines. Churchill explained that 'in this matter I am indebted to Professor Lindemann, with whom I have discussed the problem for the last two years'. He declared that 'no consideration of expense should delay remorseless experiment'. The day before this meeting the Prof wrote to Churchill to brief him further on aerial mines. Lindemann suggested that if anyone in the Swinton Committee objected to his proposals, Churchill might demand that the Prof should be heard in their support.[5] Churchill and Lindemann went on in growling discontent at the lack of urgent attention to their proposals. After Churchill had attended four meetings of the Swinton Committee he launched another paper. It incorporated Lindemann's grumbles; in a short document on the inadequacy of experiments on aerial mines, Lindemann's name appeared five times and there were other references to what was said or stated at meetings of the Tizard Committee which Lindemann had attended.

This paper, dated 2 June 1936, set off a crisis. Tizard replied in a paper for the Swinton Committee, of which he was a member in addition to being in the chair of the Air Ministry Scientific Committee. He argued that aerial mines had been considered before Lindemann became part of the Tizard Committee and pointed out that experiments had shown that aerial mines were unlikely to be effective. Tizard concluded, 'I take the strongest exception to a member of my Committee who has not succeeded in convincing his colleagues on scientific and technical questions, endeavouring to force his views, through a member of this committee [the Swinton Committee], however

distinguished.' In other words, Tizard complained that Lindemann was using Churchill as a means of defeating other scientists. A few days later, Tizard wrote to the Prof, 'No doubt you
already know that as a result of your personal criticisms to
Winston Churchill he made a written attack on the Research
Committee [the Tizard Committee] without taking the trouble
to ascertain my views first.' When, Tizard claimed, he offered a
reply to this attack, Churchill 'followed up in Committee with
other wild criticisms presumably based on information from you
. . . I don't think it is possible for us to go on collaborating
without continual friction.' He had told Swinton, now Air
Minister, of this. Evidently, Swinton had counselled patience –
serious political embarrassments threatened – and Tizard wrote
again to Lindemann early in July. He ended with a direct plea:
'do give co-operation a further trial. I am much more interested
in defeating the enemy than in defeating you!'[6]

On 6 July Baldwin's Cabinet came together to discuss with
Eden, by then Foreign Secretary, the closing stages of the crisis
in Abyssinia (as Ethopia was generally called in those days), the
stagnant international discussions over the Rhineland crisis and
the domestic problem of what to do about Churchill. Neville
Chamberlain reported that his brother Austen had told him
that he felt concerned about 'the situation of this country, of
Europe, and of the Government'. For the first time since the
end of the nineteenth century 'the House of Commons', Austen
pointed out, 'was divided on foreign policy'. Neville Chamberlain feared that Churchill and Lloyd George, whom Neville
particularly disliked, would work together and 'would accuse the
Government of not taking defence sufficiently seriously and
eventually they might insist on telling the country, or at any rate
Parliament, what they thought about it'. Austen Chamberlain,
encouraged by Churchill, called for a secret session of the House
of Commons. Baldwin suggested that Churchill 'was contem-
plating the delivery of a speech four hours in length'. Ramsay

MacDonald (now Lord President of the Council) asked 'whether the Cabinet would welcome the prospect of having to face Mr Churchill's criticisms in Parliament'. He suggested instead giving a private hearing to 'influential MPs' and, to try to avoid Churchill's full blast, a version of this suggestion was taken up. Swinton, Air Minister, though he had originally supported Austen Chamberlain's suggestion that Churchill should be added to the Air Defence Research Committee of which he was chairman, attacked Churchill. As a member of the committee 'his attitude had throughout been unhelpful . . . Mr Churchill had also been working in close alliance with Professor Lindemann.'[7]

Lindemann now set off the final crisis in the Tizard Committee. It met on 15 July 1936 to work out a progress report. The Prof had irritated the other members by announcing a few days before that he would be a candidate in the by-election for one of the two Parliamentary seats representing Oxford University. He intended to stress the inadequacies of defence against hostile bombing attack. Because of Lindemann the committee could not agree on any single report on what it had done. Lindemann insisted that he would write his own. The two independent scientists, Hill and Blackett, had now had enough of Lindemann, and both wrote to Swinton that same day. Blackett put it all in one sentence: 'My views as to the best procedure to expedite the study differ so widely from those of Professor Lindemann that I feel that further work together on the Committee will be too difficult to be fruitful.' A. V. Hill explicitly declared 'that so long as Professor Lindemann remains a member of this Committee, it will be impossible for me to serve on it'. Hill raised Lindemann's relations with Churchill, and denounced the candidate for the Oxford seat in the Commons as 'someone who intends to use any available method of advertising the unique value of his opinions'.

In fact, apart from Lindemann's clumsy bullying of scientific competitors, difference was slight. All of them wanted funds for research. A less combative Lindemann could have tried to work with the Tizard Committee in pursuit of funds. But as Hill wrote, 'Instead of being frank and open with his colleagues on the Committee, he went behind their backs.' As the Prof put it before he joined the committee, he regarded it 'purely as a blocking committee, likely to do more harm than good'. Moreover, if funds were limited, Lindemann took it for granted that he should determine priorities, and aerial mines had to come first. Churchill could use his influence and his oratory to support him. Swinton tried again to calm things, but Hill and Blackett stood firm. So Swinton, as Secretary for Air, dissolved the Tizard Committee and re-created it without Lindemann. Since Lindemann had treated the committee as useless or worse than useless, he could hardly complain; in any case, Churchill could speak up for aerial mines and support his Oxford candidacy. The latter provided another instance of a Churchill candidate forcing a split Conservative vote, and in this case letting in a capable, independent MP, Arthur Salter. Meanwhile Churchill presented his own resignation from the Swinton Committee to protest against Lindemann's extrusion but was persuaded to remain.[8]

After the Indian issue had faded, Churchill could hope for office, even sometimes expect it. The disturbance associated with Lindemann helps to explain why existing Cabinet Ministers could fear Winston Churchill as a disruptive, self-centred bully and therefore tolerate the absence of his energy and powerful abilities from the governments presided over by MacDonald, Baldwin and Baldwin's favoured successor, Neville Chamberlain. In the second half of 1935 and the first half of 1936 these fierce quarrels, well known to a small group, did not arouse public attention and excitement. What did was Mussolini's conquest of Abyssinia and the Rhineland crisis.

In early 1935 Churchill continued to struggle against Indian reform or, as he claimed, continued to defend ordinary Indians.

Together with the Prof he continued to call for experimentation on defence against bombers, on infra-red for detection and, above all, on aerial mines to destroy enemy raiders. (Then often referred to as 'invaders', a word which in 1940 had a different meaning.) New problems in foreign policy emerged and required Churchillian opinion and comment: the Anglo-German naval agreement and the growing signs of trouble between Italy and Abyssinia. In May 1935 Hitler spoke. As usual, he mingled promises of conciliation with threatening display. Baldwin, not yet Prime Minister, though the most influential member of the government, thought that Hitler's speech showed he might be ready to work for agreed limitation of air forces. In another gesture towards Britain, Hitler claimed 35 per cent of the strength of the Royal Navy; Churchill pointed out that the new ships this would involve would be stronger vessels than the older ships of the Royal Navy. None the less, 'All must welcome the friendly tone of Herr Hitler, his friendly references to this country, and the several important points which he brought forward and which form a good link upon which conversations could be opened, and negotiations, perhaps, be founded.' Even when Churchill warned of the threatening dangers of growing German strength he had to agree that 'to represent everything that has been said by Hitler as containing in it only the purposes of political manoeuvre would be, as it were, to destroy the very means of contact and of parley between one great nation and another'.

Early in June 1935 Ribbentrop, whose advice Hitler often preferred to that of his foreign minister, von Neurath, appeared in London with a peremptory 'take it or leave it' demand for an Anglo-German naval agreement embodying 35 per cent of British naval strength as Hitler had suggested. The British government took it; and, without consulting any other country, accepted the agreement. Baldwin, the new Prime Minister, backed this contradiction of the principle his predecessor, Ramsay MacDonald, had accepted a few weeks before at Stresa, that Britain, France and Italy were united in opposing German breaches of the arms limitations of the 1919 peace treaties. Churchill joined the friends of collective security in denouncing the single-handed British acceptance of German treaty-breaking, which ignored Stresa and the League of Nations.

Meanwhile, Britain was beginning to urge Italy to obey the League and renounce the breach of treaties. The ambitions of Italy in Abyssinia were becoming increasingly obvious. Churchill commented on the effect of the Anglo-German naval agreement: 'we have placed ourselves in a position where it makes it very difficult for us to remonstrate too strongly with Italy without being exposed to a somewhat severe reply that when we think our special and particular interests are involved we show but little consideration for the decision against treaty-breaking to which we have just urged the League of nations to come'. The First Lord of the Admiralty, by contrast, declared that he regarded the Anglo-German naval agreement – 'and we believe that the German government regard it – essentially as a contribution to world peace and international appeasement'.[9] Hitler certainly welcomed it because it rendered war unlikely between Britain and Germany and made Britain less likely to worry about what might happen in eastern Europe. Moreover, for Hitler, understandings reached directly with individual countries lessened the possibility of any coalition designed to restrain him.

The developing Abyssinian crisis embarrassed Churchill. The League of Nations offered a cover for his plans for anti-German combinations, but in Abyssinia Germany had no concern. A quarrel with Italy would not help the restraint of Germany. Still, it seemed more and more likely that Italy contemplated aggression in breach of the Covenant of the League. In July 1935 Churchill ended a speech on foreign policy with this conclusion: 'the one great fear of Europe is the power and might of the re-armed strength of Germany . . . the one

75

great hope is the gathering together of Powers . . . in a system of collective security under the League of Nations in order that this tremendous process of rearmament of Germany may not be attended by some lamentable breakdown of peace'. Yet earlier, though he opposed ceding British territory to persuade Mussolini to abandon aggression, he had said that if Italy had thus been bribed into peaceful ways 'the gain would have outweighed the loss'.

Strangely, bizarrely, Churchill retained his admiration for Mussolini: a few weeks before the Italian attack on Abyssinia, he glorified Mussolini as 'so great a man, so wise a ruler', who was presiding over a 'revivified Italian nation'. And later on, after the war had begun in Abyssinia, Mussolini had a 'commanding mind' and was 'a historic figure'. But, of course, freedom and democracy made sense among the white English-speaking peoples, not among ungovernable and restless foreigners. He hoped the British government would not allow the impression to spread that Britain was 'coming forward as a sort of bell-wether or fugleman to gather and lead opinion in Europe against Italy's Abyssinian designs'. Even when Italy was conquering Abyssinia, Churchill claimed it was 'a mistake' to have admitted Abyssinia to the League and 'the Abyssinians must be made to put their house in order'. Some sort of 'settlement' might still be hoped for and the League should avoid 'only look[ing] at the faults of one side without considering its responsibility for putting right abuses and great evils on the part of the other party'. In any case, the war between Italy and Abyssinia was 'a very small matter' compared with the threat from Germany.[10]

However, Churchill, like Baldwin, who had just announced the date of the general election, had to take into account the popular enthusiasm for the League which the League of Nations Union demonstrated in 1935 in the 'Peace Ballot'. More than eleven million people answered a questionnaire, whose results appeared in June. Only a small minority opposed 'economic and non-military measures' to stop one nation attacking another, while more than half of the replies approved 'if necessary' of 'military measures'. Everyone knew that support for the League and 'collective security' came from many people: the Ballot suggested that they were an overwhelming majority. With the general election approaching, all candidates but especially the Conservative Party, including both Baldwin and Churchill, had to take the League of Nations, and possible 'sanctions' in its support, more seriously than they might otherwise have done.

Italian action against Abyssinia became a great issue in British domestic politics. In August, with Italian preparations for attack going forward, Churchill went to see Samuel Hoare, his main opponent over India, now Foreign Secretary, and Anthony Eden, whom Baldwin, as one response to the Peace Ballot, had made Minister for League of Nations Affairs. Churchill 'now regarded the Indian chapter as closed' and expected to co-operate with the government. 'We should make it perfectly clear ... that we are prepared to carry out our League obligations even to the point of war with all our military resources, provided that the other members of the League are prepared to take the same action.' The critical other member was France, and Churchill accepted that the French were unlikely to provoke Italy. Thus he approved, in advance, of Hoare's speech in Geneva in September, which proclaimed that the British would do everything to stop Italy except anything actually effective. Churchill's main interest in the League was as a defence against Germany. 'If the League now collapsed in ignominy,' which was an outcome that his, and the government's, policy made certain, 'it meant the destruction of the bonds that united British and French policy and of the instrument that might in the future be chiefly effective as a deterrent to German aggression.' On 11 September Hoare addressed the League general assembly: 'The League stands and my country stands with it for the collective maintenance of the Covenant in its entirety, and particularly for steady and collective resistance to all acts of unprovoked aggression.' The repetition of the word 'collective', Hoare thought, signified that Britain would not take the lead in applying the Covenant. In fact, he made Britain seem the main advocate of 'sanctions' against Italy.[11]

Early in October 1935 the Italian attack on Abyssinia began. In that month the League agreed to an embargo on the grant of loans and on the export of munitions to Italy. The following months, all imports from Italy and exports to Italy of rubber and iron ore were prohibited. In the last discussion of foreign affairs in Parliament before the election, Churchill gave priority to the danger from Germany. He spoke, though, at length about the League. Sometimes he seemed to have become a League fanatic: 'if I am asked, "how far will you go in support of the Covenant of the League of Nations?" I shall say we ought to go the whole way with the whole lot'. As his remarks indicated with increasing clarity he felt more and more strongly that he could exploit support for the League to bring support for his own hopes: rearmament and the formation of anti-German coalitions. 'Some people say: "put your trust in the League of Nations", others say: "put your trust in British rearmament". I say we want both. I put my trust in both.' This meant that he was hoping to overcome the contradiction between those, 'progressives', who opposed armaments except for collective security in the League and those who supported rearmament to defend British interests. The Abyssinian problem was an embarrassment for Churchill. He had no interest in the defence of Abyssinian freedom, and rather than quarrelling with Mussolini preferred to sign him on as an opponent of Hitler.

Churchill's 'support' for the League made it easier for him to work for the return of the national government at the general election. At the Conservative Party Conference in the autumn, he went out of his way lavishly to praise Baldwin. Naively, he seems to have supposed that he would be brought back into government after the election.[12] Self-centred and domineering personalities often fail to realize how inconvenient they may seem to others as possible collaborators. Baldwin clearly preferred not to risk his own unemphatic dominance and seems to have had in mind that his chosen successor, Neville Chamberlain, should not have a more glamorous colleague to dim his prestige as a successful Chancellor of the Exchequer.

After the election and the meeting of the new Parliament, Churchill stayed for the meeting of the Air Defence Research Committee (the Swinton Committee) on 9 December. He prudently remained silent on Italy and the League. The next day he went abroad for a protracted sunlit holiday until 26 January, sometimes with the intellectually stimulating company of Lindemann. Churchill's holiday was damaged by another display of Randolph's tactlessness, in which Churchill's son outclassed his father, while falling behind him in intellectual brilliance. This time Randolph accepted the invitation of the 'true' Conservatives in the local association in Ross and Cromarty to stand against Malcolm MacDonald, son of Ramsay, who was a Cabinet Minister as Dominions Secretary, and the national government candidate, and therefore that of Conservative Central Office. The local association wanted something other than this prominent 'National Labour' candidate. By now, in January 1936, Winston Churchill had re-emerged as a supporter of the national government, and even of Baldwin. India was no longer a big issue and Churchill evidently supposed that his natural claims to office might now be met, as defence became more and more prominent. The fact that Churchill and his son were both in Morocco when Randolph received and accepted the invitation spread the belief that his father had encouraged Randolph. In fact, Churchill felt embarrassed and dismayed by his son's impetuous indiscretion. He gave it no support. It came to nothing. Ross and Cromarty returned Malcolm MacDonald early in February. Among four candidates, MacDonald got nearly 50 per cent of the votes, Randolph Churchill just under 14 per cent.[13] It did not make more likely Winston Churchill's return to office.

Usefully, however, his holiday enabled Churchill to avoid comment on the 'betrayal of the League' embodied in the Hoare–Laval plan. Hoare and Pierre Laval, the British Foreign Secretary and the French Prime Minister, agreed on a scheme for a partition of Abyssinia. Italy would be given effective control of most of the country, while Haile Selassie, the native Emperor, would still have something. Before it could be presented to Mussolini, the plan was 'leaked' in Paris. It was desperately unpopular in Britain, especially since candidates at the election had usually proclaimed their loyalty to the League. The Cabinet forced Hoare's resignation, but even so Baldwin faced a political crisis. He met it, in part, by promising Hoare future reinstatement in the Cabinet in return for his taking prime responsibility for the Paris scheme and by making Austen Chamberlain, for a critical few days, believe that he might become Foreign Secretary once again; in fact, Baldwin put in his friend Eden. Churchill kept away from the whole dispute. Austen Chamberlain's resentment sharpened his support for Churchill's criticisms of the government. For Churchill himself the Hoare–Laval plan would have been welcome, if accepted by Italy and then dressed up as a concession imposed on Italy by the League. Understandably, he said nothing when the future of sanctions was discussed in the Commons on 24 February 1936, in particular the proposed sanction to forbid oil supplies to Italy, though he spoke later that day on a supplementary naval estimate. In that speech, though of course favouring new naval building, he gave no support to the oil sanction.

The speaker who came after him, a Labour member, commented, 'I am sure the Government will think of the Right Hon Gentleman when they start forming their opinions regarding the

Minister for Defence.'[14] A few days before, Sir Murray Sueter, a retired admiral with strong connections with naval aviation, had moved a private member's bill to create a ministry of defence. That something had to be done to prevent the army, navy and air force simply competing, or compromising, without regard to any general plan was becoming widely discussed and accepted. At the end of 1935, Wing-Commander James, a Conservative MP, backed by many others, had urged some measures to co-ordinate defence. He argued that Baldwin and Maurice Hankey, as Cabinet Secretary the most influential civil servant, had blocked it. Frequent letters to *The Times* confirmed that informed opinion, especially among ex-officers and MPs, wanted action of some kind. (In those days letters to *The Times* provided an effective outlet for parading opinions.)

No one could doubt that the obvious person to overlook defensive preparation was Winston Churchill. He knew it himself. Thus in the debate on Admiral Sueter's bill he spoke only ten words, six of which were 'I have not said a word.' A Liberal National MP who had served at the Admiralty when Churchill was at its head observed that 'co-ordination' of defence 'was really a fight between the Departments and the Treasury. When we had a forceful personality like the Right Hon Gentleman, the Member for Epping (Mr Churchill), at the Admiralty, we got all we wanted.' No one ever questioned Churchill's forceful personality; that assumption lay behind everyone's attitude to him. When Edward Grigg opposed a ministry of defence because it would overwhelm anyone 'unless he were a man the like of whom I do not see on the horizon of this country at the present time', Churchill was promptly pointed to.

In this debate, Churchill abandoned his role of critic. Austen Chamberlain, as it were, deputized for him. Austen's hopes of a return to office had already been disappointed when Baldwin, skilfully enough, put in Eden to replace Hoare at the Foreign Office. He now launched a direct attack on Baldwin as Prime

Minister. Baldwin's confession of May 1935 that he had been completely wrong about the growth of the German air force and his meaningless refusal to defend Hoare because 'my lips are not even yet unsealed', those things Chamberlain insisted 'could not have happened if the thinking machine of the Government was working properly, if their defence organisation was really efficient'. From the progressive Conservative left there spoke the most independent of their MPs, Vyvyan Adams. He gave an early sign that Churchill might begin to appeal to League of Nations enthusiasts and to former fanatical disarmers:

> Do let us face the facts as they are in Europe today. International relations are steadily and rapidly deteriorating, and the only way for Great Britain to be strong for peace is for her to be sufficiently powerful to deter. Let us face this further fact, that the long-range danger to European peace and civilisation comes not from Signor Mussolini but from the men who are at present misruling Germany.[15]

The words could have been Churchill's.

Baldwin postponed the decision on how to modify the organization of rearmament. He was waiting until the 1936 White Paper on defence had been presented and debated: as Churchill commented, it reversed 'the usual and normal procedure' which is 'to put the horse before the cart ... but no doubt there may be very good reasons for having adopted the contrary one in this case'. We do not know the reasons. Baldwin's reticence provided and provides a screen to cover his thoughts. It might have been an example of that indecision which contemporaries assumed in him or it might, perhaps, have been an attempt to prevent Churchill from producing portentous Churchillian attacks on the latest defence scheme. On 8 March 1936 Neville Chamberlain recorded in his diary that Churchill had asked to see him. Churchill 'explained that he was in a very difficult position because S.B. [Stanley Baldwin] did not propose to announce the name of the Minister till after the debate. He wanted to make a "telling" (I understood in the form of a fierce attack on S.B.) speech if he were ruled out from the post, but not if there were any chance of its being offered him.' Neville Chamberlain, who ranked as the dominant member of Baldwin's government, claimed that the Prime Minister 'had not yet made up his mind and therefore I could not say he was ruled out'. Chamberlain confided to his diary, 'I thought it an audacious piece of impertinence to ask me such a question with such a motive.'

The day before Chamberlain's diary entry, on 7 March, Hitler had sent troops into the demilitarized zone of the Rhineland, contrary to the treaty obligations to keep that area clear of troops and military installations, and thereby set off the 'Rhineland crisis'. There was a consolation for Neville Chamberlain: the Rhineland remilitarization made it easier to keep out the favoured candidates for the new ministry, Winston Churchill and Samuel Hoare (the latter had experience at the Air Ministry and, as we have seen, had been promised a return to office). The crisis 'afforded an excellent reason for discarding both Winston and Sam, since both had European reputations which might make it dangerous to add them to the Cabinet at a critical moment'.[16] Churchill, of course, was not popular among the rulers of Germany.

Churchill's speech on 10 March in the debate on the defence White Paper won general applause from the government side and sympathy from some of the opposition. Samuel Hoare damaged his cause by ostentatious flattery of Baldwin: 'If he will impress upon the country the great urgency of the problems that face us, he will find a great body of support in the country, and among his followers there will be none more willing to give him support than a very old friend and former colleague,' Hoare himself. Churchill, Neville Chamberlain noted, 'suppressed the attack he had intended and made a constructive and helpful speech which carried the House with him'. Churchill made no mention of the Rhineland crisis except to say that 'if what we have seen in the past few days is the mood of a partially armed Germany, imagine what the tone would be when the colossal preparations which are being made are approaching their zenith, and when at the same time the limits of internal borrowing are already in sight'.

In what turned out to be a percipient analysis Churchill argued that the rulers of Germany would soon face a choice. Either they would have to stop rearming or they would have to go to war: 'Can we doubt what course the man at the head of Germany would be likely to choose?' There Churchill proclaimed in advance his divergence from Neville Chamberlain's 'appeasement' – Chamberlain, especially early in 1939, supposed that Hitler would choose conciliation. Churchill's criticism of the national government, however, was indeed mild by his standards. He claimed something that more and more people had begun to agree with, that the government should have begun large-scale rearmament much earlier. He urged subcontracting by firms making aircraft. Something had to be done to combat shortages of skilled labour. He wanted at least a skeleton ministry of munitions. He gave new, and entirely justified, warnings that Britain had no prospect of catching up with or overtaking German rearmament. This speech made it plain that Churchill had unequalled merits as a possible minister for defence.

He was not Baldwin's choice. It was, to everyone's surprise, the Attorney-General, Sir Thomas Inskip. Next day *The Times*, doubtless following a ministerial lead, remarked that others had been ruled out as 'ill-adapted to teamwork or (what is equally important) to work with this particular team' and 'above all that their appointment at this particular moment in the world's affairs might be misunderstood or misrepresented'. Chamberlain remarked in his diary that Inskip 'would excite no enthusiasm but he would involve us in no fresh perplexities'. His half-brother Austen Chamberlain set things out differently when he spoke after Churchill at the annual dinner of the Birmingham Jewellers Association: 'Mr Churchill has great courage and infinite energy and great and wide experience of the matters of defence, and there will be many in the House of Commons who regret that Mr Baldwin has not thought fit to call him to that new office, for which he has greater qualifications than any living politician.'[17]

Hitler's remilitarization of the Rhineland represented a fine calculation. After the First World War, the Treaty of Versailles had prescribed that Germany should keep no troops and erect no military constructions in the area of western Germany bounded by a line fifty kilometres to the east of the Rhine. The treaties of Locarno in 1925, freely negotiated with the German government (not a Nazi government, of course), promised British and Italian support for France and Belgium in the event of German violation of the demilitarized zone. If German forces moved into the zone as an obvious preliminary to an attack on France or Belgium, an immediate military reply was allowed; otherwise they were to appeal to the Council of the League of Nations, which would order appropriate actions to put things right. Now German troops marched in without asking permission from anyone. Hitler accompanied this display of force with a string of offers of conciliation and negotiation about objects appealing to the British: perhaps German return to the League, perhaps an air pact and agreed limitations of air forces, new, revised, improved Locarno treaties, non-aggression pacts – European appeasement. The crisis, indeed, guaranteed much talk, which helped to distract attention from another Hitlerian triumph. Again Hitler increased his power to do one of the two

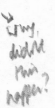

things he cared about. The remilitarization made wars easier: Germany could attack eastwards with less fear of France or attack France and Belgium with less preliminary delay.

In histories of the coming of war this crisis has often been seen as the last chance to check Hitler without war. Some suppose any counter-attack from France would have precipitated instant German military retreat from the zone. Some claim that Hitler would have been overthrown. These writings derive partly from German arguments that the cause of war is to be found in the feebleness of the democracies, partly from those who exempt themselves or their heroes from blame. During the Rhineland crisis Churchill's diagnosis was disappointingly imprecise. He did not advocate immediate and decisive action to throw the German army out of the Rhineland. He accepted, even applauded, the British government's evasive policy of futile talking and negotiation. Certainly he hoped that collective security through the League of Nations could be made to work against Germany and that the covenants of the League could somehow create a coalition against aggression, by which word Churchill always meant, above all, German aggression, though it was often politically incorrect to say so. Since the French government decided to make no individual riposte, the British determined what would happen. British opinion would, it is certain, have rejected any British leadership in counter-measures to the German display of force: Churchill did not demand them. He may have sympathized with French claims for British support; he acquiesced in the end in their effective rejection.

On 12 March he spoke to a thinly attended meeting of the Foreign Affairs Committee of MPs supporting the government: Britain had to fulfil the obligations of the Covenant of the League. He pictured, the Prime Minister was informed, 'all the countries of Europe hurrying to assist France and ourselves against Germany'. That implied an agreed Anglo-French attitude. There was no such thing, and the diplomacy of the crisis involved the French in endeavours to get as much support as they could from the British and then settling for what turned out to be protracted verbiage. Austen Chamberlain at another, better-attended meeting of MPs on the government side put it accurately when he urged them to support the government 'in trying to be the honest broker' between France and Germany. When Churchill spoke to MPs he underestimated the gravity of events. With the forces at the disposal of the League 'a wonderful chance' was now offered: 'the chances of a peaceful and friendly solution are good'. In fact, maintaining the capacity of France to keep Europe safe from aggression was unlikely to be done peacefully and impossible to be done in any way friendly to Germany.[18]

Churchill knew Pierre Flandin, the French Foreign Minister at that time, and Ralph Wigram, who served in the Foreign Office Central Department, which dealt with France and Germany. Wigram was well acquainted with Paris, having served in the embassy there. Both Churchill and Wigram certainly encouraged Flandin to press the British to do something; so did Joseph Paul-Boncour and René Massigli, respectively minister for the League and from the political section in the French Foreign Office, who came from Paris to support Flandin. Churchill invited Flandin to dinner, when he arrived in London, with Austen Chamberlain, Samuel Hoare and Robert Horne, a former Cabinet colleague of Churchill's. (In Churchill's memoirs this influential group are counted, strangely, as 'my principal associates'.)

The day after this dinner party, Saturday 14 March, one week after Hitler's reoccupation of the Rhineland, Churchill spoke with Austen Chamberlain at the Jewellers Association dinner in Birmingham. As usual for him in this crisis, Churchill set out two mutually incompatible views. France 'has taken the right and proper course of appealing to the League of Nations'. The snag about this 'course' was that it meant France would do nothing to resist the German remilitarization unless Britain was ready to help and to sponsor at least economic sanctions against Germany or even to support military confrontation. Only a very small minority in London would have dreamed of such things. Without shared British and French determination to reverse the German coup, the League was an impressive mechanism for concealing inaction by portentous talking and writing.

Churchill presented the jewellers with a typical example of his threatening rhetoric. 'If the authority of the League is destroyed, as it might well be, in the triumph of the Nazi regime, irrespective of law, events will continue to roll and slide remorselessly downhill towards the pit in which Western civilisation might be fatally engulfed.' What Churchill was striving for was a barrier to Nazi aggression based on co-operation between Britain and France and rallying many European countries. Public opinion, overwhelmingly exploding in 1935 in the Peace Ballot, meant that he could call for this only by disguising his ambition as meaning 'support for the League of Nations'. That became Churchill's foreign policy theme for the year 1936. Above all, it justified his consistent, central demand for armaments. There remained the embarrassment of Italian aggression, and after his gloomy forebodings of Nazi triumph he turned to Abyssinia, where 'the bugles should sound "ceasefire"', and sanctions against Italy should be suspended.

Churchill spoke again two days later, in the Commons. The *Times* Parliamentary correspondent reported that he 'was given a cordial welcome by a crowded House', perhaps to make up for his rejection as co-ordinator of defence. This speech was on the naval estimates, and no one in the debate made any reference to the Rhineland. Next, he spoke on the progress of the Jewish National Home in Palestine and denounced Germany's 'horrible, cold scientific persecution' of Jews, with 'people reduced from affluence to ruin, and then, even in that position, denied the opportunity of earning their daily bread, and cut out even from relief by grants to tide the destitute through the winter, their little children pilloried in schools to which they have to go; their blood and race declared defiling and accursed; every form of concentrated human wickedness cast upon these people by overwhelming power, by vile tyranny'.[19]

On 26 March the Rhineland crisis was successfully anaesthetized in what everyone agreed to be a debating triumph for the Foreign Secretary, Anthony Eden. He effectively combined firmness with feebleness. 'I want in all bluntness to make this plain to the House – I am not prepared to be the first British foreign secretary to go back on the British signature.' But 'our objective throughout this period has been to seek a peaceful and agreed solution'. There should be 'negotiations' to bring a 'happier atmosphere' to allow 'those larger negotiations on economic matters and on matters of armaments which are indispensable to the appeasement of Europe to take place. I assure the House that it is the appeasement of Europe as a whole that we have constantly before us.' Churchill applauded and agreed. 'Upon one of the most delicate and one of the most grievous topics that could possibly be discussed, there is an overwhelming consensus of opinion . . . I feel very much relieved and even exhilarated by the speech.' Things had gone wrong that might still be put right. 'An enormous triumph has been gained by the Nazi regime.' But 'I desire to see the collective force of the world invested with overwhelming power . . . then, in my opinion, you have an opportunity of making a settlement which will heal the wounds of the world.'

Neville Chamberlain, winding up the debate for the government, felt that many members of the Commons 'must have been struck and perhaps a little surprised, at the general consensus of opinion in this House' in support of the government's proposals for negotiations. Anthony Eden and Neville Chamberlain insisted that British obligations to assist France against the German breach of the Treaty of Locarno remained 'in respect of any measures which shall be jointedly decided on'. Both government speakers made it clear that the word 'jointly' meant that the British could veto any such measures. Churchill agreed with Eden and Chamberlain in seeking, in Eden's words, 'a strengthened League of Nations, an ordered Europe, a greater confidence in which nations would rely less on arms and more on law and order'. Chamberlain commented on Churchill's 'vivid picture – for he is an artist in words as well as in paint – of a state of affairs in which there should be the peaceful encirclement of a potential aggressor. You might have the peaceful encirclement of a lion if half-a-dozen people joined hands and stood all round it,' but strength mattered too. Where Churchill differed from the government at this stage in 1936 was not on foreign policy or even on the desirability of rearmament, but more on the speed and extent of British rearmament. More and more clearly he spoke in favour of the League of Nations to win support for British armed strength. Vyvyan Adams, that League enthusiast, wrote to Churchill with 'respectful congratulations' on his speech. 'Some of us lurking on back benches are hungry for chances to intervene in these Foreign Affairs debates: but nine-tenths of our appetite is satisfied when you state so perfectly what none of us could say so well.'[20]

March 1936 was a fraught and painful month for Britain and for Churchill. In Europe the German action meant, to an extent that Churchill did not seem fully to grasp, that the formation of an effective block of states to curtail German aggression had been made much less likely after the demonstration of French weakness over the German remilitarization. It was unthinkable at the time, whatever anyone later claimed, that Britain would push France into firmness over a Rhineland demilitarized zone that most in Britain thought to be a legacy of the unfairnesses of Versailles, and something that would in any case soon be negotiated away. For British opinion, all that happened in March 1936 was that the seizure of a prospective

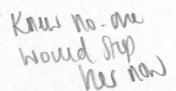
Knew no-one
would stop
her now

concession to Germany came first and negotiations came after. For Churchill, March 1936 seemed a moment when his recall to high office was possible, even likely. He showed no public signs of disappointment when it did not happen, and continued giving powerful, sometimes dramatic, sometimes amusing, speeches in his familiar and incomparable style.

CHAPTER SIX

Interfering with Industry?

BY THE SUMMER of 1936, advocacy of the League supplied Churchill with the argument which he believed to be attractive to most people in British political life. Then they might support his repeated demand for rapid rearmament against Germany. It would appeal to most Labour politicians, to Liberals and to those Conservatives who followed the Baldwin line of national cohesion. Baldwin followed vaguely progressive impulses and, as so many of the most successful British politicians in the twentieth century tried to do, endeavoured to persuade centrist Liberals to vote Conservative (some Labour politicians later did the same) rather than to throw their votes away on the Liberal Party. Churchill had alienated these people by his contempt for Baldwin's 'progressive' policies at home and overseas, especially in India. Now the League might win them over. An embarrassment for Churchill's new stance, as eloquent advocate for collective security under the League of Nations Covenant, disappeared in the summer of 1936. Haile Selassie, the Emperor of Abyssinia, had lost; what limited sanctions had been applied against Italy by the League had proved futile. French governments had been reluctant to risk war with Italy by applying sanctions that would have worked: cutting off Italian oil supplies or closing the Suez Canal. Churchill usually, though not always, shared their view. Like them he thought of Italy as a possible ally against Germany.

He preferred Laval's policy of trying to settle with Mussolini to the British government's policy of denouncing Mussolini and refusing serious measures to stop his conquest of Abyssinia. Understandably he attacked this policy for its inevitable failure. But his retrospective support for the Hoare–Laval plan, which he described in May 1936 as 'a very shrewd, far-seeing agreement', would cause dismay to the normal supporters of the League.[1]

In June, Attlee, as Labour leader, moved a vote of censure on the government after it had abandoned sanctions against Italy. Churchill told some of his constituents that he thought sanctions should have been given up long before. 'The government have now reached the same conclusion and I shall certainly support them when the issue is raised in the House of Commons.' So he did, by voting for them against Attlee's censure. Prudently, however, he did not speak in the debate. Even with a three-line Whip in force, two Conservative MPs joined the Liberal and Labour members in supporting Attlee. They were enthusiasts for collective security, and both of them might be won to Churchill's view that the humiliation of the League came from 'the improvident neglect of our defensive strength in years when every other great nation is arming steadily and resolutely.' They were Vyvyan Adams and Harold Macmillan.

In superb, brilliant speeches Lloyd George offered the most effective opposition to the government. Eden gave the best defence. In the same speech he confirmed that the Rhineland crisis had been smothered and reduced to futile talk. 'Ever since the events of 7th March we have sought to rebuild,' and 'I believe that nothing less, if I may say so, than a European settlement and appeasement should be our aim.' If Germany could make it clear that the European situation could only 'be modified by free negotiations and agreements', all might be well.

As for the Rhineland crisis, there were 'elements in the present situation which would enable us to attempt to conclude a permanent settlement based on the disappearance of the demilitarised zone'. Eden helped to make appeasement respectable. Baldwin's pious uplift made a contribution. Paradoxically, over Abyssinia, Neville Chamberlain added soothing reassurance by appearing to be more emphatic in hostility to League sanctions against Italy than Eden. Eden, by contrast, seemed a loyal friend of collective security.[2]

In midsummer 1936 Duff Cooper, then War Minister, spoke in Paris. His speech set off a brief flurry of controversy which illustrated two Churchillian attitudes to the foreign policy of that time and their limitations. Duff Cooper gave stress to the need for Anglo-French co-operation and understanding. Some League enthusiasts interpreted it as a call for an Anglo-French alliance and therefore a return to discredited pre-1914 politics. Attlee, for the Labour Party, forced a Commons debate. He pointed out, correctly, that the government claimed that they desired 'to carry out the principle of the League of Nations and collective security'. He went on to warn that 'any suggestion of an alliance of this kind – an alliance in which one country is bound to another, right or wrong, by some overwhelming necessity – is contrary to the spirit of the League of Nations, is contrary to the Covenant'.

Churchill replied by referring to the Anglo-French staff talks agreed on in March – 'the grave, sombre meeting of technical experts' – and he regretted any doubt raised about 'what, I think, is the growing consensus of opinion throughout the House as to the general direction in which we should advance'. Churchill continued to be deluded by the staff talks, whose purpose was only to persuade people like him, and the relevant sections of French opinion, to believe that the British government were ready to do something to counteract the remilitarization of the Rhineland. In fact the talks had no serious military purpose at all. Churchill had a longer way to go than he seemed to imagine to persuade the government, or the Labour and Liberal parties, that commitment to the League should mean the creation of an effective anti-German coalition. At this stage Churchill did not stress his opposition to the government's foreign policy relating to 'the appeasement of the situation in Europe', to use Baldwin's words of 23 June.[3]

Churchill, indeed, kept silent in the next debate on foreign policy, though he was in the House to vote for the government and to speak briefly (just before 1 a.m.) on Lords amendments to the Sunday Trading Bill. The week before, however, he spoke on defence. He criticized the new Minister for Co-ordination of Defence – not personally, for after all Inskip could 'put up an excellent defence for the Government, especially when . . . the "knock-about" element is required'. It was rather that he had far more to do than any person, without the backing of a department of civil servants (Inskip had only one or two assistants), could be expected to do: 'he has allowed himself to become the innocent victim of responsibilities so strangely, so inharmoniously, so perversely grouped, endowed with powers so cribbed and restricted, that no one, not even Napoleon himself, would be able to discharge them with satisfaction'. He had to work out strategy and how to produce weapons. A minister of supply was needed. Churchill concluded with a restatement, in one protracted sentence, of his theme that more weapons needed to be made more quickly:

> All I ask is that the intermediate stage between ordinary
> peacetime and actual war should be recognised; that a state
> of emergency preparations should be proclaimed, and that
> the whole spirit and atmosphere of our rearmament should
> be raised to a high pitch, and that we should lay aside a
> good deal of the comfort and smoothness of our ordinary
> life, that we should not hesitate to make an inroad into our
> industry, and that we should endeavour to make the most

strenuous efforts in our power to execute the programme
that the Government have in mind at such pace as would
make them relevant to the ever-growing dangers that gather
round us.

Neville Chamberlain, for the government, responded in his
irritable, resentful way, contrasting with the smoothly conciliatory manner of Baldwin, and noted that Churchill 'succeeded,
as he always will, in arousing cheers and laughter' by his attack
on the co-ordination of defence. A more sympathetic reaction
came from one of the wildest League enthusiasts, the Liberal
Geoffrey Mander, who actually suggested that recruitment for
the army would be helped if 'it were made clear that the services
of the army are required solely for support of the collective
system of the League of Nations and would not be used for any
other purpose'. Mander supported Churchill: 'We all know that
Germany is the Power that is threatening the independence of
countries all over Europe. I do not think that the views expressed
by the Right Hon Member for Epping (Mr Churchill) on the
danger of the menace are in the least bit exaggerated.'[4]

These were the Churchillian themes in 1936: using support
for collective security to extend support for rearmament and
calling for some regulation of industry to shift some production
from civilian to military purposes. From early in that year
Churchill contemplated the notion of some grand rally, some
great public meeting, in support of arms for collective security.
He asked Walter Citrine, the general secretary of the Trades
Union Congress, to take the lead. Here would be a sign of the
wide range of opinions, from the left wing (though Citrine was
emphatically not an 'extremist') through to the Conservative
right, which he could still claim to represent. Churchill himself
forced the great rally in support of rearmament to be postponed
until late 1936: before then arms for the League meant action to
support Abyssinian resistance to Italy, which he did not at all

wish to advocate.[5] Soon other disagreements and diversions replaced those over Abyssinia. One continued for three years – the Spanish Civil War; the other presented brief but intense excitement – the King's desire to marry a divorcee.

Churchill and Neville Chamberlain first took up their roles as the great controversialists, the protagonists of increasingly divergent responses to Hitler, in the debate over Chamberlain's 1936 budget. Should the state insist on limits on civilian production in order to release resources for rearmament? Churchill pointed out that Inskip, a few days after taking the office of coordinator of defence, had 'explained that he was working under peace conditions'. Would this permit enough weapons to be produced: could 'the gun plants and the steel plants and, above all, the aeroplane factories' fulfil the need in time? Chamberlain agreed that Churchill's demand would 'speed up the programme [of rearmament] very materially', but then he set out some contrary arguments. If industries were diverted and labour controlled, the 'principal difficulties ... will be in getting the kind of labour which will be necessary for the more skilled operations and getting the labour where it is wanted'. There would be benefits in arranging this. However,

> it would mean that you would have to cease from proceeding with a great deal of commercial and industrial work ...
> orders which would have to be cancelled would go elsewhere, and in the future you might not easily regain the markets which we had set aside ... we do not think that the situation has arrived at that point, which would justify the risks necessarily associated with such a step.

In 1937, 1938 and 1939 Chamberlain became less and less inclined to take 'risks'. In 1936 Chamberlain and Churchill had more in common than later on. At the 1935 general election Chamberlain had seemed readier for rearmament than many other Cabinet ministers, and in early 1936, when the rearmament programme was discussed by ministers, Chamberlain, supported by Eden, had come out in favour of giving priority to the creation of a force of bombers to threaten direct attack on Germany and so deter German attacks; Churchill felt the same. In his budget speech Chamberlain referred to his prediction of 1934 – 'we have now finished the story of "Bleak House" and are about to enjoy the first chapter of "Great Expectations"'.[6] Defence spoiled the prospect but, of course, Chamberlain as Chancellor did not wish to throw away his successes.

By the time Churchill delivered his elaborately prepared sentence for the Commons demanding interference with civilian industry, the Cabinet had worked out how to respond to his speeches. The government would accept the idea of a deputation of MPs to set out its thoughts in private to reduce the risks of Churchill's denouncing the government in Parliament, even in secret session as he had suggested. When he replied to Churchill in the Commons, Neville Chamberlain, speaking, he said, for the Prime Minister, announced that the government would receive a deputation.

Action followed: on 28 July 1936 members of the Lords and Commons were received by Baldwin, Lord Halifax and Thomas Inskip. Halifax, the Lord Privy Seal, represented the Lords on the government side – had Swinton, the Air Minister, done so he would necessarily have been joined by the ministers for the navy and army. Neville Chamberlain would also have been there had he not been unwell. None of the deputation, in spite of Churchill's hopes, came from opposition parties. It consisted of thirteen MPs including five former ministers and four others who had held junior office and were privy councillors. Austen Chamberlain was the most senior of these eminent persons and formally led the deputation. There were five peers, including another former minister and two of the very highest service ranks. Among these, however, Churchill dominated. He put more questions and raised more subjects than any other member of the delegation. Duff Cooper, then War Minister, in an official letter called it simply the 'Winston deputation'.[7]

The decisive issue raised by the deputation came from Churchill. He repeated the argument he had put in Parliament. War production had to be given priority over civilian production. An emergency threatened. Unless countered by British strength and by those other countries threatened by Germany, Britain and the Empire might be subjugated or destroyed. Facing these perils was the only way to avoid them. Churchill encapsulated the fundamental question relating to British policy toward Hitler: how severe and how urgent was the threat he presented?

> I plead that whatever is said, action should be taken in the sense of an emergency. I do not at all ask that we should proceed to turn ourselves into a country under war conditions, but I believe that to carry forward our progress of munitions we ought not to hesitate to impinge to a certain percentage – 25 per cent, 30 per cent – upon the ordinary industries of this country and force them and ourselves to that sacrifice at this time.

Then the 'nation would cease to be unresponsive to the national needs' and 'the socialists' might stop voting against military estimates.

Chamberlain drew essential support from Lord Weir. In January 1936 Weir had been brought in to the committee of Cabinet ministers which would make recommendations on what should be done about the first far-reaching and serious rearmament programme. As Air Minister, he had been a colleague of Churchill's at the end of the First World War. He was head of a family engineering works which flourished throughout the twentieth century. Now Weir insisted that the rearmament proposals could not be completed in the time suggested, that is three to five years, without 'semi-war conditions' which 'would necessitate interference with existing civil and export trade'. In the end, the committee noted 'that under Lord Weir's proposals supplies called for in the 3–5 years programmes are to be secured without interference with or reduction of production for civil and export trade'.[8] This decision faced Inskip when he came into office to co-ordinate defence. In April he told the Cabinet that some manufacturers had asked him whether they should give priority to defence orders over exports and domestic production and 'he had reserved his position'. After Churchill's remarks in Parliament, Inskip declared that he might have to ask for priority for defence orders over those 'for home and foreign account'. Chamberlain referred him to his reply to Churchill in the budget debate. In May Churchill wrote directly to Weir accusing him of 'lending all your reputation to keeping the country in a state of comfortable peace routine'. Weir urged the danger of 'grave effects and dislocations'.

Churchill's remarks at the meeting with the deputation produced a characteristic reply from Baldwin; by contrast to Churchill's showpieces he affected stupidity and slowness of intellect:

> We have had in our minds, very present to our minds, the point, I think, [that] has been latent in a good many observations that have been made, could we do better if we were to turn over, Mr Churchill did not say definitely to war conditions, but to some kind of half-way house? That is a question which I have thought about a good deal and mainly discussed with the Chancellor of the Exchequer [Neville Chamberlain]; it touches him so closely, and we have always felt up to now, we have felt to do that might throw back the ordinary trade of the country perhaps for many years. It has never been done in peace-time: throw it back for many years and damage very seriously at a time when we might want all our credit, the credit of the country. If the emergency were such as obviously demanded it, of course, it would have to be done, and I am

not afraid of emergency powers. I am not afraid of anything
if it has to be done.[9]

Baldwin exposed the fundamental division between Churchill
and the government: how overwhelming was the emergency
facing Britain?

The deputation had to be taken seriously. The distinction
and prestige of its members, though none was then in office,
meant that effective answers had to be given to their complaints.
Government offices prepared comments, pledges or refutations.
Churchill's demand came before the Board of Trade and the
Treasury, the dominant force of British political life, then headed
by the most important Minister of the 1930s, Neville Chamberlain. The Admiralty, the War Office and the Air Ministry, too,
prepared briefs for their political heads to enable them to deal
with the worries of the deputation. The usual British pattern
came out. Departments prepared arguments for the ministers to
enable them to silence distracting outsiders. Sir Maurice Hankey, that ubiquitous and experienced civil servant, organized
counter-strokes to support the opinions the Cabinet had turned
into policies. Some of the replies justified Churchill's unease.
The War Office noted that 'We have to work, in our negotiations with the Trade [providing supplies for the army], on the
principles of "business as usual" and the Trade are very busy
with the normal orders. As far as possible we are even trying to
meet foreign orders for munitions in order to provide for the
future healthy state of the armament industry and Foreign
Trade. These factors are naturally a handicap to progress.' The
Admiralty, backed by large and effective naval shipyards and
the British shipbuilding industry, showed complacency. Even the
Air Ministry accepted:

the policy of the Government that the deficiencies of the
Defence Forces should be made up with the least possible
interference with the export trade of the country ... the

Air Ministry regard as sound policy that our hold on the export markets of the world should be maintained as far as possible in order that should the demands of the RAF abate even temporarily the aircraft industry may be in a position to avert a corresponding diminution in work.

The chief civil servant at the Board of Trade, Sir Horace Hamilton, sent to Sir Richard Hopkins, one of two knights who dominated 'Treasury thinking', communications showing little understanding of the Churchillian conviction of the urgency of armaments. The statistical department of the Board of Trade argued, absurdly, that Churchill's demand would remove from peace production some two million persons. Two alternatives would follow: 'either a much reduced standard of living or a heavy adverse balance of payments ... loss of confidence in sterling would ensue, with its inevitable consequences not only on the trade of this country but on the prospects of an increase in world trade, which at the present time are brighter than for many years'.[10] Written less than three years before the outbreak of the Second World War, this conclusion implies inappropriate priorities. The acting chief industrial adviser, L. Browett, drafted a note for Hamilton to send to the Treasury. Again he caricatured Churchill's proposals which he said, were:

> put forward on the basis that whatever Germany has in the way of air forces, bombs, anti-aircraft defence, guns, shell, ships, tanks, machine guns, etc. etc., this country must have as much and more. If his conception of the German preparations is correct, it would mean that to carry out his programme here, the country would have to go over completely to war conditions and become, as the saying is, an 'armed camp'. This would mean that ordinary trade, whether home or export, would be completely disorganised and largely come to an end. It would also follow that the Budget would become hopelessly unbalanced.

Then, at last, the writer threw in an effective and relevant argument: 'financial power – an important and indeed vital weapon in a time of emergency – would have to be thrown in with the rest to put the country in the state of preparedness demanded by Mr Churchill'.[11]

Within the Treasury, R. G. Hawtrey, a serious economist, took a sensible view: Churchill was suggesting 'the maximum practicable (or useful)' diversion of industry and 'too much stress ought not to be laid on Mr Churchill's 25 to 30 per cent'. Hawtrey thought 'it depends upon the adaptability of the factors of production, plant, labour, skilled and unskilled, and management'. He had a tentative solution for an increase in imports and fall in exports: 'suspension of external investment along with some realisation of our existing foreign investments, would have to be relied on to fill the gap'. Sir Richard Hopkins, at the head of Supply, put forward a political view. Churchill's proposal 'is to assume a degree of forbearance on the part of the community which would only be forthcoming in the face of grave and imminent emergency'. Edward Bridges, soon to depart from the Treasury and to succeed Hankey as Cabinet Secretary, thought Churchill wanted the government to insist that there already existed a grave and imminent emergency. It is 'difficult to foretell how far it is possible to allow the defence industry programme to impinge on the skilled engineering industry without giving rise to serious economic consequences'. But he declared himself 'rather perturbed by the present tendency of the defence departments to proceed with the greatest possible haste': they 'should not let in the clutch too fiercely'.

Early in November the Treasury set out its collective view on Churchill's idea in a note for Samuel Hoare to use in the debate on defence that month. Both Sir F. Phillips, in charge of Finance, and Sir Richard Hopkins, overlooking Supply, made amendments and then approved it. Phillips asked for it to be sent to Neville Chamberlain. The central point was that a 'heavy decline in our exports at a time when imports are necessarily heavy would much weaken our financial strength, the latter being at present our own decisive advantage'. Inskip circulated a paper to the Cabinet at the end of October 1936 which set out the proposition that he was to put before the Cabinet again at the end of 1937 in more elegant phraseology:

> It is true that the extent of our resources imposes limitations upon the size of the defence programme which we are able to undertake. This is only one aspect of the matter. Seen in its true perspective, the maintenance of our economic stability would more accurately be described as an essential element in our defensive strength; one which can properly be regarded as a fourth arm in defence, alongside the three Defence services, without which purely military effort would be of no avail.[12]

Churchill intended to preserve peace by preparing for war. By this time, the summer of 1936, more and more people agreed with him, including, however reluctantly, Chamberlain and even Baldwin. Churchill wanted higher priority to be given to the equipping of the armed services. In considering this debate it should always be remembered that no one expected the defeat of France in 1940 and the desperate hazards that resulted for Britain. They both forced, and made possible, dependence on the United States. In the 1930s the independence of Britain and the Empire was an object taken for granted. If Britain went to war with Germany, France, it was assumed (at least before late 1938), would be in it. Indeed, for the British government then, the problem was that encouraging France to believe that Britain would certainly be at its side in a war with Germany might lead it to provoke avoidable or unnecessary conflicts. Thus the Rhineland crisis of March 1936 has been for the British government a matter of restraining France.

In effect, the British, including Churchill, supposed that

British power would be used as decided by Britain. Churchill advocated 'collective security under the League of Nations'. His purpose was to increase support for British rearmament. Supporters of collective security unfortunately had treated it as a substitute for British armed strength. Churchill wanted to convert these people to the belief that British armed strength would make war less likely rather than make it more likely by encouraging an arms race. Collective security certainly meant the involvement of France. That implied a long war in which British creditworthiness was critical. A strong pound in peacetime, based on limits to government spending and the maintenance of a comfortable balance of payments, would make foreign banks – especially, what mattered most, American banks – feel that loans to the United Kingdom were safe.

In 1936, then, this counter to Churchill's rearmament doctrine made sense; things changed a year later when the new Prime Minister, Neville Chamberlain, began more and more to feel that there were easier, and more congenial, ways of preventing war than preparing for it.

In the midst of these debates the more long-lasting, if the less intense, of the distractions broke forth. On 18 July 1936 army officers set off risings to seize power from the Republican government in Spain, which had come to office after the narrow electoral victory of the centre-left (popular front) in February. Riots and repression dominated Spanish political life in the 1930s. From 1934 to 1936 a right-wing government had been able to use the army to maintain order. This process reached its climax when General Franco crushed the 'workers' alliance' led by miners in Asturias by using artillery and bombing. Now, in 1936, industrial workers and landless agricultural labourers might hope for reform. Rhetorically, a section of the Socialist Party, led by Largo Caballero, called for revolution, while anarchists, far more numerous in Spain than anywhere else in the world, demanded free voluntary collaboration among equals to improve social conditions. Against these people there arose a formidable coalition of large landowners, the Church, the army and the Civil Guard, disturbed by the hostility towards them of the left, often supported by small peasant proprietors who were also alarmed by threats to property. After the electoral victory of the popular front, workers and the rural poor sometimes sought to accelerate reform by violent demonstrations or seizures of property. On the right the Falange, the fascist movement, one more reliably concerned to defend existing social hierarchies than the German Nazis, grew in numbers and encouraged violence by attacks on Socialists and anarchists and the disorderly poor.

The military expected to seize power without much difficulty. Instead the government, hesitantly, handed out arms to hastily formed militias to support the minority of the army who remained loyal and the Republican assault guards. Even so, for some months the rebels seemed likely to win and only by the end of 1936 was it evident that a civil war, potentially protracted, had begun. Unease in Britain first appeared when Mussolini and Hitler gave moral and material support to the rebels. Even so, if Franco won quickly his debts to them would not be overwhelming. The military coup could seem an interesting outside event, not something to worry about. As time went on that changed. In Britain there were two dominant interpretations of the war in Spain. One was that it was fascism in revolt against bolshevism. The other was that it was fascism against liberal democracy: evil in rebellion against virtue. These opposed interpretations developed within a few days, by the end of July 1936. The latter opinion became more and more prominent among those, a growing number, who cared at all.[13]

Unfortunately Churchill insisted that it was fascism fighting bolshevism. This was when he was trying to win supporters of the League to back his demand for British rearmament. However, League supporters tended more and more to support the Spanish government as the defenders of freedom and democracy against Franco. On 10 August Churchill gave his version of the war in Spain to readers of the *Evening Standard*: 'Fascism confronts Communism'. So, 'whoever wins in Spain, freedom and free democracy must be the losers. A revivified Fascist Spain in closest sympathy with Italy and Germany is one kind of disaster. A communist Spain spreading its snaky tentacles through Portugal and France is another, and many will think the worse.' In November Churchill told MPs of his surprise that Soviet Russia, threatened by both Japan and Germany, should have acted with 'such insensate folly' as to set off war in Spain. 'Why, but for Russian Communist propaganda and intrigues which for more than six months racked Spain before the outbreak, the Spanish horror need never have occurred. Spain might be a constitutional republic, adjusting its internal stresses by ordinary Parliamentary processes.' (Ivan Maisky, the Soviet ambassador in London, later wrote to correct him.) But, Churchill went on, there were hopeful developments taking place in Russia. Instead of the foolish conduct of fomenting revolution, Russia might play a part in preserving peace. Meanwhile, 'we must use our full strength and influence to rebuild the League of Nations, to make it strong enough to hold a potential aggressor in restraint by armed strength, and thereafter to labour faithfully to mitigate just and real grievances which, if unremedied, are likely to lead to a renewal of the quarrels, the crimes and the miseries of mankind'.[14] First, then, strength to resist Hitler, then appeasement.

One week later Churchill spoke to the Commons again. He exposed all his main preoccupations. His speech took an hour and was another of his great performances. It was part of the debate on the address of thanks for the King's speech opening Parliament. Churchill had joined with others to put on the paper the same amendment to the address as they had submitted two years before expressing disquiet over the feebleness of British rearmament. Two years on and Germany had rearmed in flagrant disregard of the treaties, the Rhineland was occupied and fortified and, under the Anglo-German naval agreement, Germany was building a large new submarine fleet. For the moment, Britain and France together might be stronger than Germany. But British and French efforts would in about a year prove insufficient to maintain that balance of force. So Britain and France should:

> gather round them all the elements of collective security . . . which can be assembled on the basis of the Covenant of the League of Nations. Thus I hope we may succeed again in achieving a position of superior force and then will be the time not to repeat the folly which we committed when we were all-powerful and supreme, but to invite Germany to make a common cause with us in assuaging the griefs of Europe and opening a new door to peace and disarmament.

Armed strength and a defensive League had to come before appeasement. Once more Churchill spoke of Baldwin's pledge of March 1934 that parity would be secured with any air force within striking distance of this country. Yet delay and procrastination continued: 'even after the Government had realised that a world of armed and arming menace was springing up around them, no measures were taken for a long time equal to the situation or to make up for the years that were lost'.

Churchill then mocked ministers' declarations that if necessary they would accept interference and controls. He quoted Inskip's 'the decision is not final' and Samuel Hoare, as First Lord of the Admiralty, claiming that the government were 'always reviewing the position. Everything, he assured us "is entirely fluid".' Unfairly, but powerfully, Churchill denounced these claims. The government, he declared, 'go on in strange paradox, decided only to be undecided, resolved to be irresolute, adamant for drift, solid for fluidity, all powerful to be impotent. So we go on preparing those months and years – precious, perhaps vital to the greatness of Britain – for the locusts to eat. They will say to me "a minister of supply is not necessary, for all is going well". I deny it.'

Baldwin, in reply, 'put before the whole House my own views with an appalling frankness'. Without a general election he had no 'mandate' for rearmament, but if he had tried an election earlier than he did, which was in the autumn of 1935, the Conservatives might have lost it. 'Supposing I had gone to the country and said that Germany was rearming and that we must rearm. Does anybody think that this pacific democracy would have rallied to that cry at that moment? I cannot think of anything that would have made the loss of the election from my point of view more certain.' Baldwin's speech clearly refers to the timing of the general election, whatever later historians may suggest. He pointed to the Fulham by-election in the autumn of 1933. Churchill's opinion diverged. For him it was a question of leadership. Baldwin should have been pointing the way rather than collecting votes for an election and, Churchill later claimed in his memoirs, so putting party before country. At the time, Churchill scored points against Baldwin and his appalling frankness.[15] His speeches always showed concern to accelerate and increase rearmament. With that constant theme he more and more stressed Anglo-French co-operation, extended by some sort of defensive grouping under the League.

His thoughts on rearmament were well informed and supported by detailed analysis, occasionally foolish, sometimes wise but always careful. Thoughts on foreign policy, the League and so forth were more nebulous and sometimes merely the incantation of popular slogans. One principle however stood out – concentration on the German threat; Italy and Japan should be encouraged to be friends. Churchill sought to get 'peace' societies to support arming Britain to stop aggressors. After Italian aggression in east Africa ceased to be the main problem, it seemed easier for Churchill to do this – especially when, for a few months in 1936, the idea of persuading all countries not to intervene in Spain won general support.

In October that year Churchill revived the plan of a great public meeting to rally cross-party support for armaments. All the groups with which Churchill had associated himself, the Anti-Nazi League, the Focus, the Peace with Freedom movement and the New Commonwealth Society, of which Churchill was president, would come together under the aegis of the League of Nations Union. Sir Walter Citrine, Churchill insisted, should take the chair. He was general secretary of the Trades Union Congress, and therefore an important member of the National Council of Labour and of the Labour Party national executive, and he was prominent at Labour Party meetings as well as at those of the TUC. With Ernest Bevin, chairman of the General Council of the TUC, he stood for many of Churchill's views – rearmament and foreign allies, and hostility to the communists. Citrine and Bevin, moreover, though opposed to Franco, were less passionate in their support of the Spanish Republican government than some trade unionists. (This was especially true, as it happens, of the Amalgamated Engineering Union, which was critical for rearmament and among whose members workers in aircraft factories were particularly concerned to help the Spanish government.) Citrine and Bevin also aroused the hostility of the AEU through their attitudes to the privileges of skilled workers. For Churchill any sort of trade unionists were of value, since he had the reputation, partly from legend, partly from the general strike of 1926, of being bitterly hostile to them. Indeed, he felt the lower classes in their 'cottage homes' should be carefully protected and looked after but should be deferential to their betters. Citrine effectively fitted Churchill's expectations. Alfred Wall also spoke at the Albert Hall demonstration at the beginning of December 1936; Churchill described him as 'a very authoritative trade unionist and a model of common sense'. Then there was Violet Bonham-

Carter, Asquith's daughter and a loyal friend of Churchill's, who represented the Liberals. Churchill could speak for the right-wing Conservatives. Lord Lytton gave authentic League of Nations Union support.[16]

This grand event, carefully prepared, proved a flop. Every speaker took it for granted, one report noted, that the entire audience was in sympathy. 'It was not . . . the none too frequent applause came generally from scattered individuals.' Large numbers of the 'peace army' were present: those who could not bring themselves to accept warlike preparation. Churchill, however, was 'in excellent form'. He ended his speech with rational relevance: 'one fifth part of the effort necessary to win a war will stop a war'. The meeting should have attracted attention and publicity to Churchill's pleas for the League, by which he meant an anti-German coalition (more easily called for than achieved) of Britain, France, Poland, Rumania, Yugoslavia, Czechoslovakia and Russia and, above all, enlarged and accelerated rearmament. It did not attract attention because the amorous problems of the new King, Edward VIII, his love for a twice-married middle-aged American, seemed more urgently important and exciting. The great meeting was on Thursday, the King's troubles became public on Tuesday. The Bishop of Bradford revealed what had been gossiped about by those who knew what was in the foreign press, by those who took part in secretive conclaves of Cabinet ministers and by leading politicians including the leaders of the Liberal and Labour parties, Citrine for the TUC and Churchill. Churchill's Albert Hall production became news of small significance compared with the King's romance. *The Times* gave the Albert Hall meeting muted coverage; the *Evening Standard* left it out; the *Manchester Guardian* eliminated everything but the King from its main newspage, apart from one column from Neville Cardus on the impending Test Match in Brisbane between Australia and England – Churchill and the League of Nations it relegated to a less important page, itself dominated by the 'constitutional crisis'. The same paper reported, from Paris, dismay that Britain 'should virtually have become paralysed as a factor in world affairs'.[17]

Churchill cared about the King, indeed, seems to have cared for the King. It was his duty, he noisily believed, to protect and defend the King. What that meant was keeping him on the throne whatever he decided to do about Mrs Simpson. If the King did not insist on marrying her, that would be best, because of possible objections at home and in the Empire. If he did insist, then let there be a morganatic marriage, in which Wallis Simpson would be a 'consort' without ever actually becoming queen. The King should remain king. Churchill inclined to believe that public opinion shared his strongly held convictions and would support him if the issues were not fudged, for instance, by party managers. In particular, he imagined, wrongly, that he could better assess opinion than could Baldwin. Citrine found it difficult at the Albert Hall assembly to prevent Churchill from raising the issue in his speech. That week Churchill insisted twice in the House of Commons that the King should not be forced into a quick decision and that Parliament should be able to consider any eventual outcome before it was finally determined. That weekend he issued a long statement, printed in the newspapers. The suspicion developed that he was seeking again to turn Baldwin out and to force a general election on whether or not the King could marry without abdicating the throne. That would require Churchill to be invited to form a government. These were no more than suspicions, without solid evidence, but they helped to explain the events of Monday 7 December 1936.

That day Churchill presided over a lunch given by the Anglo-French luncheon club with Paul Reynaud as guest of honour. Reynaud had recently become a minister and would take charge of Finance in November 1938. Later, he would be

the last Prime Minister of the Third Republic in March–June
1940. Churchill gave the toast. 'The sympathies of every man
and woman, not only in England, but I believe in all the friendly
nations of Europe, will go out to a sovereign who is under most
grievous stresses.' There were, it was reported, murmurs of 'God
bless him' from every side. Thus fortified, Churchill went to the
House of Commons. In a reply to a question of Attlee's, Baldwin
had described his handling of the royal predicament; he was
obviously doing everything to avoid divisive controversy at home
or in the Empire, especially, of course, in Canada, South Africa,
Australia and New Zealand. Calm and order prevailed; Baldwin's brief narrative reflected and emphasized his own sympathetic tact. Churchill rose and, for the third time, asked for an
assurance that 'no irrevocable step—' only to be interrupted
with cries of 'speech' in protest against his use of question time
and there were direct cries of 'No!' and 'Sit down!' The Speaker
ordered Churchill to 'confine what he has to say to a simple
question'. Churchill pressed on amid cries of 'Order!' to ask for
'no irrevocable decision', and the Speaker intervened again to
silence him since he 'insists on going beyond a simple question'.
Churchill appeared 'pale and patently taken aback'. One
observer of the scene asserted that Churchill had 'experienced
the most striking rebuff of modern parliamentary history',
another that he had 'probably never been so drastically rebuffed
in his political life'. A close associate of Baldwin's remarked later
that he had overheard Churchill gloomily declaring that 'his
political career was finished'. If true, Churchill quickly shrugged
off this gloom. The report the French embassy telegraphed to
Paris the next morning seems more likely to be accurate.
Churchill had faced protests from every part of the House, the
French ambassador in London reported. 'Visibly very discouraged, he declared to one of his friends that he would not
intervene again in any way in this debate.'[18]

Later that day, indeed, Churchill addressed the 1922

Committee of Conservative MPs on defence and said nothing about Edward VIII and Mrs Simpson. His careful and well-ordered remarks were fully reported in a paper sent to Inskip. Churchill discussed in turn the state of the three services. About the navy he was complacent: 'we could pride ourselves on having a fleet which was well prepared and well equipped'. Battleships, he claimed, would be able to beat off aerial attack: the Second World War later showed this to be a questionable claim. On the army, he considered the possibility of enemy airborne invasion and urged the creation of strong mobile units (these would certainly have been reassuring in the unexpected situation of the summer of 1936). Correctly, he pointed out that Britain had fallen behind in the quality of armoured fighting vehicles.

But Churchill paid most attention to the air force. By this time, the end of 1936, statements of British weakness in the air compared with Germany had become uncontroversial. French airfields would help. This was one of the reasons why it was vital to be close friends with France: a more controversial point since, to many at the time, that might make agreement with Germany less likely. Those present at this meeting, and there was a large attendance of MPs, thought it a good speech and it was 'well received'. An MP who reported the occasion noted his own opinion that there were many people who felt disturbed by the disparity of British and German air power. On this single day, therefore, Churchill had shown how he could be totally insensitive to the beliefs of his audience and how he could, on the other hand, formulate, express and emphasize their notions.[19] Much of his audience will have been present both in the Commons when he seemed incredibly foolish and, later on, at the 1922 Committee when he seemed perceptive and well informed.

At the end of the week Baldwin announced to the Commons his recommended solution to the problem of the King: either he must give up marriage to Wallis Simpson or he must renounce the throne. At last Churchill accepted and supported Baldwin's decorous dealings and so at last fell in with the overwhelming judgement of MPs of all parties. After an interval of more than an hour for the House to think about Baldwin's recommendation, Attlee spoke for the Labour Party, Sinclair for the Liberals and then Churchill, speaking, as so often, as a political force in his own right. As soon as his intention became clear, to support Baldwin, there was cheering and his brief speech was punctuated by 'hear hears' and more cheers. As he ended 'loud cheers' broke out.[20] All was forgiven – but not forgotten. 'Edward VIII' confirmed 'India': Churchill could not be counted on for loyalty to his party leader. Baldwin's style meant he would feel more resentment than he showed. Yet as a minister Churchill would have fitted more easily into a Baldwin Cabinet than into one of Baldwin's successor, Neville Chamberlain. Chamberlain interfered far more obviously and energetically than Baldwin in the conduct of ministers.

CHAPTER SEVEN

'Appeasement'

CHURCHILL'S FIRST SPEECH in 1937 followed an invitation to address the Leeds Chamber of Commerce. The tastes of Leeds men of trade seem to have been eclectic. Churchill's invitation to Leeds came after the belated withdrawal of Ribbentrop, then German ambassador in London. Ribbentrop acted as a dedicated Nazi, was close to Hitler and had already won for himself contemptuous dislike in London. Like Churchill he had a high opinion of himself and like Churchill could be decidedly self-centred. His talents, however, were infinitesimally small compared with Churchill's. Churchill was always worth listening to and often amusing; Ribbentrop was neither. The Leeds Chamber of Commerce, when Ribbentrop claimed enforced absence, welcomed instead the most prominent advocate of collective resistance to German expansion. Churchill stood in for the ambassador, who, Hitler had hoped, would have confirmed what the Führer thought to be implied by the Anglo-German naval agreement of 1935 – British abandonment of eastern Europe to Germany. Churchill received 'vehement appeals' and betook himself to Leeds, where a 'record attendance' at the annual dinner was expected. Many more, he was told, had asked to be present at the dinner on 25 January than had done so for Ribbentrop.

One of the MPs for the City of London, another guest, whose urgings may explain Churchill's presence, spoke first. Then Churchill told the Leeds worthies that he detested both fascists and communists. He would shun both. Britain had to arm and be strong and join with other countries in the League, which 'weaves together all forces of peace in the world'.[1] These positions represented problems for 1937. Now the Soviet Union played a prominent part in the League. Now communists stood for anti-fascism. Now Moscow directed them to work with anyone who would fight fascism. That could include liberal capitalists and even those people, until recently denounced as social fascists, who claimed socialism to be possible without 'proleterian revolution'. Communists should help to create 'popular fronts' by working with leaders of anti-fascist groups instead of seeking to destroy their parties. Churchill regarded 'popular fronts' with suspicion. Like most British conservatives he had viewed with dismay the electoral success in France of Léon Blum's 'popular front' of radicals, socialists and communists. Before long, however, he was won over by Blum's obvious concern to maintain and expand French military strength. Early in 1937 he praised Blum's government as 'composed of very able men' which had proved capable of 'rallying the whole strength of France to the cause of National defence'. He even gave a grudging, tentative tribute to French communists who had 'placed many restraints upon themselves' in the interests of France 'as the opponents of German Nazism'.[2]

By contrast, Churchill had certainly not become reconciled to the popular-front government in Spain. General Franco had by now created in rebel-held Spain a respectable military–clerical dictatorship: murderous repression was more discreetly carried out there than it was by the revolutionary supporters of the government. As Churchill put it, 'peace and order reign over the broad areas of Nationalist Spain and industry and agriculture pursue their course. Trains run. Food and petrol can be freely purchased,' though he accepted that 'prompt and ruthless' killings maintained this orderly calm.

Early in 1937 Cabinet ministers met to discuss a suggestion from Eden and the Foreign Office to make 'non-intervention' a reality rather than a disreputable fraud. Eden's memorandum suggested that whatever Hitler and Mussolini wanted could not be in British interests: 'the character of the future Government of Spain has now become less important to the peace of Europe than that the dictators should not be victorious in that country . . . Germany and Italy have made it clear to the world that the object of these Powers is to secure General Franco's victory whether or not it represents the will of the Spanish people.' Eden suggested that the powers allegedly committed to 'non-intervention', among whom Italy, Germany and the Soviet Union were vigorously intervening, should be told that the Royal Navy would be made available to enforce non-intervention and so compel these countries either to stop intervening or to give up the pretence of support for 'non-intervention'. The Cabinet turned him down. Hoare, as head of the Admiralty, led the opposition. He began by claiming that 'we were getting near a situation where, as a nation, we were trying to stop General Franco from winning. That was the desire of the Parliamentary Parties of the Left; but there were others, including perhaps some members of the Cabinet, who were very anxious that the Soviets should not win in Spain.'[3] Churchill, at that time, was among the most 'anxious'.

Churchill believed that if a Spain ruled by Franco should emerge from the civil war it would not damage British interests because of the power of the British navy, especially if working with the French navy. No one ever contemplated the disaster of 1940, when France fell under German control. Churchill insisted that the Spaniards would display ingratitude to their German and Italian helpers and would assert defiant independence, and that, in any case, Anglo-French naval strength and the long, exposed Spanish coastline would leave little alternative. So it would be quite safe to allow the 'Reds' to be defeated. Churchill's attitude to Spain did not advance the causes he had at heart. Though indifference to the Spanish conflict existed, those who cared about Spain were usually the sort of people whose support for rearmament and a League of allies against aggression Churchill was hoping for. Overwhelmingly they believed that the Spanish government, in resisting Franco, was defending freedom and democratic government against the forces of fascism and tyranny. Churchill narrowed the range of his appeal; his posture emphasized his upper-class conservatism. He may have been misled by his contacts with Citrine and Bevin, both of them eminent trade unionists who regarded communists with the highest suspicion. Churchill probably did not grasp that the Amalgamated Engineering Union, the most important for arms production, disliked Citrine and Bevin and the Trades Union Congress and especially Bevin's Transport and General Workers Union, which had no objection to limiting the privileges of the skilled workers of the AEU. This sort of thing was not a special interest of Churchill's, yet the AEU used the government's support for non-intervention as a reason, or excuse, for refusing to co-operate in providing arms for a reactionary pro-fascist British government.[4]

Another problem created by Churchill's attitude to the war in Spain is hypothetical and cannot be established by documentary evidence. In 1936, 1937 and early 1938 Soviet foreign policy involved supporting collective security and working with any anti-fascist forces: hence the support given by national communist parties to 'popular front' governments. An alternative policy remained available and contacts kept it alive in case it seemed best to pursue it. That was to build up Soviet military strength and meanwhile keep out of war by tolerating or even encouraging German expansion elsewhere. It culminated in the Nazi–Soviet pact of 1939. There are signs of discontent in Moscow with British and French attitudes to Spain, even before the Munich agreement of September 1938 gave strong grounds for mistrust. Churchill's attitude to Spain may have suggested that even the most vigorous and eloquent opponent of Nazi Germany could not be counted on as a reliable 'anti-fascist'.

Paradoxically, Churchill had not reconciled his understandable anti-communist emotions with the role he ascribed to Stalin's Soviet Union in the anti-German alliance that he wished to develop from 'collective security'. He tended, as usual in Britain, to take it for granted that Hitler's Germany and the Soviet Union could be assumed to be mutually hostile under all circumstances. In consequence, also, he consistently underestimated the difficulties of co-operation between the Soviet Union and the countries on its borders. In retrospect, we may feel that only a determined and completely trustworthy opponent of Nazi Germany had any chance of extracting from Stalin acceptable conditions for such collaboration. Churchill fitted best. Spain did not strengthen his claims.

A day or two after his return from Leeds, Churchill joined in a brief debate started by a private member's motion complaining of the continuing inadequacy of British defences against air attack. Oliver Simmons moved the motion. He was an expert aeronautical engineer, prominent in the Royal Aeronautical Society. Inskip, Minister for Co-ordination of Defence, spoke with several interruptions from Churchill, yet when Churchill himself spoke he treated Inskip with careful courtesy, though of course agreeing with Simmons by noting as usual the failure to come anywhere near the parity with the German air force that Baldwin had promised.[5]

Churchill's 1937 themes – a word he relished – continued from January. They were Spain, rearmament and foreign policy: neutrality in Spain tilting to Franco, rearmament to be maximized; foreign policy based on an anti-German coalition, legitimized by the Covenant of the League. Then, that year, the thought of a possible recall to office came up once more. Now it was Baldwin's retirement in May 1937 and the succession to him as Prime Minister of Neville Chamberlain, who was less inclined than Baldwin to be conciliatory towards socialists, which produced this possibility. Churchill told his wife in February that it would be good to have had the uncertainty cleared up. He said that he did not care.[6] Probably this was as sincere as any ambitious, self-confident politician can ever be about prospects of office. That year Churchill had to work especially hard to finance his indulgent style of life; office would reduce his immediate income. The problem the new Prime Minister, Neville Chamberlain, presented was that he believed in himself; he knew he was right and so, of course, had a duty to carry through his views and decisions. Though far less assertive in dialogue, he was as convinced as Churchill himself of the correctness of his ideas. For the historian, the significance of 1937 is that their policies then diverged.

Churchill, it seems, did not notice in 1937 the extent of this divergence. He was unaware of Chamberlain's growing determination to keep him out of his Cabinet. Thus he could reasonably expect to be called in to help in organizing rearmament. Certainly that year his opposition to the government diminished in ferocity. But there may be no connection. There was one display of better relations with the new Prime Minister that Churchill could not avoid. Austen Chamberlain's death in March 1937 left him clearly the most senior and experienced of Conservative politicians. When he proposed at the end of May Neville Chamberlain's election as Conservative Party leader, just after Chamberlain had succeeded Baldwin as Prime Minister, a formal obligation dominated. Just the same, Churchill did it impressively, and included his own tribute: when the government 'were at length convinced of the urgent need to rearm . . . no-one was more active than Mr Chamberlain . . . in pressing forward the policy of rearmament'.

A more convincing display that Churchill at that time really did support Chamberlain's foreign policy exploded at the Conservative Party conference in Scarborough in October. Complaints were now things of the past. 'At present the Government is making a great effort for rearmament.' Now the government should be supported 'in its policies of defence and world peace'. Ministers 'possess the confidence of the Empire in the sober and resolute policy which they are pursuing – a policy not meddlesome or provocative, and not cravenly indifferent to wrongdoing or to the fate of world causes'. The Conservatives welcomed all this with 'loud and prolonged cheers'. Much of this demonstration was support for Eden. Baldwin had brought Eden into the Cabinet to confirm his government's devotion to those vague entities the 'principles of the League', replacing Samuel Hoare after he had been led astray by Laval. More specifically, Churchill thought Eden (and the government) to have espoused co-operation with France as the basis of European security.

On 25 May Churchill had spoken at a banquet of the New Commonwealth Society in front of a large number of important people and heads of foreign embassies in London. Officials at the French embassy thought one part of his speech should be sent to the Foreign Ministry in Paris. Churchill saw the mutual defensive commitments of Britain and France, reinforced by staff talks, as the principal basis of British security and British existence in the coming years.

The Royal Navy and the French army ranked above all rivals and even the two air forces will probably act in the most efficacious manner to discourage anyone who might be tempted to make war on us. Then this union of French and British democracy, in discouraging aggression, will be powerfully aided by the growing force of Russia. And we see developing and increasing the understanding, the sympathy and the goodwill of the citizens of the United States.

So 'I feel the firm hope that we can cross the dangerous years in which we find ourselves without falling into the abyss and again reach firm ground in the future.' These remarks were greeted by prolonged applause. Yet Churchill did not understand that the undertakings to France and the staff talks were no more than a means of doing nothing, and of persuading the French to do nothing, to counter the German remilitarization of the Rhineland in March 1936. Spain, he said, could be settled by European action and 'a regime that is neither Bolshevist or Nazi set up'. So 'this is no time to abandon the cause of the League of Nations, or to despair of true international comradeship and cooperation'.[7] Here is serious self-deception. Even Churchill failed to grasp at that time that Hitler would choose struggle rather than safety, war not disarmament.

Spain continued to separate Churchill from those who might sympathize with his support for the League and sometimes to separate him from reality. In April 1937 crisis came over the Basque country, where Franco's insistence on a unified, central-ized Spain aroused the opposition to his rebellion there of devout Catholics. Franco declared a blockade of Bilbao; 'non-interven-tion' meant that British ships should not carry weapons or munitions, but what about ships peacefully bringing food into that besieged port? Should the Royal Navy ensure their safe passage into Bilbao? On 7 April Hoare, as First Lord of the Admiralty, told the Cabinet that the blockade was effective. The British navy could force a passage for merchant ships but Hoare successfully argued that this would mean a violent breach of 'non-intervention' in the Spanish civil war. Franco threatened to attack any ships approaching Bilbao, and the Cabinet met in emergency session to decide what to do. Hoare took the lead once again. Franco, he insisted, 'was anxious to avoid antagonising us'. So Franco 'wished to avoid a clash'. The Cabinet decided therefore that, while British ships should not be molested on the high seas, they should be advised not to approach Bilbao 'in view of risks against which it is at present impossible to protect them'.[8] The Basque authorities affirmed that British ships could safely go into the coastal waters approaching Bilbao, whatever Franco claimed. On 14 April Attlee, for the Labour Opposition, moved, in a passionately worded speech, a vote of censure against the government. 'British ships are worried that the Government cannot protect them. They are to all intents and purposes told that they must not go to Bilbao. General Franco may not be able to make an effective blockade but the British Government will oblige him by doing so.'

Sir John Simon pleaded the government's case, Sinclair followed for the Liberals. Then Churchill spoke. 'I refuse to become the partisan of either side. I will not pretend that, if I had to choose between Communism and Nazi-ism, I would choose Communism.' These words did not suggest much comprehension of the civil war in Spain. Later in the speech he produced his own 'appeasement policy'. The closest parallel came later in Samuel Hoare's much denounced 'golden age' speech early in March 1939. If only Britain, France, Italy, Germany and Russia would co-operate, Churchill declared, how much better things would be. He set out his 'daydream' of how this might be contrived. The great powers might abandon non-intervention 'in favour of a policy of combined intervention in Spain'. Secretly they would agree to 'propose to the Spaniards a solution' resulting in a 'hybrid Government' in Spain of people who have not been 'involved in the ferocity of this struggle'. Among the mutually suspicious great powers of Europe this would introduce a 'new theme'. Hence it might be with this common purpose 'that clenched fists would relax into open hands of generous cooperation, that the reign of peace and freedom might come, and that science, instead of being a shameful prisoner in the galleys of slaughter, might pour her wealth abounding into the cottage homes of every land'. Here was Churchill's notion of appeasement. Churchill, of course, voted with the government against Attlee's motion of censure; the Duchess of Atholl and Vyvyan Adams, usually Conservative supporters of Churchill, did not.[9]

On 19 July 1937 another Churchill speech on Spain actually won favourable comments in German newspapers, an uncommon reaction to Churchill under the Nazis. In a debate on foreign policy, Churchill concentrated on Spain. He repeated his explanation of the military revolt:

> safety and order had largely lapsed in Spain ... constitutional parliamentary government was being used as a mere mask, a screen, to cover the swift, stealthy and deadly advance of the extreme Communist or anarchist factions, who saw, according to the regular programme of Communist revolutions, the means by which they could obtain power. It was when confronted with the situation like that that this violent explosion took place in Spain.

By then this was the view of a small minority in Britain. But Churchill's main concern was the mounting of howitzers in places under Franco's control where they could threaten the British naval base at Gibraltar. His conclusion was not that the British should help the government rather than General Franco; it was, on the contrary, that relations with Franco should be closer. A few days later he extracted an answer from Inskip about these guns. First, though, the Speaker claimed that Inskip might not be capable of answering, a point which justified Churchill's comment on the 'serious and grave' responsibilities borne by Inskip as Minister for Co-ordination of Defence, with his departmental support limited in Churchill's words to 'two private secretaries and three lady typists'. Inskip, however, did his best to reassure Churchill about the guns near Gibraltar.[10]

Support for Franco could go too far for Churchill and even

for the Admiralty in London. At the end of August Italian submarines began to attack ships sailing towards government-held Spain: 'pirate' submarines was the name usually employed. One sank a British ship, the SS *Woodford*. Worse still, one fired a torpedo which narrowly missed a British destroyer, HMS *Havock*. The French demanded a conference to work out measures to suppress the 'pirates'. The British agreed, and at Nyon it was decided that British, French – and Italian – warships would patrol the Mediterranean and attack 'pirates'. It proved easy since Mussolini, recognizing that his submarines could not be relied on for correct identification of their targets, called them off even before the Nyon conference began. Churchill expressed pleasure on the 'very considerable achievement' of Eden, the Foreign Secretary, in bringing 'stern and effective measures . . . to bear upon an evil doer, without incurring the risk of war'.[11] Far more than Eden, Churchill thought it worth while to try to restore Anglo-Italian friendship. On that point he agreed with Neville Chamberlain, while there were already signs of strain, still invisible to the public, between Eden and Chamberlain generated by differences about dealings with Italy.

Chamberlain was clear-headed, rational and determined. He had succeeded to Baldwin's majority in the House of Commons, but he wanted his own majority – that is to say, to win the next election. To do that he had to clear one great, expensive obstacle to domestic progress: the need to rearm. If only Hitler could be persuaded to limit armaments, all would be well. In 1937 it was clear that rapid German rearmament had caused economic problems inside Germany. Yet Hitler could surely be offered a peaceful solution to Germany's legitimate grievances. It seemed difficult, however, to find out what Hitler wanted; that fact impeded rational discussion and the search for peaceful compromise and the appeasement of Europe.

In October there emerged an unexpected chance to find out. Lord Halifax, as a master of foxhounds, got an invitation to attend a hunting exhibition in Berlin. The Foreign Office, still with Robert Vansittart as its official head and Eden as Foreign Secretary, showed neither enthusiasm nor hostility in response. The department of the Foreign Office dealing with Germany increasingly felt, as did Vansittart, that talks seeking European peace, 'a general settlement', should be postponed until Britain became militarily stronger. Meanwhile Germany should be 'kept guessing'. That is to say, Britain should not promise it would intervene militarily if Germany attacked Austria or Czechoslovakia but should not announce that it certainly would not do so. Chamberlain wanted to accelerate negotiations with Germany, not to delay them. Eden sometimes sympathized with him about Germany but certainly resented the usurpation of his position as Foreign Secretary by Halifax, who was someone outside his control. Eden would not have been pleased by the observation passed on by Chamberlain's press secretary to the German embassy in London, that 'Halifax was, in the opinion of Chamberlain, the most important statesman and politician England had at the present time'. Thus Eden insisted that Halifax should only listen and not propose anything to anyone in Germany. Vansittart particularly objected to Halifax going on the long journey from Berlin to Berchtesgaden to meet Hitler.

Chamberlain encouraged Halifax to visit Hitler even in his Bavarian retreat. Sir Nevile Henderson, British ambassador in Berlin, encouraged Halifax too. If Britain made adequate concessions, 'Germany will keep her word, at any rate for a foreseeable period. And particularly so, if we take it for granted that she will keep her word ... we should not oppose peaceful evolution any more than we could condone forceful expansion.' Halifax passed this letter on to Chamberlain with his own comments: 'I am not happy over the F.O. attitude over Czech S or Austria ... I hope that we should not feel bound to (in Henderson's words) oppose "peaceful Evolution" – rather liberally interpreted perhaps.' Halifax told Hitler that on Danzig,

Austria and Czechoslovakia 'we were not necessarily concerned to stand for the status quo as to-day . . . If reasonable settlements could be reached with the free assent and goodwill of those primarily concerned we certainly had no desire to block.' Chamberlain was pleased by Halifax's conversation, which he thought 'a great success because it achieved its object, that of creating an atmosphere in which it was possible to discuss with Germany the practical questions involved in a European settlement'. As he wrote, 'I don't see why we shouldn't say to Germany, give us satisfactory assurances that you won't use force to deal with the Austrians and Czecho-Slovakians and we will give you similar assurances that we won't use force to prevent the changes you want if you can get them by peaceful means.' There were great efforts needed to arrive at 'satisfactory conclusions', yet 'all the same the obstacles don't look insuperable'.[12]

The Halifax visit began Chamberlainite appeasement. From then until 2 September 1939, Neville Chamberlain pursued this policy. Here was the caesura, the moment when Churchill's policy and Chamberlain's diverged. They began to pursue peace by different means. Chamberlain sought the closest contact with Hitler which could be attained. Rational discussion would prevent disaster. Reasonable German grievances could be assuaged even if this meant the weakening of potential coalitions that might deter Hitler from violence. Churchill looked for the most powerful armed coalition against him. Contacts with the Führer should not discourage potential partners.

Surprisingly Churchill did not notice that his plans and Chamberlain's had begun decisively to separate. He was, of course, unusually busy with his writing. A more important reason was that Anthony Eden did not make public his complaints about the Halifax excursion. Indeed Eden did not differ from Chamberlain at that time on Germany, though his view of Mussolini's Italy distinctly differed: there Chamberlain's opinion corresponded more to Churchill's than did Eden's. Churchill, however, deceived by the Anglo-French staff talks of 1936, regarded Eden as a reliable advocate of Anglo-French military co-operation. Most important of all in making Churchill tolerant of Halifax's journey was Chamberlain's encouragement of a French visit to London and his success in soothing his French interlocutors. The day after Halifax's return, Camille Chautemps, the French Prime Minister, who had recently succeeded Blum, and Yvon Delbos, the Foreign Minister, were invited to London and promised an account of the Halifax visit.

Neville Chamberlain showed skill and imagination as a political manager. He believed that it was worth while persuading the largest possible number of people to support his policy. Of course, if they got in the way and frustrated his wishes they would have to be outmanoeuvred or ignored. But it was best to carry his Cabinet and as many as possible of the MPs who had been elected to support the national government. Churchill's support, if available, was easier to deal with than his denunciations. It is true that Chamberlain did not have Baldwin's skill in generating misty confusion over his thought, but he showed himself effective in deploying arguments to win over particular listeners even if they were not the arguments that dominated his own thought. He did not spare himself in winning assent.

Halifax told the Cabinet that 'the Germans have no policy of immediate adventure. They were too busy building up their country ... Nevertheless he would expect a beaver-like persistence in pressing their aims in Central Europe: but not in a form to give others cause – or probably occasion – to interfere.' Of Czechoslovakia Hitler had told Halifax, 'She only needed to treat the Germans living within her borders well and they would be entirely happy.' Halifax put the same point to Chautemps, Delbos and Charles Corbin, the French ambassador in London, when they met on 29 November. Chamberlain claimed that British public opinion did not think their country should be 'entangled in a war on account of Czechoslovakia, which was a long way off and with which we had not a great deal in common'. But there would be support for 'a reasonable and peaceful settlement between Germany and Czechoslovakia. People here were of the opinion that the Sudeten Germans were not getting fair treatment from the Czechs.' So the Czechs should be generous to the Germans living within their borders. Delbos insisted, the Foreign Office memorandum reports, that:

> it was not less necessary to give advice to Germany. Our efforts should be directed to both sides. He feared, however, that what Germany really wanted was to absorb the Sudeten territory, and not that the Sudeten Germans should receive better treatment. The absorption by Germany of Austria and part of Czechoslovakia would ... mean German hegemony, and a new appetite on the part of Germany for further conquest.

Delbos added that Austria should not be neglected. Eden, who identified himself with Chamberlain at this time much more than was later claimed for him, not least by Churchill, remarked that no one had given any pledges to Austria, in contrast to Czechoslovakia. Delbos pointed to the various declarations made in favour of Austrian independence.

Thus Chamberlain presented a dress rehearsal of the appeasement arguments he deployed in 1938. If the French could be brought with him, so much the better. Surprisingly, they were. Corbin, the ambassador, sent his impressions to the Foreign Ministry in Paris. Chamberlain had dominated the meetings, he wrote, speaking with a clarity which he compared with the confused declamations of Ramsay MacDonald and the silences of Baldwin. Relations between Eden and Chamberlain were excellent, Corbin claimed, and rumours to the contrary had no foundation. (This was at the end of 1937; early in 1938, when Eden began to get in the way over Mussolini, Chamberlain replaced him with Halifax.) First of all, the ambassador

went on, Chamberlain stressed the need for the closest co-
operation between Britain and France – though it was true that
it was Eden, not Chamberlain, who claimed that there was no
British prejudice against the Franco-Soviet alliance and said that
the French could tell Moscow of his assertion, as he would
himself tell Maisky, the Soviet ambassador in London. So,
Corbin concluded, 'in this particularly delicate domain as elsewhere, a spirit of realism dominates the policy of Chamberlain
and his ministers'.[13]

Persuading the French of the virtues of the British government was something Churchill would find creditable. To Chamberlain's annoyance Attlee for the Labour Party forced a
discussion of foreign affairs in the Commons, just before the
Christmas adjournment of 1937. Churchill spoke and favourably
assessed the Halifax visit. He had been 'personally anxious about
Lord Halifax's visit to Germany' because 'if it were thought that
we were making terms for ourselves at the expense either of
small nations or of large conceptions which are dear, not only to
many nations but to millions of people in every nation, I think
that a knell of despair would resound through many parts of
Europe'. However, all was well because of the 'reaffirmation of
British and French solidarity for mutual safety and for the
discharge of our duties under the Covenant'. Churchill attached
'the greatest significance' to relations with France, 'founded
upon the power of the French Army and the power of the
British Fleet'. France and Britain, 'in spite of their tardiness in
making air preparations, constitute so vast and formidable a
body that they will very likely be left alone undisturbed, at any
rate for some time to come'. There now existed a great measure
of unity in attitudes to foreign policy. 'There are differences
about this horrible Spanish civil war, but more and more I think
we all feel that, in some way or other, the influence of Britain
must be made continuously effective to bring out some mode of
life, some way of living between these two sides who have torn

their Motherland in pieces.' Churchill ended this speech by repeating that 'for five years I have been asking the House and the Government to make armaments'. But British armaments alone would not be enough, so Britain had to support the League. By doing so, 'we secure a measure of unity at home among all classes and all parties, which is indispensable to the efficiency of our foreign policy as well to the progress of our defensive preparations'. Moreover, 'we consecrate and legitimise every alliance and regional pact which may be formed for mutual protection'.[14]

Both Chamberlain and Churchill, then, looked forward with hope to 1938. Their reasons were not the same. Chamberlain and Halifax looked forward to what history has since labelled 'Chamberlainite appeasement'. Churchill looked forward to a balance of armed force which would deter Nazi aggression. They both of course wished for peace. Their methods of winning it differed. At the end of 1937 Churchill failed to measure their divergence. Christmas 1937 promised not much goodwill but perhaps plausible prospects of peace. Nineteen-thirty-eight floodlit the difference between Churchill and his supporters and the Chamberlainite appeasers. In the autumn of 1938 Chamberlain and his supporters endeavoured to obscure that clarity.

By the end of 1937 Churchill had established his position as the most eloquent early exponent of the danger presented by Nazi Germany. Rearmament was urgent, especially in the air. More and more people from all parties and none began to agree. Baldwin's 'confessions' strengthened Churchill. In November 1934 Baldwin had asserted that Germany had less than half the strength of the RAF and that in November 1935 'we shall still have a margin of nearly 50%', though he added that he assumed 'no acceleration in Germany'. However, Hitler startled his British interlocutors in the spring of 1935 by claiming that Germany already had air strength equal to the RAF. In

May 1935 Baldwin claimed that his figures had been correct in November 1934, but:

> where I was wrong was in my estimate of the future. There I was completely wrong. I tell the House so frankly, because neither I nor any advisers from whom we could get accurate information had any idea of the exact rate at which production was being, could be and actually was being speeded up in Germany in the six months between November and now. We were completely misled on the subject. I will not say we had not rumours. There was a great deal of hearsay, but we could get no facts.

The 'hearsay' had reached Churchill, particularly by way of Desmond Morton, who in the 1930s was head of the Industrial Intelligence Centre of the Committee of Imperial Defence, and from the Foreign Office by way of its permanent head, Vansittart, and Ralph Wigram, the head of the Foreign Office Central Department which dealt with Germany. (Some historians have exaggerated the 'secrecy' of what they provided and the furtiveness with which they did it. Churchill was a senior member of the Privy Council: Vansittart certainly thought him a justifiable recipient of what was common knowledge in the British embassy in Berlin and Wigram was not acting in defiance of his wishes. Morton agreed with Churchill's desire to make rearmament the overriding priority and told him so. But what he conveyed about German armed forces was, of course, known to the German authorities and there is no sign that he revealed any secret sources.) The Foreign Office and Vansittart had, of course, information bearing on German hopes and intentions, and were increasingly uneasy about German rearmament. They felt that the Air Ministry in London underestimated the danger. The Air Staff wished to maximize spending on the air force but the ministry, as part of the government, tended (as goverments will) to allege that everything necessary was being done.

Churchill was certainly correct when he asserted that German production of aircraft exceeded that of British factories. In each year, 1934, 1935, 1936 and 1937, while Churchill demanded urgent action, German factories turned out more than two and a half times the number of aircraft made in Britain. This was a large disparity and Churchill's occasional exaggerations, such as his belief in 1935 that the German air force would soon be ten times as strong as the RAF, were unnecessary. In 1938 action began to be taken in Britain and new German aircraft were slightly less than twice as numerous as British. At the end of 1939, after war had begun, British production actually exceeded German. Debates between Churchill and the government involved the number of squadrons and first-line strength. These were shifting and controversial measures with many variables: numbers in squadrons could vary, as could reserves of aircraft and crew, not to mention their quality and that of the mechanics who serviced the aircraft. However, it was clear that whatever 'parity' signified it certainly did not exist between the British and German air forces, although Churchill exaggerated the proportion of combat aircraft as distinct from trainers that the German air force acquired.[15] Baldwin's admission that he had been wrong aroused less discontent in May 1935 than his 'appalling frankness' in November 1936. In May 1935 many still hoped for 'arms limitation' and an 'air pact'; by November 1936 these hopes had diminished. Both occasions served to emphasize Churchill's concern for national defence.

Less certain than the advertisement of Churchill's vigilant attention to national safety is how far his sustained campaign for rearmament especially in the air had any effect on government action. The government worried about how to respond in public debate, but how far the Treasury, the CID, the Air Ministry or Inskip, the co-ordinator of defence, changed anything they did in response to Churchill's persistence is less evident. His emphasis on 'parity' helped persuade the government to try to increase the 'first-line' strength and the number of squadrons available for combat. This could lead to hollow façades, as a member of the Air Council in the Air Ministry commented in 1938: 'We have during the past few years been building up a front-line Air Force which is nothing but a facade. We have nothing in the way of reserves or organisation behind the front line with which to maintain it.' Many more were produced of an aircraft which proved disastrous in service in 1940, the Fairey Battle, in order to maintain total aircraft output; the Air Staff knew it to be nearly worthless as early as 1936.[16] After the summer of 1936 Churchill received detailed information about the weaknesses behind the façade from a serving air force officer then attached to the directorate of training in the Air Ministry. This was Squadron-Leader C. T. Atkinson, who approached Churchill on his own initiative. Later he introduced Group Captain L. L. MacLean, a staff officer in an RAF bomber group. Churchill sometimes used this information in speeches, sometimes in documents sent to ministers or their advisers. Though he did not reveal his sources, they must have been evident to his correspondents. A letter he passed on to Maurice Hankey, Secretary to the Cabinet and to the Committee of Imperial Defence, included notes on a conference at Bomber Command headquarters. Hankey replied with a long careful letter explaining his unease about these leaks. Churchill responded in two snappish, angry sentences in which he complained about receiving 'a long lecture' and then, 'You may be sure I shall not trouble you again in such matters.' Hankey, of course, disliked criticism of the mechanism of government, much of which he had created, but Churchill's snarl shows how easily he could make enemies.

The great issue separating Churchill from the governments after 1932 was the urgency of rearmament. Should the idea of national crisis be disseminated? Was preparing for war the best way of preventing it? Chamberlain, supported by Lord Weir, blocked compulsion being applied to industry as a dangerous inference with ordinary trade; their most effective argument was that economic strength made Britain powerful. In Churchill's opinion loud stress on the desperate urgency of arms production would defeat the obstacles which shortages of skilled labour presented. Trade union concerns about more flexible use of labour would then be overcome with the help of the TUC, whose influence he exaggerated. (Weir preferred to national agitation quiet action by individual factory managements who, after all, would locally be offering increased employment.) By the end of 1937 Chamberlain had settled on appeasement as the best means of preventing war. In 1938 he exploited fear of the power of the German air force to justify his policy. In this way, Churchill's insistence on the dangers of German bombing gave arguments to opponents of his foreign policy.[17] In fact, the Germans never developed an effective strategic bombing force, as the British and Americans did after 1942. The Blitz of 1940 came nowhere near to justifying the fears expressed, most eloquently by Churchill. The German air force was less impressive than its façade. For instance, one of Churchill's complaints pointed to the multiplicity of types of aircraft in production in British factories. In Germany, the Heinkel heavy bomber, HE177, became the only one to be produced. Endless technical problems meant that fewer than a dozen ever came into service. Churchillian criticism was not permitted in the Third Reich. Whatever its faults and exaggerations, it compelled ministers, serving officers and civilian officials to examine what they were doing.[18]

At the end of 1937 the prospects for peace in Europe seemed more promising. If Hitler confined himself to parades and patriotic displays he could be tolerated. To the British, after all, Germans were especially partial to military show. Chamberlain knew what he would do if Germany sought change. Peaceful evolution would make resistance unnecessary. Churchill could go on a protracted holiday after Christmas unconscious of Chamberlain's new determination to appease. In 1938 and 1939 Hitler demonstrated that he would prefer military strength to peaceful prosperity. If military power had to be used to permit its continued expansion, then so be it.

CHAPTER EIGHT

A 'Grand Alliance'?

CHURCHILL BEGAN 1938 in France, after spending Christmas and the New Year at Blenheim. He stayed in Paris with Eric Phipps, the British ambassador. Blum came to lunch on 3 January and Alexis Léger, the chief official at the French Foreign Office, the next day. Then he went on to the South of France. He worked on *Marlborough*, and paid his respects to the Duke of Windsor, the former King Edward VIII. Lloyd George and Eden came to lunch, forming a trio which aroused Neville Chamberlain's suspicions. Soon after, Eden hurried home to be told that the Prime Minister had asked President Roosevelt to postpone his plan to ask a committee of smaller states to consider the problems of the world. Eden got Chamberlain to withdraw this message, but it made no difference, since Roosevelt himself dropped the idea. This event, whose implications Churchill exaggerated in his Second World War memoirs, began the process which led to Eden's resignation, which Churchill, after the war, treated as an awesome catastrophe. In fact, Eden was not the 'strong young figure' standing up against appeasement that Churchill later described. His policy towards Germany was hesitant, and amounted to doing nothing definite either to resist or to conciliate.[1]

Churchill, however, correctly represented the immediate

excitement among contemporaries evoked by Eden's resignation as Foreign Secretary. Chamberlain and Eden certainly disagreed about whether it was worth conciliating Mussolini, but Eden had not opposed appeasement of Germany and the Cabinet seemed genuinely surprised by his dispute with the Prime Minister. Contemporaries, though, treated Eden's departure as the start of a wholly new policy. This was because Eden had, at every stage, successfully supplied high-minded utterances to conceal lack of substance. Above all, he favoured the League of Nations. Though it never became clear what action he thought should follow support for the League, he proclaimed his adhesion to its principles. He resigned on 20 February 1938. On the 22nd, the Commons debated foreign affairs. The day before, in his resignation speech, Eden had spoken with boring caution; Churchill now supplied the drama and attributed to the former Foreign Secretary's departure far more portentous implications than Eden himself claimed for it. He told the Commons: 'All over the world, in every land, under every sky and every system of government, wherever they may be, the friends of England are dismayed, and the foes of England are exultant.' Chamberlain and his colleagues had entered upon 'a new policy'. The old policy was an effort to establish the rule of law in Europe and build up, through the League of Nations, or by regional pacts under the League of Nations, effective deterrents against the aggressor. 'That is the policy', he affirmed, quite wrongly, 'which we have followed. Is the new policy to come to terms with the totalitarian Powers in the hope that by great and far-reaching acts of submission, not merely in sentiment and in pride, but in material factors, peace may be preserved?'[2]

Churchill took up the policy he claimed Eden to have followed, and he might have expected the support of those, in Parliament and outside, who had trusted in Eden's virtues. He did not get it. Instead of a demand for the policy alleged to be his, Eden called nebulously for 'national unity': everyone should

R. A. C. PARKER

work together and forget or diminish differences. About thirty back-benchers on the government side abstained on the vote of censure moved by the Labour Party after Eden's resignation. Vyvyan Adams voted against the government. Conservative Whips had made extra efforts. However, as the French ambassador in London reported to Paris, 'Conservative MPs who took an interest in foreign affairs were prominent amongst the dissidents,' while Chamberlain's support came mainly from 'obscure members who had never spoken at Westminster and who had no clear opinions'. These sheep who faithfully followed Chamberlain could be turned round in private party confabulations if, but only if, they thought the Prime Minister was leading them to electoral disaster. Conservative dissidents could perhaps have formed a group to support Churchill's version of Eden's objectives and won the support of what Lloyd George described as the 'millions of people in this country ... who look to him [Eden] to continue to give them guidance and inspiration'. They did not get inspiration from Eden, only trite conventionalities.[3]

Moreover, some articulate and prominent politicians among independent-minded Conservative members continued to aim their opinions in divergent directions. Robert Boothby, speaking after Churchill in the debate, explained that Eden's resignation meant a 'fundamental change of vital importance'. Now a 'static and negative policy' would change in Chamberlain's hands 'to a positive and dynamic policy'. Victor Cazalet's suspicions were aroused by Churchill's eulogies of Eden. He told Baldwin, Eden's patron, that he 'smelt a rat, or at any rate, a mouse' on account of Eden's recent meeting with Lloyd George and Churchill: 'three prominent gentlemen have all been on the Riviera together'. Cazalet added that 'a combination of Lloyd George and Winston was fatal to any attack on the Government'.[4] Leo Amery was delighted by Eden's departure from the government. He reckoned that Eden had prevented good relations with Italy ever since 'the Abyssinian business'. 'Naturally,' he noted, 'Winston will exploit the situation to the full, and will perhaps expect me to back him. I doubt whether I can do that.' He thought Churchill knew, during the debate on the Labour motion, 'that there was no hope of any cave worth mentioning' – that is, any group of Conservative MPs who would systematically oppose Chamberlain. Amery felt some of his own views had at last been accepted, and declared, 'Neville's speech is the first breath of fresh air on the Government front bench for many long years.'[5]

Soon Hitler unleashed another big crisis by invading Austria on 12 March 1938. Kurt von Schuschnigg, the Austrian Chancellor, had met Hitler the month before and submitted to demands which the Führer believed would progressively erode Austrian independence. Then Schuschnigg, to defend Austrian independence, announced that a plebiscite would be held to reaffirm it. The question he posed was worded so as to make certain a vote of 'yes' to Austrian independence. Conservative Catholics and Social Democrats could be relied on for an anti-Nazi vote. Hitler first threatened invasion to get the plebiscite cancelled and then decided to invade anyway. Italy, Britain and France were committed to maintaining Austrian independence; at least they had promised to consult together about 'any measures to be taken in the case of threats to the integrity and independence of Austria', as Chamberlain had put it. Faced with the accomplished fact of its destruction, Mussolini refused even to consult with Britain and France (winning Hitler's effusive gratitude), and in London and Paris verbal protests were drawn up which made no difference. Chamberlain said that the British government had explained that they would 'strongly disapprove . . . of violent methods', but 'nothing could have arrested this action by Germany unless we and others with us had been prepared to use force to prevent it'.[6] Hitler had now begun to unify Germans in a great German state, without negotiation or discussion, simply by armed force. It seemed probable that he would soon seek similarly to 'solve the problem' of the German population within Czechoslovakia.

What should be done? There were three choices. One was to let the Third Reich do what it liked in eastern Europe and to give Hitler a 'free hand' in the east. The snag was that such a British withdrawal from Europe would leave Germany strong enough to dominate Europe, and Britain would in the end have either to arm against the European continent or rely on Hitler's goodwill to keep British independence. The second possibility was to help to arrange peaceful change to Europe sufficient to turn Hitler, or Germans who could control him, into peaceful ways, and make him ready for rational, orderly solutions to German grievances. Then all nations could disarm and civilian production and trade would bring prosperity. The problem with this apparently rational course was that Hitler might prove to be untrustworthy, and uncontrollable by reasonable Germans. Moreover, British conciliation of Germany might make other countries feel they would be wise to make their own bargains with Germany, and it might make rational Germans admire Hitler's success. The third option was for Britain to arm and make firm alliances with any country ready to resist armed German aggression. Then Hitler might restrain himself or rational Germans might restrain him. The problem here was that alliances against Germany might make Hitler more, rather than less, dangerous and make more Germans inclined to support him. Moreover, disarmament would be ruled out if Britain and Britain's allies built up their armed strength.

On 14 March Churchill expounded the third option. Attlee, for the Labour Party, demanded 'a return to League principles and League policy' to build up 'a world of law and a world of justice'. Sinclair, the Liberal leader, wanted to 'support France if she, in the pursuit of her undertakings to Czechoslovakia, finds it necessary to uphold the independence of that country'. But above all 'let us base our policy firmly on the principles of the Covenant of the League of Nations'. Churchill, too, invoked the League. He was accustomed to doing so to support rearmament; now the League justified a precise foreign policy. 'I affirm that the Government should express in the strongest terms our adherence to the Covenant of the League of Nations and our resolve to procure by international action the reign of law in Europe.' Co-operation between Britain and France provided a base. 'That is the beginning of collective security. But why stop there? Why be edged and pushed further down the slope in a disorderly crowd of embarrassed states? ... Why should we delay until we are confronted with a general landslide of those small countries passing over, because they have no other choice, to the overwhelming power of the Nazi regime?'

Churchill may well have been influenced by an able and charming young relation, Shiela Grant Duff. A letter from her arrived when he was away in the South of France. When he saw it he marked it 'to read again'. Grant Duff discussed the countries of eastern Europe that were pursuing 'an equivocal policy which will allow them to come in on the winning side if there is war, but if only we could prove to the eastern neighbours of Germany that we are the winning side, the war might be prevented altogether. Churchill finished his speech to the Commons:

> If a number of States were assembled around Great Britain and France in a solemn treaty for mutual defence against aggression; if they had their forces marshalled in what you might call a Grand Alliance; if they had their staff arrangements concerted; if all this rested, as it can honourably rest, upon the Covenant of the League of Nations agreeable with all the purposes and ideals of the League of Nations; if it were sustained, as it would be, by the moral sense of the world; and if it were done in the year 1938 – and, believe me, it may be the last chance there will be for doing it –

then I say that you might, even now arrest this approaching war![7]

Churchill had indicated what he called 'a positive conception, a practical and realistic conception'. 'His speech greatly impressed the House,' according to *The Times*, a journal strongly in favour of Chamberlainite conciliation. Rab Butler, the Foreign Office Minister in the Commons, remarked that Churchill was 'listened to with rapt attention'. *Punch*, then a representative organ of the middle classes, noted that Churchill was 'frequently cheered'. By adding to 'the virtually unanimous support' of the opposition parties 'a very large and daily growing section of Conservative opinion', the more sober *Economist* reckoned, Churchill had ensured that 'his view now represents the view of a majority of the nation'.[8] The left in politics hearkened to Churchill. In *Tribune*, the weekly of the far left of the Labour Party, Aneurin Bevan, already a prominent MP, came close to adulation. Chamberlain, he wrote,

> compares most unfavourably with Mr Winston Churchill who is now enjoying the full flower of his diverse talents. Chamberlain puts in the organ stops so that only a thin listless trickle of sound is allowed to issue forth. Churchill on the other hand pulls out the stops and allows the argument to speak through him in a diapason of majestic harmony. His speech on Monday made a profound impression on all who heard it. His demand for a start to be made now against the onrush of the dictators found an unusual measure of support in all parts of the House. So cogent and convincing was his argument that the time has arrived to assert the power of the free democracies against Hitler through the agency of the League that the absence of any reference to the situation in Spain showed unmistakably the strong support that Franco has in the ranks of the Tory Party.

Bevan thus noted the problem which, more than any other, weakened Churchill's appeal to anti-Conservatives: his lack of enthusiasm for the Spanish government's struggle against Franco's rebellion.

Hitler's use of force sharpened interest in the idea of a British 'popular front', a cross-party, national opposition to appeasement. In early 1937 G. D. H. Cole, a scrupulous, honest academic on the left of the Labour Party, wrote a lengthy contemplation, *The People's Front*, for that 1930s association of high-minded advanced progressives the Left Book Club. 'The moment Great Britain is ready to act, the European Pact of Mutual Defence can be made, with overwhelming support from the countries not yet under Fascist control. Europe can cry halt to Fascism; and Fascism will have to halt, because the forces arrayed against aggression will be manifestly too strong to be challenged. Great Britain holds the key of European peace.' Churchill thought the same. 'I, as a Socialist,' Cole explained, 'am fully prepared to collaborate in preventing war with non-socialists, who believe that it is possible to preserve the institutions of liberal democracy.' Churchill appears twice in Cole's book. Once he supplies a precedent for Labour Party approval of moves towards a popular front when Cole evokes the appearance on the same platform with Churchill of Walter Citrine, the TUC general secetary. Then, unnamed, Churchill shows how hesitant was Cole's own recent acceptance of the idea of all-party opposition to appeasement:

> I used to believe that it was essential, in order to build up the Labour Party into a solid force for Socialism, to avoid all collaboration on political issues with people who did not call themselves Socialists. I was even hesitant about supporting such non-party bodies as the League of Nations Union, in which I might find myself sharing a platform with someone many of whose views seemed to me sheerly detestable and pernicious, in spite of his willingness to give at any rate lip-service to the League idea.[9]

For a long time left-wing socialists thought resistance to fascism impossible under a capitalist regime. Fascism, Marxist history demonstrated, was an outcome of 'imperialism', itself a necessary consequence of 'capitalism'. Hence, on the left, some supported a different kind of front from the 'popular front', the 'united front', which would bring together everyone struggling for socialism, including communists. Cole dedicated his book to Sir Stafford Cripps. Cripps, with his lucid, logical mind, often well distant from reality, alternated fronts, advocating with dogmatic conviction whichever front he favoured for the moment and so irritating the Labour Party leadership, an irritation tempered by Cripps's charm and personal courtesy. In the same issue of *Tribune* that contained Aneurin Bevan's eulogy of Churchill, Cripps asserted that the path of salvation lay through proletarian rule: 'Let us redouble our efforts for victory for the British working class, for by that victory alone can we now save our Spanish and Czechoslovakian comrades and our own lives and homes.' The following month Cripps, supporting the 'emergency conference' on Spain, accepted the idea of 'a Popular or Democratic Front', which would mean 'that any idea of real Socialism would have to be put aside for the present'. But he soon excluded Churchill: 'In the minds of those who support a Peace Front the position of Spain is the keystone. That in itself excludes from their ranks the Winston Churchills and the Edens of this world. They stand condemned.'[10]

Another writer, on the far left, indeed then a 'fellow traveller', John Strachey, responded to Churchill's speech. On 16 March *The Times* published a letter from Robert Boothby, an MP intermittently close to Churchill but somewhat two faced – on 12 March he had written to Chamberlain 'as a whole-hearted supporter of your foreign policy'. Boothby asserted that the nation had to be rallied round a 'clear cut foreign policy'. He suggested a 'pact of mutual assistance between those Powers which are resolved to offer effective resistance to further aggression in Europe' and a specific pledge to support France in defence of Czechoslovakia. There should be no agreement with

Italy unless foreign troops and arms were withdrawn from Spain. A few days later Boothby wrote to Churchill. Strachey, a friend of Boothby's – they shared a certain cultivation and raffishness – had talked to him. He told Strachey that Churchill was 'in general sympathy' with Boothby's case. Strachey then asked 'if he could tell his friends that there was a movement among supporters of the Government in favour of a firm stand against aggression and I said yes'. It got into the *Evening Standard* with rumours, which Boothby disowned, about intrigues in the Cabinet. Thoughts of an anti-appeasement coalition lingered. That particularly rebellious Conservative MP Vyvyan Adams was spoken of in public by a Labour MP as 'one who justifies' some other Labour MPs 'in talking about the Popular Front'.[11]

Churchill's uncertainty about the Spanish Civil War remained an obstacle to any claim he could make to lead all anti-appeasers. Through taking a position of 'even-handed neutrality', he managed to get the approval of Sir Henry Page Croft, a former diehard over India, and now the noisiest supporter of Franco. On 17 March 1938 another former diehard, the Duchess of Atholl, now a passionate supporter of the Spanish government against Franco's rebels, wrote to Churchill. He had invited her to join the national committee of the Focus Anti-Nazi group: 'I shall be very glad to do so if the Committee will be prepared to discuss what can be done to prevent an insurgent victory in Spain.' Churchill sent back an embarrassed evasion: 'Spain is one of the topics we shall have to discuss at our meetings, and, of course, I cannot tell what the reaction will be upon that question until discussion among all the parties who belong to our Focus has taken place.'

Spain brought together a 'popular front' on 23 April 1938. At the Queen's Hall in London there met a 'National Conference to Save Spain, Save Britain, Save Peace'. Conservative, Liberal and Labour MPs joined in. Stafford Cripps observed at the time that 'the real question to be decided is whether the chance of altering the foreign policy of this country and of calling a halt to Fascist aggression within a practicable period of time is worth the abandonment for the time being of real working-class control. I say for the time being, since such a point could not be considered as a permanent alignment but only as a temporary cooperation to save democracy and peace.' Saving Spain and working-class control ranked low in Churchill's priorities.[12]

Hitler's aggressive display of contempt for international respectability did, for a moment, make Chamberlainite appeasement difficult to pursue. It precipitated a brief struggle for dominance in the Conservative Party. Churchill had a fundamental political problem, which Lieutenant-Commander Fletcher, a Labour MP who strongly sympathized with Churchill, pointed out in the House of Commons after he had heard Churchill's speech. 'We had a great speech, as usual, but what did he do to achieve his objects? He cannot influence the Government Party because he advocates those views about the League and collective security and he has no influence with those in our parties who advocate these views, because he remains a Member of the Government Party.' Fletcher was right that Churchill, however much he disagreed with the government, never intended to go into full-scale opposition to the Conservative (or national) government. He had to appeal to Conservatives, to induce a sufficient number to feel that his policies should be pursued and that he should be in the government to help to pursue them. Of course, if his feelings appealed to Labour and Liberal supporters their adoption by a Conservative government would help the party at election time, and his presence in government would then help to bring national support for foreign and defence policy. Fletcher's comments on Churchill's speech implied that he should leave the Conservatives and set himself up as an independent prophet: the alternative of joining the Liberals would seem farcical, given Churchill's past, and Labour would be unsuitable for an orator who, one month before, had told a

London audience that 'the follies of the Socialist opposition are beyond description'.[13] But an independent prophet can do little unless he can influence the government party in the House of Commons, so there was, in the end, no alternative to Churchill's continued adhesion to the party of which he had been so prominent a member since 1924.

Moreover, Churchill's policies were not the same as those of the Liberal and Labour oppositions. The day after Churchill's speech there appeared a manifesto with many eminent Liberal and left-wing supporters: Fletcher was there, together with Maynard Keynes, Gilbert Murray, Henry Wickham Steed, Violet Bonham-Carter, Norman Angell, G. D. H. Cole, Josiah Wedgwood and other progressive luminaries, to whom two Conservative MPs, the Duchess of Atholl and Vyvyan Adams, added themselves. They called for Churchill's policy with one addition, well outside his wishes: that 'our naval pre-eminence' should enforce non-intervention in Spain or that the whole policy of non-intervention should be scrapped. Over Spain, Abyssinia, Manchuria, Churchill's attitudes were not those of the devout adherents of League principles. There survived, too, on the left some who believed that the League should mean disarmament and who objected to Churchill's success in persuading the League of Nations Union to preach rearmament and armed alliances. Churchill's correspondence contains a printed copy of a speech from a member of the Union denouncing 'a reversion to power politics' which 'would automatically divide Europe into two hostile camps' and 'inevitably lead to war'.[14] However, now that German threats dominated British fears, 'collective security' in its new Churchillian guise as a camouflage for an armed alliance could hold the support of many old enthusiasts for the League.

Churchill himself understood that he could impose his policies only by winning support from Conservative MPs and Conservative ministers. He and the other most critical person in any popular front took that for granted. In March 1938 Churchill wrote to Attlee about Robert Cecil's plan for an inter-party group to sponsor a campaign for the League and rearmament. He suggested that Attlee should leave it to 'unofficial members of your party, as otherwise it would look as if there was a significance quite beyond anything which an educative campaign implies'. Attlee agreed: 'exactly the same reasons as you state seem to me cogent'.[15] These two leading politicians understood each other without difficulty. To others Churchill was explicit. The next general election could be as late as autumn 1940. Sir Richard Acland, a high-minded, rich but egalitarian Liberal (who annoyed Churchill after 1940) sent a long, elaborate letter to him. He explained that Churchill was building up a personal following which would enable him 'to present Mr Chamberlain with an ultimatum in the form I can break you unless' he changed his policy. Churchill replied concisely and clearly: in the present Parliament 'The Government have a solid majority, and Chamberlain will certainly not wish to work with me. If of course the foreign situation darkens, something in the nature of a National Government may be forced upon us.'

From Manchester, Churchill's devoted Conservative follower, James Watts, thought that 'a revolt in Parliament run by all those who care for decency and equality [he was, of course, a pre-Thatcher Conservative] and who are alive to the menace to the world from German frightfulness, would surely rally the country to fight for its liberties as one family'. Churchill answered conclusively, 'There is no chance whatever of any action in Parliament being effective. The present majority will remain dumb to the end.' It was not that Churchill's case was weak; it was that Chamberlain's self-confidence and skill in presentation and political manoeuvre were overwhelming. Soon the Labour Party leadership itself crushed the popular front. On 13 May 1938 the National Executive issued a portentous, elaborately argued document. 'We cannot accept that such a combination, even if it were practicable, would lead to the early defeat or break up of the "National Government" . . . A new situation might arise, of course, if any considerable number [of MPs] were to rebel against the Prime Minister's authority. At the present moment however there are no signs of such a rebellion.'[16] The 'National Government' referred to was the Conservative-controlled sham of 1931.

Certainly, Churchill's 'Grand Alliance' was attractive enough to worry Chamberlain. He had to pretend to think about it sympathetically, to claim to be reluctantly compelled to reject it. In fact of course, as the French ambassador in London, for whom the future of Europe depended on British policy, fully understood, a revolution in Chamberlain's thinking was highly unlikely. On 13 March the Prime Minister confided to Hilda, one of his two intelligent and well-informed sisters, his first reactions to the German seizure of Austria. He was cross; Hitler was once again making it difficult for him to act reasonably. 'Force is the only argument that Germany understands,' and only alliances could produce it. Still, 'I am not going to take the situation too tragically . . . if we can avoid another violent coup in Czechoslovakia, which ought to be feasible, it may be possible for Europe to settle down, and some day for us to start peace talks again with the Germans.'[17] Two days later, after Churchill's speech, Chamberlain spoke to the Foreign Policy Committee of the Cabinet. He did not think that 'anything that had happened should cause the government to alter their present policy; on the contrary, recent events have confirmed him in his opinion that the policy was the right one, and he only regretted that it had not been adopted earlier'. But there was a problem: 'recent events have greatly disturbed public opinion'. Accordingly, 'the government's policy would have to be explained and justified to public opinion even more carefully and thoroughly than would otherwise have been necessary'.

The Prime Minister claimed that the only permanent salvation for Czechoslovakia was to find a settlement Germany would accept. Provided Germany could get what it wanted by 'peaceful methods there was no reason to suppose that she would reject such a procedure in favour of one based on violence,' he told the Foreign Policy Committee on 18 March. Halifax argued that close association with France or Russia would render it 'more difficult . . . to make any real settlement with Germany'. Chamberlain briefed the editor of *The Times* the day before the full Cabinet. He took his habitual pose: 'he said he had come clean round from Winston's idea of a Grand Alliance to a policy of diplomatic action and no fresh commitments'. The Cabinet got a report from the Chiefs of Staff explaining that an attempt to defend Czechoslovakia against aggression would fail, and that a long war would be needed to get German forces out again. Halifax nevertheless told the Cabinet that Chamberlain and he had considered the proposal that Britain should promise to join in guaranteeing Czechoslovakia 'with some sympathy'.[18]

Chamberlain made sure that Churchill himself felt he was being taken seriously. He had 'a long conversation with Winston'. He wrote to his sister setting out Churchill's view 'at that time in favour of a joint guarantee to Czechoslovakia, by UK, France, Yugo-slavia, Rumania, Hungary and any other Balkan States that might be induced to come in'. He had told Churchill that 'I had been revolving the same idea in my mind and was much attracted by it, but that before coming to any decision I should have to examine it much more thoroughly and in particular get military advice upon it'. Chamberlain's letter to Hilda, after an outburst of self-congratulation on the 'eclatant success' of his statement of Britain's post-Anschluss policy ('I never remember a speech by a British minister at a critical time which has won such universal approval in Europe'), largely concerned Churchill. He retailed some gossip. Churchill, he claimed, had for a while convinced one of Chamberlain's

Cabinet ministers that the Prime Minister had agreed with his plan. When this Minister asked Chamberlain his true opinion 'about Czecho, I told him that I had begun by wanting to help her, but that the more I had examined it, the more I was convinced that it was impracticable'. Once again Chamberlain paraded his allegedly open-minded appraisal, his care in deciding that he should not make promises to resist German aggression and his scrupulous caution in going for conciliation rather than confrontation. 'Winston, whose wishes often become indistinguishable from his thoughts, told many people that I agreed with him.'

The letter to Hilda was begun at Cliveden, where Chamberlain had stayed the weekend – perhaps a less sinister spot than many progressives assumed at the time. He continued the letter after he was back in Downing Street, and set out his views on Churchill, patronizingly amiable but with barbed asides. It was on 24 March that Chamberlain gave to the House his much heralded statement on British policy over Czechoslovakia. 'You may be amused to hear that on Wednesday I sent for Winston and told him that as we had already had a talk in the Lobby, I didn't want him to have to wait until I spoke in public to know how my mind had finally settled.' There follows, from Neville Chamberlain's pen, remarks which probably reflect his conceit rather than Churchill's simplicity. 'Winston was terribly pleased at being thus taken into confidence, and he did not attempt to argue, though he intimated that his speech was already made and would not be altered.' Chamberlain thought Churchill's speech next day had, in fact, been softened because of this conversation; reading the speech suggests that Chamberlain's capacity for self-delusion was at least as strong as Churchill's. Churchill 'assured me', he wrote, 'that he had not and would not intrigue against me, that he was no suitor for office now, though at one time he would have liked to be in, that his attitude towards the Govt even though critical would be "avuncular"'.

He commented, 'He doesn't want office as long as he knows he can't have it, and though he won't intrigue himself, he doesn't mind others doing it provided they are successful. But all the same, I can't help liking Winston although I think him nearly always wrong and impossible as a colleague.' Evidently Chamberlain would keep him out as long as he could.[19]

Chamberlain's commentary on Churchill was prompted by an earlier letter from Hilda. She wondered 'how much truth there really is in these constant rumours of discontent in your own party and "caves"'. (For nearly a century after Bright's speech in 1866, 'cave' or 'cave of Adullam' applied to a group of members forming a secession from their party.) 'Do you think', Hilda went on, 'there is any body of men who are intriguing, or at any rate hankering after another leader? I can't believe it, certainly in the country one hears no whisper of such an idea, but the House of Commons is a funny place and I suppose Churchill's oratory does secure him a certain amount of attention and perhaps support.' Perhaps she had in mind the recent letter to *The Times* of Ronald Tree, an MP who was rich enough to be independent, but was a very junior office-holder as PPS to Robert Hudson, himself a minister outside the Cabinet. Tree suggested extending the 'National Government to include members of the trade unions on the Left and Mr Churchill on the Right, at the same time bringing Mr Eden back into the Cabinet.' And Chamberlain's sister had perhaps also noted the public remarks of a Cabinet minister, Lord De La Warr, that 'this country was determined to make a firm stand against aggression'.

Chamberlain continued his letter to his sister: 'to answer the question in your letter, everyone in the House enjoys listening to him and is ready to cheer and laugh at his sallies, but he has no following of any importance'. Sadly Chamberlain seems to have been correct, at that time, so Churchill would not be forced into office by the Conservative Party. 'As to the "dissentients" in the Cabinet, pay no attention to any rumours. There is no wish to have any other leader.' In other words, Chamberlain did not fear threats of resignation from his Cabinet.[20]

Chamberlain obviously intended to keep Churchill out of his government and believed he could do so. Churchill probably did not realize the force of his hostility. After all, he did not think that he was always wrong, or that he was an impossible colleague; probably he was unaware of his own forcefulness when he wanted to get his own way. That month, March 1938, indeed saw Chamberlain triumph; his European policy, which involved restraining France and conciliating Germany, he kept going until September 1939. It was from the outside that Churchill had to preach to the Cabinet and persuade it to change Chamberlain's policy. The support of Labour and Liberal politicians helped increasingly to give him the appeal that attached to someone who could unite much of the nation. But Cabinet ministers and Conservative MPs were the audience he had to convince. That would remain true at least until the next election, which could wait until the autumn of 1940; Chamberlain hoped by then to have won peace and disarmament and to be acclaimed by the world and by grateful British voters.

On 24 March, speaking to the House of Commons, Chamberlain successfully rejected Churchill's demands for a Grand Alliance to resist Hitler, and, as he had planned, 'explained and justified' his policy of conciliation. Churchill himself described it as 'a very fine speech'. It showed skill and care. Chamberlain defined and defended appeasement. He reminded his hearers that 'peace is the greatest interest of the British Empire'. But he did not preach surrender. Britain would fight if its vital interests were menaced, and fight for 'our liberty and the right to live our lives according to the standards which our national traditions and our national character have prescribed for us'. Once again, he made obeisance to the idea of a European alliance: 'there was much to be said for a proposition of that kind'. But, for the left, he noted that it 'does not differ from the old alliances of pre-war days', however much it might be wrapped up in the League Covenant. For the right he adroitly changed the subject. Britain 'must be strongly armed for defence and for counter-offence'.

Then Chamberlain moved to the central issue. Should Britain promise to go to war if France went to war to defend Czechoslovakia, or should Britain promise to defend Czechoslovakia against aggression? This, he felt, would be a sacrifice of sovereignty. The decision to go to war would be made for Britain by foreigners. Then he produced a carefully constructed paragraph designed to show that Britain was not abandoning Europe to its fate. If war broke out no one could tell who might become involved: 'this is especially true in the case of two countries like Great Britain and France, with long associations of friendship, with interests closely interwoven, devoted to the same ideals of democratic liberty, and determined to uphold them'. This amiable, if non-committal, reference to France had been forced on Chamberlain and Halifax by their colleagues. Left to himself, Chamberlain liked frankly to set out his thoughts. Often he was induced by members of the Cabinet to be less combative, to conceal or camouflage his thoughts and so to prevent unease or hostility among Conservative MPs. This sugar-coating of the government's refusal to support France even succeeded in winning thanks from Blum, who at that moment found himself briefly at the head of the French government and wrote in his own hand to Chamberlain to say on behalf of his colleagues and himself 'how much we have been touched by your declaration concerning the links joining your country and ours'. On the other hand, as the Berlin press noted, 'England does not guarantee Czechoslovakia.'

Chamberlain explained his objection to the Soviet proposal for a conference. He correctly described it as a plan to resist aggression rather than to remove the causes of aggression: 'it would aggravate the tendency towards the establishment of

exclusive groups of nations'. He defended non-intervention in
Spain, however flawed, as preventing general war. Then having
raised issues embarrassing to Churchill, he, as it were, gave
way to him by apparently taking over his rearmament policy.
Chamberlain played high cards in Churchill's strongest suit. He
announced accelerated rearmament. 'The existing programme',
he said, 'has been carried out with the intention of interfering as
little as possible with normal trade.' That principle would go, he
alleged. Employers and trade unions would be consulted. Production 'will be substantially increased'. 'With a full sense of the
responsibility which in such times must rest on the shoulders of
those who administer the affairs of this great country, I affirm
my conviction that the course we have decided to pursue is the
best and, indeed, the only one which is likely to lead us to our
goal' of peace.[21]

In his response to Chamberlain's statement, Churchill called
for 'deterrents against aggression': arms and alliances. Surely
Britain and France had now formed a defensive alliance. 'Why
not say so . . . treat the defensive problems of the two countries
as if they were one'. This point Chamberlain had dodged. For
he did not want an Anglo-French alliance which might make
the French feel able to protect Czechoslovakia and so weaken
the pressure that he hoped they would put on that country to
satisfy the spokesman of German claims there, Konrad Henlein,
leader of the Sudeten German Party. Churchill asked for an
assurance to be given to Czechoslovakia that a German attack
would be resisted by Britain as well as France. He assumed that
France and Russia would resist and that Germany was therefore
unlikely to attack Czechoslovakia in 1938. But his worries were
wider, and he needed the Grand Alliance to counter them. The
Grand Alliance he defined as France and Britain in 'decided
action', which would rally 'five States as well as Czechoslovakia'.
He named Yugoslavia, 'a most powerful and virile state', Bul-
garia, Rumania, Greece and Turkey, 'all of whom have powerful

armies'. Then he brought out again the familiar demand for a ministry of supply, a ministry of defence and an act to enable the government to 'divert industry, as far as necessary, from the ordinary channels of commerce so as to fit our rearmament in with the needs of our export trade, and yet make sure that rearmament has supreme priority'. Chamberlain had learned to make gestures to avoid real change and had pre-empted the last demand. Churchill concluded with yet more oratorical majesty:

> I have watched this island descending incontinently, feck-lessly, the stairway which leads to a dark gulf. It is a fine broad stairway at the beginning, but after a bit the carpet ends. A little further on there are only flagstones, and a little further on still these break under your feet . . . Now is the time at last to rouse the nation. Perhaps it is the last time it can be roused with a chance of preventing war, or with a chance of coming through to victory should our effort to prevent war fail.

This speech proclaimed the need to resist German aggression. It had its weaknesses as a means of arousing the nation, especially its 'progressive' high-minded sections. There was little about Spain, just a passage suggesting that Franco-British collaboration would somehow generate mediation; it was non-committal about Italy; and the Soviet Union was taken for granted as a supporter of resistance to Hitler. The great theme was to unite south-eastern Europe in an anti-Nazi bloc. A speaker in the debate detected 'through the rolling rhetoric of the elder statesman the rattle of the sabre of the subaltern of cavalry'. Perhaps it would be more to the point to detect the infantry officer of the First War. Here he was counting up numbers of divisions, containing, no doubt, men capable of defending trenches with their muskets, but ill equipped for modern war. If he took for granted the USSR, he was showing dangerous ignorance of the problem of getting the countries of south-east Europe to co-operate with the Russians or vice versa. Still, perhaps his plan for British patronage of an anti-German Europe might have made co-operation easier.[22]

Members from all sides showed their awed admiration for his speech. The next speaker found it 'very difficult to follow' Churchill, 'who so moved the House in the great peroration to which we have just listened'. James Griffiths, the eloquent Welsh Labour member, noted that 'we always listen to him with respect. Any time he speaks we learn a good deal.' Replying for the government, Sir John Simon admitted that 'of course we have to consider and pay great attention to the speech made by the Right Hon Member for Epping'. But Chamberlain won the contest. Next day, *The Times* felt able to announce his victory. 'All suggestions of a revolt in the Conservative Party were entirely dissipated by the Prime Minister's speech.' If there had been a vote:

> it is doubtful if a single supporter would have dissented. Yet only a few days ago there were rumours that 50 or 60 MPs were dissatisfied with Mr Chamberlain's handling of the international situation since the German occupation of Austria. Mr Churchill's contribution to the debate was naturally regarded as a deciding factor. When it was realised that he was critical without being hostile, the alleged 'cave' against the government disappeared into thin air.

A friend to Churchill, and an old associate in the fight over India, 'Top' Wolmer, evaded the issue. He was the son of the Earl of Selborne, well connected with eminent Conservatives, and became known as 'the embodiment in the House of the Conservative Party's conscience'. 'There is everything', he declared, 'to support the policy which the Prime Minister is pressing at the present moment of trying to get a settlement which will be a lasting settlement. But if the attempt fails, I hope and believe that our Government will pursue a policy on the lines' Churchill had advocated 'in that great speech which he delivered tonight'. To try conciliation and then to take up confrontation meant believing, as Wolmer said, 'that the resources of the free nations are immeasurably greater than the resources of the dictator States'. It is often said that British weakness led to appeasement; confidence in British strength, in the resources potentially available to a united and determined nation, counted at least as much. Try Chamberlain first; then, if that fails, try Churchill. The self-confident masters of the mighty British Empire often failed to understand that this dilatory process might lose potential friends and allies among those fearful of German power. Chamberlain's promise to accelerate rearmament helped to reassure.[23]

Chamberlain's closest associates continued to take Churchill very seriously. Sir Louis Spears, an old associate and friend of Churchill, hoped to take Churchill on a timely visit to Czechoslovakia. In April 1938 he sent a disconcerting letter to Churchill expressing the hope that he would not object to an extra companion on the visit, Sir Joseph Ball – 'he is very anxious to see the same things as you are on behalf of the Prime Minister and he is absolutely discreet'. Ball, officially, was head of the Conservative Research Department. In addition, he was Chamberlain's agent for intelligence and clandestine propaganda, and used his former service in MI5 to advantage. Spears assured Churchill that Ball did not know that Churchill was coming on the trip to Prague. This is impossible to believe. Ball, among other nefarious activities, arranged telephone taps, and it is likely that Churchill was a victim; certainly, the telephones of the Czech legation will have been tapped. Churchill did not go to Czechoslovakia.[24]

The day after the debate of 24 March, Churchill went out to Paris to stay from Friday to Monday at the British embassy. Sir Eric Phipps, the ambassador, arranged for him to see nearly everyone who counted in determining French policy, Edouard Herriot, Paul Reynaud, Léon Blum, Joseph Paul-Boncour, P.-E. Flandin, Edouard Daladier and Alexis Léger. Phipps kept an eye on him and arranged that those 'meetings will not unduly excite the French'. He urged the French, he claimed, to pour 'liberal sprinklings of salt' on Churchill's remarks during his 'hectic and electric weekend'. Churchill 'strongly advocates a close Anglo-French alliance with staff talks, military and air, and also the joint attempt by France and Great Britain to galvanise the Central European and Balkan Powers to join together in resisting German pressure'. Thus Churchill tried to get the French to support his campaign to change British policy; unfortunately, French governments could not do it. The British took it for granted that French support would be there for Britain when it was wanted; meanwhile France could be bullied into pursuing whatever policy the British chose. If French governments did not like it, there was nothing they could do except venture the hair-raising gamble of assuming British support for actions the British government asked them not to take.[25]

In mid-April Churchill announced a series of meetings to make people 'realise the increasing danger ... and the need for a united national effort to cope with it'. They were to be in Manchester, Sheffield, Birmingham and Bristol, and in Churchill's Epping constituency. It should have been a great historical event, another Midlothian campaign. It failed. Before he started, Churchill identified himself once again with the Conservative diehards. He denounced Chamberlain's latest triumph of conciliation, this time his treaty with Eamon De Valera which transformed the Irish Free State into Eire, an independent Irish republic. Churchill vehemently protested against the British renunciation of the right to use, in war, the treaty ports, naval facilities at Queenstown (Cobh), Berehaven and Lough Swilly. In 1941, after the fall of France, he was unexpectedly proved correct. But in 1938 he seemed archaic and antediluvian. Vyvyan

Adams, perhaps in the division lobbies the most active Conservative opponent of government policy, told the Commons that he disagreed with Churchill, 'who has made . . . a series of great speeches . . . I think that recently he has very rarely been wrong' – but he thought him wrong now. Churchill, *The Times* commented, 'disappointed some new-found admirers'.[26]

He began in fine style in Manchester, at the Free Trade Hall, on 9 May. He spoke on behalf of the movement for the 'Defence of Freedom and Peace' and the League of Nations Union. He was introduced by Sir Arthur Haworth, the local head of the League of Nations Union, a Liberal. After Churchill's 'frequently applauded' speech, a Labour alderman (Toole) and a Conservative councillor (James Watts) proposed a vote of thanks. Both were prominent in their local party organizations, and Watts came from a family of Manchester merchant princes with a magnificent warehouse, crammed with cotton garments, displaying in Piccadilly in central Manchester the full splendours of the revived Renaissance. Joseph Toole, the Labour alderman, made the point directly. He 'wondered why the government could not find room for such brains'.

Churchill put forward his alternative League policy in a mature and developed shape. Now the USSR had its place: 'we should certainly not go cap-in-hand to Soviet Russia, or count in any definite manner upon Russian action. But how improvidently foolish we should be when dangers are so great, to put needless barriers in the way of the general association of the great Russian mass with resistance to an act of Nazi aggression.' Then as a 'third stage' he added, as eventual recruits to the alliance, Poland, the Baltic States and 'the Scandinavian powers'. He brought in the Far East and praised Chiang Kai-shek, supported as he claimed by Soviet help, and referred to the threat to the Japanese presented by the Soviet Far Eastern army. He condemned 'the shameful intrusions of Dictator powers' in Spain 'under the deceitful masquerade of Non-Intervention', though his solution for Spain offered little hope: 'our country ... may yet find the means of mediating between the combatants'. Apart from Abyssinia, every concern of the League zealots got an outing and the eclipse of Eden, as the hero of the right-minded, advanced a little further. 'We must gather together around the joint strength of Britain and France and under the authority of the League all countries prepared to resist, and if possible to prevent, acts of violent aggression. There is the path to safety. These are the only guarantees of freedom. There, on the rock of the Covenant of the League of Nations alone can we build high and enduring the temple and the towers of Peace'.[27]

Conservative Central Office kept an eye on all this. James Watts wrote to the Conservative Party Chairman to reassure him that the Manchester Conservative Party was not moving out of line. He assured him before the speech that he had 'no reason to believe Mr Churchill would make any attack on the government or on the Prime Minister'. There was less and less need for Chamberlain and his friends to worry. On 13 May Churchill and Archibald Sinclair conferred at lunch with Henlein, the Sudeten German agitator. Professor Lindemann, who spoke perfect German, was there and made notes. Henlein took them in by masterly deception; Hitler himself had encouraged his visit. Henlein, then forty years old, had been a bank clerk and a gym teacher. When not acting as the 'leader', in uniform and jackboots, he had a mild and quiet manner and insisted that he was a moderate, reasonable man, not a true Nazi, even a loyal citizen of democratic Czechoslovakia. G. E. R. Gedye, a clever journalist who had interviewed him and observed him, wrote that he was 'gifted with a curious persuasiveness which, while one talks with him, makes one feel that it would be a personal insult to cast doubt on his statements'. Gedye, though, made one notable mistake. Of Henlein's visit to Churchill, he commented, 'I doubt if he cut much ice with Winston.' Unfortunately, he did.

R. A. C. PARKER

Henlein managed to persuade Churchill to imagine that agreement was possible which will 'enable him and his followers to act as loyal members of the State prepared to defend it against aggression from whatsoever side it might come'. Churchill told Chamberlain, 'I was very much pleased with the result of this talk,' and Chamberlain agreed that 'it was encouraging rather than the reverse'. In consequence Churchill talked nonsense to his Bristol audience on 16 May. 'The prospects of a good, friendly settlement between the government of Czechoslovakia and the German population in that country are far better than I had expected. I see no reason why the Sudeten Deutsche should not become trusted and honoured partners in what is, after all, the most progressive and democratic of the new States in Europe.' In Sheffield on 31 May he showed that the British government, too, had deceived him, with many others. He believed that the British government had given support to Czechoslovakia against attack in the crisis of 20–21 May, when for a time some German military movements were treated by Prague, wrongly, as preliminaries to armed incursions. He took the view that this should make the Czechoslovak government carry on negotiations with Henlein and his aides 'without the slightest delay'. He also concentrated on the old theme of rearmament, though making obeisance to League opinion on Spain: at Birmingham on 2 June it excited his 'indignation' when he saw shameful interference disguised under the mocking terms 'non-intervention' by Germany and Italy.[28]

Apart from a different emphasis on Spain, especially in complaining of the bombing of British ships in Spanish waters, and in calling for a new organization of arms supply, Churchill's policy was now the same as the government's: together with the French to force the Prague government urgently to make a bargain with Henlein's party. Because Henlein had persuaded Churchill that he was a reasonable man who could make his own decisions and not act, as he did, simply as a puppet of

Hitler's, Churchill explained in print, 'I am sure that the essential elements of a good and lasting settlement are present,' and insisted that there should be no 'obstinacy' or 'obduracy' from the Czechs. Shiela Grant Duff sent a bitter reproach: 'The Germans and the Sudeten Germans claim to have your support against the Czechs.' Churchill seems also not to have grasped how well informed was Ewald von Kleist, an emissary of that section of the German military who believed general war would ruin Germany. He told Churchill on 19 August that Hitler would use force against Czechoslovakia after the Nuremberg conference in September unless restrained by fear of Britain and France. In one way, it is true, Churchill responded admirably by writing a letter to Kleist insisting that a German attack on Czechoslovakia would bring Great Britain into war. Churchill communicated with Lord Halifax, who weakened the effect by repeating the 'may or may not' declaration on 24 March. As late as 5 September, Churchill was ready to say, if only in a piece of journalism, 'things appear to be taking a far more favourable turn in the European arena'.[29]

In these fraught months the most violent denunciation of any speech of Churchill's had nothing to do with foreign policy. He was accused, of all things, of 'orthodoxy'. On 4 May *The Times* published a 'Blast' from Wyndham Lewis, the quarrelsome painter and writer, whose (distinctly good) portrait of T. S. Eliot had just been rejected by the Royal Academy. Lewis was the most expert British exponent of Cubism, and had founded and led the Vorticists. According to him, Churchill had pronounced to the Royal Academy a 'passionate advocacy of platitude'. The protests of artists would be drowned if such 'an eminent ex-Minister of State could be found to turn on the hydrant ... of romantic Parliamentary rhetoric'. Churchill spoke at the Royal Academy dinner – one of the rare social occasions when he and Neville Chamberlain were both present. Shortly before the day of the dinner, newspapers reported the resignation from the

Academy of Augustus John as a protest against the rejection of the Wyndham Lewis portrait. *The Times* reminded its readers of some precedents. Stanley Spencer had given up his association with the Academy after some of his own pictures had been turned down. Sickert had resigned to protest against the rejection of statues by Jacob Epstein.

Churchill gave the Academy a sparkling, amusing speech. He was glad that the Prime Minister 'has found time and vitality to come here tonight'. Chamberlain could not have come 'if the same intense standards prevailed at Downing Street as at Burlington House. Fancy what his life would be if, for instance, two or three of his leading Cabinet colleagues tendered their resignations because I presented some oratorical work at Westminster and he was alleged to have received it with inadequate appreciation.'[30] Was Churchill, or Chamberlain, consciously aware at that moment that such Cabinet resignations were the only way of ending appeasement?

CHAPTER NINE

Munich

IN THE EARLY summer of 1938 Churchill had softened, for a time, his rhetorical leadership of opposition to appeasement. Deluded by Henlein, he hoped for and even expected a peaceful negotiation to settle the claims of German-speaking Czechs. He openly acknowledged that 'Parliament and the public have approved the circumspect and restrained position which Mr Chamberlain and His Majesty's Government have adopted.'[1]

His status as a potential leader of all anti-fascists, however, grew when he became more combative towards Franco. At the same time, while thus appealing to the left, he kept the sympathy of Conservatives by demanding that British warships should protect British ships from the violence of foreigners. On 21 June 1938 Philip Noel Baker, an authentically 'progressive' MP, attacked the Chamberlain government's total inaction over the bombing of British ships in Spanish harbours; Franco's aircraft, or aircraft belonging to his foreign helpers, were bombing ships in government harbours. Next day two more British ships were bombed, near Valencia. Attlee opened an attack on the government's refusal to go beyond protests. Now Churchill joined in. He urged the Prime Minister to use his influence with Mussolini to get him to stop these bombings. With evident relish, he urged Chamberlain to insist on a return from his tireless efforts to win

Mussolini's friendship. If Chamberlain failed to persuade Mussolini to restrain these attacks, then Franco should be told, 'If there is any more of this we shall arrest one of your warships on the open sea.' After Churchill spoke there came an impassioned utterance from Chuter Ede, for the Labour Party; like many of the prominent Labour MPs of those days, he served under Churchill in the war, and then under Attlee after 1945. He denounced the failure of the government to use the Royal Navy to 'fulfil their historic task of saving British lives' and asked if the Commons, 'which in former days included men of the names of Drake, Raleigh and Grenville', had 'fallen so low now that a Spanish pirate can order British ships on their lawful occasions to put back to port'. Churchill did not vote in the subsequent division. Eventually Franco agreed that, if investigation showed the attacks to be deliberate, compensation should be paid.[2]

Duncan Sandys, Churchill's son-in-law, combined the duties of a second lieutenant in the Territorial Army in the artillery, attached to the 51 (London) anti-aircraft brigade, with membership of the House of Commons as a Conservative MP. At the end of June 1938 his dual roles set off a complicated, elaborate, sometimes mildly farcical set of Parliamentary issues. To consider them, two select committees examined witnesses. They questioned the Prime Minister, the Attorney-General, the Secretary for War, the Minister for Co-ordination of Defence, the Chief of the Imperial General Staff, the General Officer Commanding the anti-aircraft defence of the United Kingdom, the GOC Eastern Command and various colonels, majors, and so on. It started with Duncan Sandys's unease about the inadequate equipment of his unit. He enquired of the adjutant of his battery, who briefed him after Sandys promised only to tell Leslie Hore-Belisha, the War Secretary. Sandys wrote to Hore-Belisha asking for a conversation and said that unless he were reassured he might have to put a question to Parliament. Hore-Belisha, learning that Sandys had gained access to secret information, informed the Attorney-General, who drew Sandys's attention to the Official Secrets Act and to the imprisonment that breaches of them could incur. Sandys complained to the Commons, which set up a select committee to consider possible clashes between the duties of MPs and national security.

Two days later, on 29 June, Sandys provided a new sensation. He had been ordered to appear next day – wearing his uniform and his ceremonial sword – at a military court of enquiry. This time the Committee of Privileges was directed to look into this new derogation from the standing of MPs. This committee condemned the military tribunal. Then the committee – and Sandys – were embarrassed to discover that, whoever was to blame for the order to Sandys, the tribunal could not be blamed, for it had never met or even been appointed, and never came into existence. The select committee on the Official Secrets Act took over the whole issue and eventually produced reports which were discussed in the House in December 1938 and April 1939.[3]

Unexpectedly the 'Sandys storm' also reinforced Churchill's support among the left. Two Labour members, Lieutenant-Commander Fletcher and James Chuter Ede, saw in the affair an attempt by an autocratic government to suppress criticism and especially Churchill's denunciations of the inadequacies and ineptitudes of government efforts to rearm, which obviously rested on revelations to him of deficiencies made by members of the defence services. Fletcher asserted that 'the government wanted to put an end to a practice which inconveniences them'. They had turned on Sandys, but 'I think that they have been flying at higher game in taking the action that they have done. They have shot at a pigeon hoping to bring down a crow.' Much later, at the end of 1938, in yet another debate on Sandys and secrets, Chuter Ede suggested that Lord Gort, the Chief of the Imperial General Staff, became interested only when someone told him that Sandys, whom he had never heard of before, was Churchill's son-in-law. Then, Ede claimed, he and the government saw a chance of making Churchill less tiresome.[4]

Once again, from the further left, *Tribune* backed Sandys and Churchill. Harold Laski declared that the Sandys case had 'a fundamental importance' and even that 'our liberty is at stake'. Aneurin Bevan, one of the best orators of the day, ranking with Lloyd George as second only to Churchill himself, turned furiously on A. P. Herbert, the joker, in the House of Commons. Alan Herbert poked fun at Churchill to compensate for the growing boredom which he claimed the Sandys storm had evoked in the outside world. He frequently contributed to *Punch* and his expert legal series of 'misleading cases' is still not forgotten. Now he derided Churchill's role as prosecuting counsel for Sandys, combined with his role as one of the judges on the Committee of Privileges. He added another metaphor. Churchill seemed 'to be attempting to combine the incompatible functions of centre forward and referee. One minute he is bounding forward to the attack, kicking goals in all directions, and then next minute, dignified, but still bounding, he is blowing his whistle.' He threw a poisoned dart. 'I am not quite clear how he manages to reconcile, I will not say with his conscience, but with considerations of taste and dignity, sitting at all upon that Committee.' He got applause from the sort of Conservative MP, not always the brightest, who believed that subalterns should not think and should do what they were told, and from those who disliked Conservatives sceptical of the government's infallibility.

Supporting Churchill, Bevan spoke. 'It seems to me an extraordinary suggestion, and one which violates all the canons of humour to which the Hon Member [A. P. Herbert] has given so many years of requited toil, to suggest that a man is more concerned for his son-in-law than—' At that point Bevan was interrupted by a Conservative member. In later years Laski and Bevan both suffered Churchillian denunciation. Churchill hated criticism, which Bevan supplied during Churchill's wartime government, and so became a 'squalid nuisance'. Laski became the butt of one of the silliest of all Churchill's speeches when, in 1945, the Prime Minister denounced his alleged plan to set up a socialist Gestapo.

In the 1937–8 Parliamentary session, the Commons debated foreign affairs thirty times, and members asked 1,533 questions. In the thirtieth debate Chamberlain announced that Lord Runciman (a rich shipowner, then the owner of Eigg in the Hebrides) would go to Czechoslovakia 'in response', Chamberlain claimed quite untruthfully, to a request from Czechoslovakia. The Prime Minister declared that 'we all feel that the atmosphere is lighter and that throughout the Continent there is a relaxation of that sense of tension which six months ago was present'. Churchill was there but did not raise objection. Chamberlain's complacency was chronic: Churchill's at most an intermittent disorder. It was left to another authentic progressive, Eleanor Rathbone, to speak up for the Grand Alliance: 'I cannot help believing that the Right Hon Gentleman the Member for Epping [Churchill] is right and that his view is the view held by many Hon Members, namely, that it is not too late to rally the peace-loving nations within the League.'[5] Perhaps it was appropriate for Churchill, who had been the close associate of Lloyd George in social reforms, to have won the approval of two of the leaders of civilizing reform in the twentieth century: Miss Rathbone, the campaigner for family allowances, and Aneurin Bevan, who later presided over the foundation of the National Health Service.

Hitler soon threatened a new crisis. International aggression may be launched by surprise or with noisy, demonstrative, advance preparations. The strength of Czech defences forbade a sudden spring. Hitler chose intimidation to isolate Czechoslovakia before moving to 'smash' that state. Doubtless Runciman's mission encouraged him. In a way that Churchill apparently did not grasp, it represented the anxiety of Chamberlain to push

Edward Beneš, and the other Czechoslovakian leaders, into accepting whatever was needed to keep Germany quiet. At the beginning of August news arrived in London of the formidable German military manoeuvres that were being prepared. The Foreign Office news department, in the second week of August, let it be known, as the diplomatic correspondent of *The Times* put it, that 'the elaborate preparations now being made in Germany for the autumn manoeuvres and the evidence of accelerated fortifications on the Western Frontier, have aroused unusual attention in diplomatic circles in London'. Soon after, it came out that the German army was to have six weeks of 'training'. One million men were being mobilized, 600,000 regulars and 400,000 reservists; by mid-September there would be more. Later in August a great parade was put on for the visit to Germany of Admiral Horthy, 'Regent' of Hungary. It was the biggest German military show since the time of Emperor William II.[6]

Evidently Hitler intended to impose a solution of the Czech–German dispute. Churchill – and Chamberlain – began to understand. They resumed their normal attitudes. Chamberlain wished to persuade Hitler peacefully to accept whatever he wanted, Churchill to counter German threats and to prevent the triumph of force. As German troops mobilized, Churchill saw 'an impending trial of will-power which is developing in Europe'. He gave up a lucrative lecture tour in the United States. Ewald von Kleist brought further evidence. On 27 August Churchill told his constituents, 'We are all in full agreement with the course our government have taken in sending Lord Runciman to Prague. We hope, indeed we pray, that his mission of conciliation will be successful.' More realistically, he responded to the calling out of 'vast German armies' by suggesting 'that outside forces, that larger and fiercer ambitions may prevent a settlement, and that Europe and the civilized world will have to face the demands of Nazi Germany' and 'the invasion of a small country'. He remained, in public, conciliatory and gentle towards Chamberlain: 'foreign countries should know and the government is right to let them know that Great Britain and the British Empire must not be deemed incapable of playing their part and doing their duty as they have done on other great occasions which have not yet been forgotten by history'. In fact, Chamberlain had already begun to meditate about flying to visit Hitler to bring him pacifying concessions. Chamberlain and Churchill now diverged in thought even more than Churchill guessed.[7]

Churchill discussed the increasingly fraught crisis with Halifax, the Foreign Secretary. Halifax told a meeting of Cabinet ministers on 30 August that 'Mr Churchill had referred to the possibility of a joint note to Berlin from a number of Powers.' Halifax thought this would lead to 'embarrassing questions as to our attitude in the event of Germany invading Czechoslovakia' – in other words, that it would bring suggestions that Britain should promise then to go to war, a pledge that Chamberlain, Halifax and most Cabinet ministers did not wish to give.

The day after this meeting, Churchill saw Halifax again for half an hour, and conveyed a letter suggesting deterrents against Hitler's violence which would not 'commit you to the dread guarantee' to Czechoslovakia. Some naval movements and mobilizations and a joint note by Britain, France and Russia threateningly, if vaguely, pointing out that a German invasion of Czechoslovakia 'would raise capital issues for all three powers'. President Roosevelt should be persuaded 'to do his utmost upon it'. Churchill suggested that the note would give 'the best chance to the peaceful elements in German official circles to make a stand'. Two days later Halifax got another letter. This time Churchill passed on from Maisky, ambassador of the USSR in London, a suggestion of Maxim Litvinov, Soviet Foreign Minister, that the Council of the League of Nations should be brought in to consult together over the danger of war.[8] The effect on Halifax was to help to make him 'unsettled', as Chamberlain put it: Chamberlain believed in his policy, Halifax became less confident. Halifax decided to order the British ambassador to warn Hitler that a German attack would bring France to help Czechoslovakia and that Britain 'could not stand aside'.

From Germany Nevile Henderson sent excited messages declaring that a warning would 'drive Hitler straight off the deep end' and 'be fatal to prospects of peace'. Samuel Hoare returned, by the overnight train from Perth, from Balmoral, where he had been shooting with King George VI the day before. He was in time to help Chamberlain to avoid angering Hitler before what was expected to be his decisive speech at the Nuremberg Party Rally on 12 September. Churchill came to 10 Downing Street on 10 September and told Chamberlain and Halifax that 'we should tell Germany that if she set foot in Czechoslovakia we should at once be at war with her'. Chamberlain, supported by Hoare and Simon, however, overruled Halifax, and a message went to Henderson that evening telling him he need not arrange to present any warning to Hitler himself.[9]

The full Cabinet approved on the morning of the 12th: Chamberlain noted that Eden, whom he had seen on 9 September, 'had concurred in this view'. Halifax told this Cabinet that the letter in *The Times* that morning from Eden 'had been published with the full concurrence of the prime minister and himself'. Prominently printed in *The Times*, it set out the government position: 'it is a dangerous illusion to assume that once a conflict had broken out in Central Europe it could be localized', and 'in any international emergency that threatened the security of France this country would be found at the side of the French Republic'. Churchill's categorical pledge to go to war with Germany if Germany set foot in Czechoslovakia did not appear in Eden's letter. Eden had taken the trouble to deliver his letter to *The Times* offices himself – the editor, Geoffrey Dawson, found Eden there on Sunday at 7.30 in the evening, waiting for his return from a weekend absence.[10]

Hitler's speech on 12 September, as expected, denounced Czechoslovakia and Beneš. Rioting followed in the Sudeten German areas, with eleven deaths there reported by next evening. Henlein's followers put up extreme demands for immediate satisfaction. Chamberlain decided to propose his secret plan to Hitler, after he had told some of his senior ministers. The full Cabinet learned of it only after he had asked Hitler to receive him; he informed the French government, later still, after Hitler had agreed.

In the later editions of the *Daily Telegraph* of 15 September the rival policies of Churchill and Chamberlain confronted each other. Readers who opened the paper in the middle where the most portentous events were set out – small advertisements still occupied the front page – found Churchill on page twelve and Chamberlain opposite on page thirteen. 'Can Europe Stave Off War? Joint Warning By Powers The Strongest Hope' headlined Churchill; 'Mr Chamberlain To Meet Hitler. Attempt To Find Solution Of Czech Crisis' stood out in even bolder type.

Churchill assessed the situation correctly: 'everything is ready or will be ready in the next ten days, for a converging attack on Czechoslovakia with troops and weapons which the Nazi party believes to be overwhelming. All that remains is for some bloody incident or actual revolt, to be created at the moment prescribed by Hitler, and for the signal to advance to be given.' He prescribed action and the language to express it: 'the ordinary smooth and balanced phrases of diplomacy with all their refinements and reserves, are of little use in dealing with the fierce chiefs of German Nazidom. Only the most blunt, even brutal language will make its effect. Moreover, whatever words are used must carry with them the conviction that they are spoken in deadly earnest.'[11]

Chamberlain got only slightly heavier type for his headlines, but from now until the meeting at Munich he made the news in a way impossible even for his most effective critic. Three flights to confront Hitler made by the Prime Minister within two weeks, single-handed, still seem sensational even at the start of the twenty-first century. Berchtesgaden, Godesberg and Munich for conferences with Hitler, with Daladier for France and Mussolini for Italy present only once with subsidiary parts, put Chamberlain at the centre of world history. Critics discussed and argued; Chamberlain acted, dramatically. He was good at the 'media'. He understood filming and knew how to pose for the cameras; he was a skilled broadcaster; he had effective publicity agents. Churchill's talents, colossal as they were, were old-fashioned: he needed a stage and audience for his best performances – the House of Commons or a public platform; broadcasting he took to slowly. Eden, commanding more public esteem than any competitor, by degrees eroded his appeal by being boring and conformist. The press noted that Churchill and Eden 'are the only two men holding unofficial positions who are known to have taken part in the discussions of the past few days' – that is to say, discussions in Downing Street in the days leading up to the week of Chamberlain's first flight, when policy was being made.

Early on 14 September both of them telephoned Halifax, each acting independently of the other as usual. Halifax told neither that Chamberlain had already asked Hitler to receive him; the Prime Minister wanted it kept secret in order not to lessen the theatrical excitement of his action. Halifax circulated the remarks of Eden and Churchill to the Cabinet. Churchill pressed 'with all the urgency that he could command' that France, Russia and Britain should at once send a joint warning to Berlin to 'save disaster'. He was convinced that 'it did not increase the danger in which we already stood and was more likely to dispel it'. Characteristically, Eden used less firmness and spoke more opaquely. He did not suggest a joint note but, 'if we and the French chose to secure corresponding action by Russia, he did not think there would be any objection to that'.[12] The Cabinet paid no attention at all. At its meeting that morning most ministers first heard of Chamberlain's startling scheme and, understandably, could think of nothing else.

Churchill had had no hint of Chamberlain's plan to descend on Hitler out of the skies to rearrange Europe with the dictator. In September 1938 he was, like everyone, surprised by how far Chamberlain would carry appeasement. Churchill's erratic son, Randolph, wrote to him that day with sound advice: 'Please in future emulate my deep-seated mistrust of Chamberlain and all his works and colleagues ... When they are with you they are careful to talk in honourable terms; if I have read them more truly it is because their underlings are less discreet with me.' It was correct, of course, that Churchill always took it for granted that he should discuss public affairs principally with the men at the top. His own mental attitudes made that seem to him the obvious course, and his high status and immense prestige made it easy to do. Thus he went to see Halifax at the Foreign Office again on 19 September after Chamberlain had come back from Hitler's mountain retreat at Berchtesgaden. Halifax after all had once been a junior minister serving under Churchill. He was the most important individual in determining whether or not Churchill could change British policy. Chamberlain could hardly live through the resignation of a second Foreign Secretary.

Less glamorous than Eden and less popular with the public, Halifax, just the same, was intellectually able and fitted perfectly the respectful, deferential British society of the early twentieth century. He was a 'gentleman', polite, modest, unostentatious, in a way denied to Churchill. He 'loved country pursuits', hunted, enjoyed village cricket and showed all the mannerisms of a firmly established hereditary landlord. He could maintain upper-class standards of living without the energy and industry required from Churchill. He gave the impression, quite misleadingly, that he found high office a time-consuming bore.[13] With the support of Halifax, Chamberlain could manage his Cabinet; without it, he could not. But Halifax was not a resigner, so his impact on the party outside was limited. In the end, in fact, he kept Chamberlain afloat by forcing him to shift his policies enough to keep sufficient party opinion behind him. Though Halifax looked down on the 'public' and its 'opinion', he sometimes shared in its evolution, mainly because he was far less confident in his own opinions than Chamberlain. All this was demonstrated at the end of September 1938.

By the time of Churchill's next conversation with Halifax, Chamberlain had talked to Daladier and Georges Bonnet, the French Prime Minister and Foreign Minister, in London. Chamberlain set out for the French the plan the British Cabinet had just accepted – to persuade Czechoslovakia to allow the German-inhabited districts to transfer to Germany. Before Churchill's visit to Halifax, the full French government had agreed. Halifax evidently pointed out to Churchill that several French ministers hoped to avoid having to help Czechoslovakia. It was a pattern of appeasement: French appeasers excused their concessions by blaming them on British softness; the British blamed the French. Potential Churchillians in London and Paris could be checked.

The day after his talk with the Foreign Secretary, Churchill flew to Paris. Both the British and the French governments had to be told to stand firm and resist. By his own later account, he induced the two most energetic anti-appeasers in the French government to stay rather than resign: Paul Reynaud and Georges Mandel. Phipps, the British ambassador in Paris, now a convinced appeaser, reported that Churchill and Spears, 'who are now in Paris are busy giving bad advice to M. Osusky [the Czech representative in Paris] and to certain French politicians'. Spears was a valuable companion for Churchill: he spoke perfect

French. Indeed he was as much at home in Paris as in London, although an MP in Westminster. He knew everyone that mattered in Paris. Next day Churchill issued a statement to the press, published by newspapers on 22 September: 'The nation should realise the magnitude of the disaster into which we have been led . . . complete surrender . . . if peace is to be preserved on a lasting basis, it can only be by a combination of all the Powers whose convictions and vital interests are opposed to Nazi domination.' He urged that Parliament should be recalled and, using his favourite adjective, 'duly informed upon these grievous matters'. Chamberlain was at Godesberg, where Hitler dismayed him by insisting on immediate German military occupation of the German areas of Czechoslovakia, without any legitimizing dilatoriness.[14]

Churchill's press release had a wide circulation; the more or less eminent persons who met him and privately grumbled with him, for the time being, counted for nothing. What mattered now was what Chamberlain decided and whether or not he could get his Cabinet to agree. Since Churchill commanded no coherent, substantial group of Conservative supporters, his political strength derived from public utterance.

Chamberlain had flown to Godesberg, having arranged that Hitler should peacefully gain what he had asked for. Undoubtedly he felt angry when Hitler asked for more. He controlled himself and continued to work for peace. The easiest way, of course, was to arrange that Hitler should get what he now demanded without his being compelled to fight for it. Chamberlain knew the method of doing it. First persuade the Cabinet in London, then win round the French with appropriate inducements by way of hints of future support or threats of present British inaction; after that bully the Czechs, and peace would be his.

Saturday 24 September gave Chamberlain a hard day. He had not had much sleep. He left Godesberg for London after an amiable farewell to the Führer, who repeated that this was his 'last territorial demand'. Chamberlain had lunch with Halifax, then met his inner group of ministers, followed by the full Cabinet. Everything went well and the Cabinet adjourned at 7.30 p.m.: time for a meal and early bed for the great peacemaker. There had been no dissent from his proposals.

Next morning, the 25th, Chamberlain received a 'horrible blow'. His Foreign Secretary, Halifax, of all people, disagreed with him. Alexander Cadogan, Vansittart's successor as the senior official of the Foreign Office, an apparently calm, placid bureaucrat whose angry passions were kept for his diary, had attacked the Foreign Secretary's acquiescence in Chamberlain's plans. Edward Halifax endured a sleepless night of worry. On Sunday morning he led a revolt of the Cabinet. A majority refused to press the French and the Czechs to accept Hitler's new demands. French ministers had already been invited to London; now Chamberlain did not succeed in persuading them to lead the way to surrender and subsequently failed to persuade the British Cabinet that this was what the French really wished to do. That day Churchill put out another statement to the press. 'There is still one good chance of preserving peace' – Britain, France and Russia should declare that a German invasion of Czechoslovakia would bring war with them all. This should be communicated to 'all neutral countries . . . particularly to the Government of the USA'. Lord Cecil and Lord Lytton went to Downing Street to tell No. 10 that the League of Nations Union 'supported wholeheartedly Mr Churchill's statement'. Leo Amery and Robert Boothby demanded the same threat, and Attlee, for the Labour Party, wrote to the Prime Minister to urge him to leave no doubt in Hitler's mind that Britain would unite with France and Russia to resist a German attack on Czechoslovakia.

Chamberlain felt he had to do something to warn Hitler; he did so as cautiously and politely as possible.[15] At midnight –

these were crisis meetings – that Sunday, Chamberlain suggested to the Cabinet that he should send Horace Wilson, his most trusted aide, first, to appeal to Hitler to discuss the method and timing of a peaceful German advance into the Sudetenland. Then, if that did not work, and only after this appeal had failed, he should warn Hitler that active French efforts to help to defend Czechoslovakia would bring Britain in. Russia was not to be mentioned. On Monday morning, the 27th, General Gamelin, the French Commander-in-Chief, came to London and, surprisingly, said that France would take some sort of offensive action if Germany attacked Czechoslovakia. That afternoon Churchill came to Downing Street and talked to Chamberlain and Halifax. Churchill was delighted. 'We three were together', he wrote later, and 'in the crisis, we all seemed very much together'. He was deluded by Chamberlain's apparent amenability. But what Chamberlain did after the meeting was to order Horace Wilson, still in Berlin, to tell Hitler that if the French attacked Germany to help Czechoslovakia against German invasion then Britain would come in. Eventually Wilson did so, as he told Chamberlain, 'in what I hope was the tone you would wish'. There was no mention of Russia.

From the Foreign Office that evening came a communiqué to the press, approved by Halifax. If the Germans attacked Czechoslovakia, 'France will be bound to come to her assistance, and Great Britain and Russia will certainly stand by France.' This remark was the closest any British government statement came to a proclamation of the Churchillian Grand Alliance at any time. Chamberlain was angry, 'much put out' in Halifax's words. Once again, Halifax had shown independence and an inclination to follow his Foreign Office advisers; there is no reason to believe that Churchill had brought about this sensational gesture. Later in the day Chamberlain issued his own press statement. It declared that Hitler could be sure that he could get what he wanted without war; the British government would see to that. Chamberlain made his proposal 'in the same spirit of friendliness as that in which I was received in Germany'.[16]

Returning, Horace Wilson suggested that the British should accept Hitler's immediate occupation of Czech territory. Halifax and the Cabinet refused. Chamberlain, dodging the Cabinet and its awkward attitude, sent off his own appeal to Hitler and an appeal to Mussolini for his support to persuade Hitler to accept a façade of negotiation. On 28 September Parliament met. War seemed imminent. Children were conveyed out of big towns to be billeted in safer homes, trenches were dug and gas masks issued. That morning the mobilization of the fleet was announced. Hitler had set out his terms; the British government, the Czechs and the French had rejected them. Would Hitler give way to Chamberlain's private and public appeals?

When Chamberlain rose in the Commons just before three in the afternoon, Hitler's answer had not come. The longer the delay the more likely the coming of war. After more than an hour of sombre narrative from the Prime Minister, he was interrupted by the thrusting of a document into his hand. 'I have something further to say to the House yet. I have now been informed by Herr Hitler that he invites me to meet him at Munich to-morrow morning'. He suggested the House adjourn 'for a few days, when, perhaps, we may meet in happier circumstances'. In the next five minutes, Attlee spoke to welcome the news, amid general cheering. Sinclair wished Chamberlain 'god speed'; so did Lansbury, the Labour pacifist; and Maxton agreed for the small number of Independent Labour members. Only Gallagher, the one communist MP, protested against the dismemberment of Czechoslovakia. *The Times* reported that 'there was a loud cheer when Mr Churchill went up to the Prime Minister and cordially shook his hand'.[17]

Next day Churchill mostly spent in the lavish comfort of the Savoy Hotel – a frequent haunt of the anti-appeasers. First lunch, with speeches: Churchill wanted to send a telegram to Chamberlain in Munich to deter him from imposing more concessions on the Czechs. He hoped Eden and Attlee would sign. Both refused. Eden wanted to seem moderate and judicious, which meant evading subordination to Churchill, while for Attlee there was no merit in association with any Conservative unless a serious split in the Tory Party could be won and of that there was still no sign – the drama of 28 September made that party seem solid. In the evening the Other Club dined at the Savoy. Two Cabinet ministers were there – Walter Elliot and Duff Cooper – and they found themselves bullied into quarrels with other diners. All this mattered not at all.[18] What mattered, for the moment, were the discussions in Munich.

Munich pleased only one of its leading actors: Neville Chamberlain. Daladier felt shame at the desertion of France's most faithful ally; Mussolini knew that his apparently important role as a mediator was a sham; Hitler resented his own failure, for the moment, to eliminate and take Czechoslovakia into his control. He had had to put up with too much fuss and interference from Chamberlain. It is true that he gave up very little of his proclaimed demands. His prestige swelled; the army plotters, if their plots were ever real, could now not justify Hitler's overthrow.

What mattered for Chamberlain was not the size of Hitler's booty, it was that he had taken it peacefully, after 'negotiation', and not by force. Certainly Hitler would have preferred an armed seizure; Chamberlain thought the Führer had turned peaceful because of his own tactful, prudent diplomacy. Perhaps, Chamberlain pondered, Mussolini had helped; Chamberlain could not know that the Italian Duce had been told what to propose by the Germans. Others in Britain thought the communiqué or the mobilization of the fleet had checked Hitler; Chamberlain thought those events had endangered his efforts. What thrilled Chamberlain was his talk alone with Hitler the morning after the Munich agreement on Czechoslovakia had been made. The Führer explained his hatred of the bombing of civilians. He was ready to abolish long-range bombers and even to join in a treaty to do so which would include the USSR. He eagerly signed a paper which Chamberlain had written. Munich and the Anglo-German naval agreement (of 1935) were 'symbolic of the desire of our two peoples never to go to war with one another again. We are resolved that the method of consultation shall be the method adopted to deal with any other questions that may concern our two countries.'[19]

The two eminent scholars who have written distinguished studies of Chamberlain, Keith Feiling and David Dilks, argue that he did not fully believe it. He had won a 'breathing space', but that might be all. War might have been delayed, not necessarily averted. Alec Douglas-Home, then Lord Dunglass, who went to Munich with Chamberlain, insists in his memoirs that Chamberlain deliberately prepared this document to give it the fullest publicity back home, so that if Hitler did not keep his word his guilt would be obvious. They are all wrong. Chamberlain reckoned he was on the way to 'peace for our time'. To pursue his policy he had to deny it. He knew his duty and resentfully understood that in the cause of humanity he had to put up with scepticism and misunderstanding. First came Cabinet ministers. Duff Cooper resigned in protest against the Munich surrender. Elliot, Oliver Stanley and De La Warr demanded increased rearmament. Halifax did not want to rule it out. Moreover Halifax wanted to bring Eden and Labour Party leaders into the Cabinet to create a united national effort. Even Samuel Hoare wished to have Eden back in the government. Chamberlain did not want 'as partners men who would sooner or later wreck the policy with which I am identified'. He kept them all out, and of course Churchill would have been worst of all. For Chamberlain Munich should bring disarmament, not united national efforts towards full-scale rearmament.[20]

The debate in the House of Commons, spread over four days early in October, was, in his own words, 'a pretty trying ordeal' for Chamberlain. He did not get the praise he thought due, even though several speakers echoed Victor Raikes's prediction that 'he will go down to history as the greatest European statesman of this or any other time'.

Chamberlain's long report to his sister Ida, composed the week after, concentrated on Churchill:

> Winston was carrying on a regular conspiracy against me with the aid of Masaryk, the Czech Minister. They, of course, are totally unaware of my knowledge of their proceedings; I had constant information of their doings and sayings which for the nth time demonstrated how completely Winston can deceive himself when he wants to and how utterly credulous a foreigner can be when he is told the thing he wants to hear. In this case the thing was that 'Chamberlain's fall was imminent'!

Chamberlain's interpretation of telephone intercepts is confirmed by a message from Masaryk in London to Prague on 1 October. 'Churchill advises emphatically after consultations with several people' that vital Czech defences should not be handed over to the Germans for at least forty-eight hours. 'He is convinced that there is a growing reaction here against the treachery towards us.' Chamberlain explained to his sister that 'the papers published a good deal of rumour about impending resignations'. Though 'much of it was false', he 'had to fight all the time against the defection of weaker brethren'. He worried especially about Oliver Stanley and Harry Crookshank, both of whom were the sort of person highly influential in the Conservative Party of those days. Stanley 'had constant qualms which required repeated interviews', and Crookshank, a minister outside the Cabinet, actually sent in his resignation and had to be talked out of it by the Chief Whip and Chamberlain himself.

Certainly Chamberlain encountered problems and he had to change the emphasis of his policy from developing the struggle for disarmament to an increase in the urgency of rearmament. However, either Masaryk or Churchill or both evidently deluded themselves with false hopes.[21]

The debate in the House of Commons began with Duff Cooper's resignation speech, which won sombre thanks from the new Czechoslovak leader General Syrový and which, for Churchill, was 'admirable in form, massive in argument and shone with courage and public spirit'. Duff Cooper set up the alternatives Chamberlain had himself repeatedly posed: 'The Prime Minister has believed in addressing Herr Hitler through the language of sweet reasonableness. I have believed that he was more open to the language of the mailed fist.' Chamberlain's problems came from the anxiety of most MPs, not least Conservative ones, to construct more and more 'mail' for the British fist.

The House of Commons 'filled to the doors' to hear Eden's first speech in Parliament since his resignation. To *The Times* 'he seemed willing to scratch but reluctant to kill' – he continued his detachment from Churchill, though he did not disagree with him. He demanded 'a foreign policy upon which the nation can unite – I am convinced that such a policy can be found – and a national effort in the sphere of defence very much greater than anything that has been attempted hitherto'. Churchill rose in a crowded house two days later, just after five o'clock on Thursday 5 October. On one point the hypnotic effect of Henlein on him had not yet worn off – he claimed that the Czechs, 'told they were going to get no help from the Western Powers, would have been able to make much better terms than they have got'. On another point he was proved wrong, but it was a matter that for a moment provoked high political interest and brought close some kind of popular front. It was the talk of an immediate general election – as Churchill put it, an 'inverted khaki election' to get political capital for Chamberlain out of his maintenance of peace.[22]

Dissident Conservatives feared that the party would set up Chamberlainite Conservatives against them in the constituencies. They became urgently interested in possible electoral support from Labour. Harold Macmillan brought in Hugh Dalton, from the Labour Party, who came to meet Churchill, Eden and others in Brendan Bracken's house late on 3 October. The idea faded after Chamberlain put off a general election; probably he wanted his policy to bring peace and prosperity as an electoral preliminary. This assemblage of anti-appeasers also discussed the content of the Labour Party amendment to be moved against Munich; the Conservatives wanted something a Conservative could vote for, or at least abstain on. At the end of the fourth day of the debate, about thirty abstained.[23]

The meat of Churchill's speech, strong, well-spiced meat, was in two propositions. The first, 'we have suffered a total and unmitigated defeat', he repeated later on in the words 'we are in the presence of a disaster of the first magnitude which has befallen Great Britain and France'. The other theme he put in these words: 'An effort at rearmament the like of which has not been seen ought to be made forthwith, and all the resources of this country and all its united strength should be bent to the task.'

In its leading article the next day, *The Times*, the powerful organ of appeasement, muffled and absorbed its great opponent. 'Mr CHURCHILL stands for one-half of Mr CHAMBERLAIN'S declared policy – that of bringing the nation to the highest pitch of civil and military preparedness for any danger that the future may hold.' The rest, the editor declared, was now only history. This half was now embodied in Munich. Here was part of the process by which Chamberlain found himself compelled to disguise his policy and conceal his hopes. When he concluded the debate, the Prime Minister disavowed his own words after his return from Munich. He was asked, he said, how he could reconcile his declared belief in 'peace for our time' with the continuance or acceleration of the present programme of arms.

> I hope Hon Members will not be disposed to read into words used in a moment of some emotion, after a long and exhausting day, after I had driven through miles of excited, enthusiastic, cheering people – I hope they will not read into those words more than they were intended to convey. I do indeed believe that we may yet secure peace for our time but I never meant to suggest that we should do that by disarmament until we can induce others to disarm too. Our past experience has shown us only too clearly that weakness in armed strength means weakness in diplomacy, and if we want to secure a lasting peace, I realise that diplomacy cannot be effective until the consciousness exists, not here alone, but elsewhere, that behind the diplomacy is the strength to give effect to it.[24]

Churchil disseminated gloom:

> The Prime Minister desires to see cordial relations between this country and Germany. There is no difficulty at all in having cordial relations with the German people. Our hearts go out to them. But they have no power. You must have diplomatic and correct relations, but there can never be friendship between the British democracy and the Nazi Power, that Power which spurns Christian ethics, which cheers its onward course by a barbarous paganism, which vaunts the spirit of aggression and conquest, which derives strength and perverted pleasure from persecution, and uses, as we have seen, with pitiless brutality the threat of murderous force. That Power cannot ever be the trusted friend of the British democracy. What I find unendurable is the sense of our country falling into the power, into the orbit and influence of Nazi Germany and of our existence becoming dependent on their good will or pleasure.

Churchill spoke prophetically. His forebodings ran so clearly counter to what Chamberlain hoped and expected, and indeed to what most people believed, that they made a high sensation. 'I venture to think that in future the Czechoslovak state cannot be maintained as an independent entity. You will find that in a period of time which may be measured by years, but may be measured only by months, Czechoslovakia will be engulfed in the Nazi regime.' Chamberlain, by contrast, predicted for Czechoslovakia a secure national existence 'comparable to that which we see in Switzerland today'.[25] It was less than six months after Churchill and Chamberlain spoke that fast-moving German army detachments moved into Prague. Hitler chose the winner of this contest between these two formidable antagonists. In March 1939 he gave the prize to Churchill.

CHAPTER TEN

Munich to Prague

HITLER, ONLY HITLER, could prove that Munich meant permanent peace. He would have to renounce aggression and disarm if he was to confirm Chamberlain's triumph over Churchill. Early symptoms did not suggest a new Nazi dictator, a pacified, rational, reformed Hitler. At Saarbrücken, soon after the Munich debate in London, he complained that 'it would be well if people in England gave up certain airs and graces of the Versailles epoch. We will not tolerate admonitions to Germany as by a governess.' A few weeks later, he publicly attacked Churchill. Duff Cooper, Eden and Arthur Greenwood, who had condemned Munich for the Labour Party, he denounced too, but he concentrated on Churchill. On 6 November 1938 Churchill sent out one of his press statements to express surprise that 'the head of a great state should set himself to attack British Members of Parliament'. He correctly suggested that 'such action on his part can only enhance any influence they may have'. Unfortunately, he threw in one of those misplaced, clumsy, foolish asides which sometimes marred his pronouncements: 'I have always said that if Great Britain were defeated in war I hope we should find a Hitler to lead us back to our rightful position among the nations.'

An unabashed, belligerent Hitler spoke his mind again a day

or two later to his old Nazi comrades in Munich and continued to advertise Churchill as his most alarming foe. The Führer saw 'only a world which is arming, a world which is threatening'. So he had to protect Germany and arm faster, because 'I am not going to take orders from British Parliamentarians.' For the moment, all was well: 'in France and Britain men who want peace are in the Government'. But German safety was fragile. 'Tomorrow those who want war may be in the Government. Mr Churchill may be Prime Minister tomorrow.' Then Hitler showed that he took the trouble to read Churchill's speeches. 'Those who want to destroy the Nazi regime but have no quarrel with the German people will first have to annihilate the German people.' After all, Hitler was an arch democrat. 'If ever a man represented a people, my dear British members of parliament, I am that man. Mr Churchill may have an electorate of 15,000 or 20,000. I have one of 40,000,000. Once for all, we request to be spared being supervised like a pupil by a governess.' (At the same time, by coincidence, French observers felt that London specialized in providing governesses to direct French policy; in those days the British felt it normal to issue orders to foreigners. Both Chamberlain and Churchill planned, in their divergent ways, to ensure a Europe suited to British interests.)

Soon these vocal displays of irritation were followed by a public demonstration of Nazi barbarity. On 7 November a German diplomatist in Paris was murdered by a Jewish youth, maddened by German persecution of his family. The *Angriff*, the German Propaganda Ministry's newspaper, captioned photographs which showed among others Churchill, Duff Cooper and Attlee with the words 'Jewish murderers and their instigators'. There followed bloodshed, burnings and destruction in German cities as Jews, their properties and their synagogues were attacked; the police did nothing.[1]

So Churchill appeared yet more vividly as the leading

opponent of Hitler. Moreover, 'peace in our time' seemed less and less certain. Everyone agreed that Britain needed to be stronger. In consequence, it became easier for those Conservative MPs who had followed Churchill's line over Munich, and refused to vote in its support, to survive the displeasure of the devout members of Conservative constituency associations. Of course, if Chamberlain, as turned out to be true, dared not risk a general election during the brief period when Munich brought widespread acclaim, they would suffer embarassment rather than the risk of 'deselection' as candidates. Conservative MPs who had dissented from Munich took full advantage of Chamberlain's apparent retreat from his initial belief that he had constructed a peaceful Europe. Now they would proclaim their fullest support for the Prime Minister's policy of rearmament and soothe their most vocally Chamberlainite constituents.

After Top Wolmer abstained on the vote to approve the Munich agreement the president of his constituency association, the Aldershot division of Hampshire, 'almost had a fit of apoplexy' and threatened to resign and withdraw his subscription with 'many other influential supporters'. Unless Wolmer explained himself, he should be asked to give up his seat as MP. Sir Godfrey Fell, the local party chairman, worried by the widespread disapproval among local Conservatives, urged Wolmer to 'reassure them that, although you did not approve the policy of Her Majesty's Government over the Munich Agreement, you will support them to the full in their determination to make this country so strong that its voice on the side of justice and equity in international relationships will carry the weight it should'. That presented no problem to Lord Wolmer. Chamberlain himself was not worried: his sister Ida was one of Wolmer's constituents and wrote to her brother, 'I do not see how I can continue to support him.' Neville replied, with characteristic confidence, 'I should, if I were you, take no steps to show your disapproval of Wolmer ... Leave them alone and they'll come home and bring their tails behind them!'[2]

Boothby, helped by his charm and his concern for the local fishing industry, secured a unanimous vote of confidence in East Aberdeenshire and 'the hope was expressed that Mr Boothby would succeed in "gingering up" the Government with regard to rearmament'. Lord Cranborne, who had resigned with Eden in February 1938, and abstained after Munich, told South Dorset Conservatives at Weymouth that his future policy was 'rearm, rearm, rearm', and secured their confidence. The Abbey division of the Westminster Conservative Party unanimously expressed confidence in Sidney Herbert's 'determination to cooperate with the Government in the speeding up of our defences'. Duff Cooper found his constituency executive committee able to 'respect his action' in resigning, though they were 'in complete agreement with the action of the Prime Minister'. They were confident that Duff Cooper 'will direct his efforts and ability to the preservation of unity in the party and will support the Government especially in the strengthening of the defences of the country'.[3]

The pattern was plain, and Churchill was notoriously the most long-standing, persistent advocate of stronger defences against Hitler. Even so, his denunciation of Munich attracted enormous attention and caused some Epping Conservatives months of unease about their member's vigorous criticisms of the Prime Minister. He was reinforced in resisting their restlessness by the steady support of the chairman of the West Essex Conservative Association, Sir James Hawkey. Churchill's line was clear. Whatever his party did he would fight the seat he held at any future election. The week after his denunciation of Munich, he wrote to Hawkey to get him to assemble the association so that he could 'consult it', and drafted a letter for Hawkey to send out to rally support. Soon after, Buckhurst Hill, one of the local branches of the West Essex party, resolved that, while supporting Churchill over armaments, 'we feel increasingly uneasy at Mr Churchill's growing hostility to the Government'.[4]

The West Essex meeting on 4 November 1938, held in London, accepted with few dissensions a skilfully worded resolution of confidence in Churchill, which urged him to 'continue his work for national unity and national defence'. There was one especially energetic and persistent opponent: Colin Thornton-Kemsley, who had been a devoted supporter of Churchill, as he said, for fourteen years. He spoke at length at this meeting before he was voted down. So, Thornton-Kemsley recorded in his memoirs, 'encouraged by the support of a large majority at this meeting, Mr Churchill continued to follow an independent and critical course. This further incensed the critics, of whom I was now amongst the foremost.' Thornton-Kemsley wanted to force Churchill to separate himself from the party and declare himself an 'independent' member. Apparently, he had had some encouragement from Conservative Central Office, who wanted to make it seem that Chamberlain could not be challenged, if only to help Chamberlain to reassure Hitler. On the other hand, they did not want a by-election: Churchill might win! Thornton-Kemsley worked methodically. There were twenty-six branches of the central council of the Conservative Party in Churchill's constituency. Thornton-Kemsley planned to get his supporters into dominant positions in a sufficient number of branches to win control of the central body.[5]

Characteristically, Churchill responded by a series of magnificent, magniloquent speeches. By the time of Hitler's seizure of Prague in March 1939, he had spoken half a dozen times in his constituency. In December, at the Royal Forest Hotel in Chingford, he responded to an ingenious attack Chamberlain had unleashed in Parliament, which provides further evidence that these two were not unevenly matched in debate. 'I have', Chamberlain declared, the greatest admiration for my Right Hon Friend's many brilliant qualities. He shines in every direction. I remember once asking a Dominion statesman, who held high office for a great number of years, what in his opinion was the most valuable quality a statesman could possess. His answer was judgment. If I were asked whether judgment is the first of my Right Hon Friend's many admirable qualities I should have to ask the House of Commons not to press me too far.

Churchill's response filled an entire speech of denunciation of government policy, a policy which he correctly asserted had been heavily influenced by Chamberlain. 'I will gladly submit my judgment about foreign affairs and national defence during the last five years in comparison with his own.' He retrospectively examined his opponent's record. His complaints were sound – except for the assertion about Hitler's Germany that: 'three years ago we might have had a lasting settlement with Germany if real energy had been shown'. Then he went on,

It is on the background of these proved errors of judgment in the past that I draw your attention to some of the judgments which have been passed upon the future, the results of which have not yet been proved. The Prime Minister assured us quite sincerely that he had brought back from Munich a basis on which a real settlement of Europe could be obtained. He told us that he believed that after Herr Hitler had gained the Sudeten region he would have no more territorial ambitions in Europe. Well, how does that stand now?

Three months later Hitler gave the definite answer.[6]

Thornton-Kemsley boldly went into the attack after this speech. His final denunciation came at a dinner at the Chapel Hall, Nazeing, where he spoke at length and rallied support from officers of other local branches. Churchill scornfully dismissed his constituency critics:

Because half-a-dozen grasshoppers under a fern make the field ring with their importunate chink, whilst thousands of great cattle repose beneath the shadow of the British oak, chew the cud and are silent, pray do not imagine that those who make the noise are the only inhabitants of the field, that, of course, they are many in number, or that, after all, they are other than the little, shrivelled, meagre, hopping, though loud and troublesome insects of the hour.

In his memoirs, written much later, when criticism of Churchill was almost unknown, Thornton-Kemsley recanted: 'One of the grasshoppers under the fern was, for the rest of his life, bitterly to regret his part in this futile insurrection.' He was away when Churchill denounced the grasshoppers in March 1939 because he had become a by-election candidate in Scotland. Early in April, when he arrived as a new MP at Westminster, the Conservative Chief Whip, David Margesson, 'suggested that it would be well to drop the difference with Winston. This made sense, and I readily agreed, for the events of the past three weeks had justified Churchill's warnings.'

Shortly before that Churchill wrote a crushing letter to Douglas Hacking, the Conservative Party Chairman, correctly accusing Conservative Central Office of having encouraged Thornton-Kemsley. Churchill threatened that an alternative Conservative association would be formed if attempts to take over the existing body in his constituency proved successful. He pointed out that Kemsley had succeeded in small, remote, rural branches of the association, and that the branches representing most Conservatives in the constituency supported the Churchillian position: at least 75 per cent, he claimed. After Hitler's seizure of Prague that figure must have been greatly swollen. Indeed, Churchill did not trouble to send this letter, since it was obviously now only of interest to historians.[7]

At the end of 1938 three by-elections tested opinion on Munich and appeasement: Oxford in October, Bridgwater in

November, and Kinross and West Perthshire in December. All were straight fights between Chamberlainites and anti-appeasers. The government won two, anti-appeasers one.

The Oxford Conservatives chose as candidate a clever, rumbustious, assertive young candidate, Quintin Hogg. He stood for Chamberlain – just as clearly as he stood for Churchill in 1945. For high-minded, anti-fascist, virtuous rectitude, there stood, suitably enough, the Master of Balliol, Sandy Lindsay. The Liberal candidate, as Chamberlain flew to conciliate Hitler, said he would withdraw if the Labour candidate also did so to make way for someone above party. The Labour candidate, Patrick Gordon Walker, had stood in 1935 and withdrew now with resentful reluctance. Indeed, he did not wholeheartedly approve of any cross-party co-operation against appeasement – 'it will mean an alliance, in fact if not in name, with the most dangerous and reactionary elements in the Conservative party': presumably he meant Churchill. At first, the Labour National Executive, worried by communist enthusiasm for the popular front, supported his refusal, but eventually allowed Frank Pakenham (later Lord Longford) and Richard Crossman to persuade it to let the local Labour Party decide.

They were energetically supported by Roy Harrod, the distinguished Christ Church economist, who wrote repeated letters to Churchill urging a broad anti-appeasement national coalition. Churchill did not respond with enthusiasm. To Lindemann, who was a colleague of Harrod's at Christ Church, he commented, 'Harrod has written all this stuff to me, which seems very silly, but do talk to him about it in an amicable manner.' To the second letter from Harrod in October 1938 he replied with his own evasive courtesy: 'I am deeply interested in all you tell me in your letter of the 15th.' In response to the third, suggesting a weekend meeting of 'dissident Conservatives, and Liberal and Labour leaders' in order to 'offer a constructive policy' he wrote, 'the moment is not yet ripe ... but I think your personal activities can do nothing but good'. Harrod's personal activities meant keeping contact with Labour, especially Hugh Dalton. Churchill refused Harrod's appeals to support Lindsay. He insisted that he could not support an anti-Conservative candidate.

Lindsay himself wrote to Churchill on 6 October, a few days before he decided that he would be a candidate in the by-election. In Oxford, he explained, 'we are planning a campaign to think out and get across a foreign policy for democracy'. He asked for Churchill's 'advice and help' and enquired if 'you could possibly come down and talk to us'. Nearly two weeks later Churchill told him, 'I have not the time at present to come to Oxford, as you kindly suggest, and I know you will understand my inability to do so.' In fact, he refused to join any movement directed against the government. Only under the cover of the League of Nations, of which Neville Chamberlain was a 'Vice-President', would he join with members of opposition parties to advocate a changed foreign policy. The only Conservative MP actively to support Lindsay was Harold Macmillan, whose Stockton constituents had good reason to regard him as an effective spokesman for their interests. Quintin Hogg won the seat. He was an articulate candidate, effectively supported by the local Conservative Party, while the Liberal and Labour constituency parties were lukewarm in support of Lindsay. However, in an exceptionally high poll, Hogg's majority was half that of the less glamorous candidate of 1935.[8]

The second by-election where Munich was the main issue, at Bridgwater in November, proved simpler than the one at Oxford. The local Labour Party was weak and short of money, and the stronger Liberals were readier to pursue popular fronts. Liberals were encouraged by Sir Richard Acland, Liberal member for a neighbouring constituency and a steady advocate of combined opposition to appeasement. Moreover the independent candidate he suggested, Vernon Bartlett, who had experience as a journalist and broadcaster and a friendly personality, readily won support. His Conservative opponent, a young member of a local landowning family, lacked the talents shown by Quintin Hogg in Oxford. On polling day a very high turnout gave Bartlett half as many votes again as the Liberal and Labour candidates had had in 1935 and destroyed what seemed a safe Conservative majority.[9]

Kinross and West Perthshire relieved the government of fears of another electoral defeat for Munich. Here, the Conservative MP since 1923 became the anti-appeasement candidate. This was the Duchess of Atholl. She was no feminist but had been the first woman to hold ministerial office, albeit a very junior post, in a Conservative administration. From a notable Perthshire family, she married into one of the most splendid Scottish titles. However, if there is such a thing as a typical duchess, it was certainly not she. She was able, a first-class musician and a talented writer. She was dogmatic, intellectually self-confident, believing that by reasoned argument she could determine the attitudes of contemporaries. Rather than ducal in manner, she gave the impression of a small, assertive, domineering headmistress. She cared passionately for a succession of political causes. For some time her generous concerns did not weaken the respect of Conservative activists in her far-flung and beautiful constituency. She worried about the oppression of women in India and concluded that self-government and the weakening of British rule should be opposed. So she stood beside Churchill as a right-wing Conservative suspicious of Baldwin's softness and his deference to Ramsay MacDonald. Her denunciations of labour conditions in Stalin's Russia caused no offence, and her support in 1935 for League sanctions against Italy after the invasion of Abyssinia entirely fitted government policy. But in 1936 her sustained suspicion of Italy began to create a little unease on the right, and the following year her conduct started to worry many Conservatives. She visited Spain with the left-wing Labour MP Ellen Wilkinson and took up the cause of Spaniards oppressed by Francoist reaction, energetically supporting the raising of aid to refugees from Franco's armies.

By 1938 she had become notorious as the 'Red Duchess' as she denounced the sham of 'non-intervention' and aligned herself with communists as well as Liberal and Labour objectives. In April that year she wrote to Chamberlain threatening to abandon the Conservative Whip to protest against the government's tolerance of Italian troops in Spain; Chamberlain took the initiative and himself ordered the Whip withdrawn. That summer she wrote a readable and persuasive defence of the Spanish government which as a paperback 'Penguin Special' became a bestseller. She attacked appeasement and – typically – set out and published her reasons to demonstrate how right she was to denounce Munich.

In November a general meeting of her local party approved the selection of a different candidate for the next election. The Duchess replied by resigning her seat and so forced a by-election in which she defended her attitudes as an 'independent'. The local Conservatives, who thought the Duchess had neglected Perthshire livestock and worried too much about Franco and Hitler, put up a cattle expert as their candidate. The Liberal candidate, Mrs Macdonald, plunged in eagerly to exploit the prospective split in the Conservative vote. It needed the personal intervention of Sir Archibald Sinclair, the Liberal leader, to cause her, full of disappointment, to stand down in favour of the Duchess, who now embodied everything the Liberals stood for in national policy. The local Liberal Party machine moved hesitantly in her support; official Conservative canvassing and motor cars she was, of course, denied. Shortage of cars turned out to be especially important since the weather on polling day, 21 December, combined abundant snow and ice; turnout was low.

Katherine Atholl, on the other hand, had powerful support

from outside. The member for the neighbouring constituency, Robert Boothby, let her down at the last moment, because, he told her, he was worried about his constituency party. Churchill, however, weighed in with unconditional help. He wrote her a letter of support and, it is said, telephoned her every day. Perhaps Churchill thought her sufficiently 'conservative' for him to waive his rule against opposing a 'Conservative' candidate. 'You stand', he proclaimed,

> for the effective rearmament of our country and for an end to the procrastination, half-measures and mismanagement, which have led us from a safe position into a state of woeful unpreparedness and danger ... Outside our island your defeat at this moment would be relished by the enemies of Britain and of Freedom in every part of the world. It would be widely accepted as another sign that Great Britain is sinking under the weight of her cares, and no longer has the spirit and will-power to confront the tyrannies and cruel persecutions which have darkened this age.

She lost, just the same, by 1,300 votes. Chamberlain, as he wrote, 'was overjoyed ... a grand wind-up to a very difficult session'. These by-elections showed clearly enough, as he realized, uncertainty among his partisans combined with determined enmity from his opponents. The country, it appeared, was divided half and half over Munich. Churchill probably got it right when he attributed the defeat of the Duchess to Scottish Tories who 'regarded her vehement sympathy for the Spanish Government as a proof that she was almost ready to carry Bolshevism into Britain, to confiscate their property, pollute their churches and, if necessary, cut their throats'.[10]

During these months of waiting to see if Hitler had been pacified or if he would forcefully seize control over more territory, Churchill concentrated his efforts on demands for the creation of a ministry of supply which, he wrote to the Duchess of Atholl, 'would be a welcome symbol of earnestness and energy which could not fail to make an impression upon foreign countries, many of whom are beginning to think, some with pleasure, others with dismay, that British democracy is losing its will to live'. A few weeks after Munich, Churchill declared, 'I see nothing for it at the moment except to await the results of Chamberlain's hopes and experiment'. When Parliament reassembled on 1 November, he played no part in the opening debate on the central preoccupation of politics in those days – international affairs. Once again, the bold Conservative MP Vyvyan Adams proclaimed Churchillian principles. 'It does seem to me a most absurd thing, in this hour of our national danger', that Amery, Eden and Churchill are outside the administration.

> So far from causing Herr Hitler to go to war, I believe that the inclusion of these Right Hon Gentlemen in the Government would cause to think twice a man who understands the use of force and respects those who would be able, if necessary, to use it. In what vital particular over the last five or six years has the reading of German motives by the Right Hon Member for Epping been proved wrong?

His forceful clarity made a contrast with the next speaker, Boothby, who soothed his constituents by proclaiming that Chamberlain 'deserves the profound gratitude of the people of this country for what he did'.[11]

In November 1938 a Liberal moved an amendment to the address after the opening of the new session. It regretted the absence from the 'Gracious Speech' of any mention of the creation of a ministry of supply. Churchill made one of his vigorous but rather rare interventions. He found 'some difficulty in making another speech in favour of a Ministry of Supply'. He reminded Chamberlain that he had adjured him not to be 'deterred from doing right because it was impressed on him by the devil'. Soon he said something new: 'If only 50 Members of the Conservative party went into the Lobby tonight to vote for this Amendment, it would not affect the life of the Government but it would make them act.' Historians have noted that only Churchill himself and two others did what he urged: his faithful disciple Brendan Bracken and the rebellious Harold Macmillan. Churchill, some assert, was an unheeded, solitary figure. That is not true. However, this rhetorical outburst is odd, if characteristic. Probably it was just that, a sensational piece of emphasis, designed to attract attention. He cannot seriously have expected his demand to lead to the voting he called for. He made no effort to discover in advance what his possible allies in the House of Commons might do, and no effort, apart from the speech itself, to persuade them to support him. As usual, he thought that cogent argument, grandiosely presented, could change conduct. Churchill was not at all the sort of politician who employs personal contact and direct persuasion of individuals or small groups. As Ronald Tree, himself an anti-appeasement Conservative MP, noted, Churchill 'seldom came to the House of Commons except to speak in debates on foreign affairs. When he did, he sat in a corner of the smoking-room with a few of his intimates, drinking whisky-and-sodas, and making no attempt to solicit adherents to his side.'

If Churchill's challenge to Conservative members was more than an oratorical outburst it was not a well-chosen moment. An amendment to the address would have the Whips in a state of extra vigilance over party discipline. This would be especially true since, as the Liberal seconder of the amendment, Major Owen, pointed out, the 'best man for the job' – of Minister of Supply – 'is ineligible because he dissents from and criticizes the Prime Minister's policy'.

A demand for a ministry of supply could indeed be regarded as a demand for Churchill's entry into the Cabinet. The speaker who followed Churchill in the debate, Arnold Gridley, though he opposed the new Ministry, paid lavish and emphatic tribute to Churchill's work as Minister of Munitions in the First World

War. One speaker, Moore-Brabazon, declared that he might have to vote 'no' to a motion that he agreed with, and Duff Cooper pointed out that sympathy for the motion could be shown only by those defying their party. Some Conservatives abstained in the division. Amery, Duff Cooper and Wolmer voted with the government against Churchill. So too did Eden.[12]

Eden's vote in this division demonstrated again that he and Churchill were not allies and did not co-operate. They did not combine to attack appeasement and weaken Chamberlain. They worked separately and so made it easier for the Prime Minister to exclude them both from the government. During the months from his resignation in February 1938 until March 1939, Eden thought of himself as a far more likely successor to the prime ministership than Churchill. Alliance with Churchill, he thought, would make his ambitions less attainable. He hoped to lead the government, or at least to reappear as Foreign Secretary, with Chamberlain either disposed of, or contrite and controllable. Churchill would be an encumbrance rather than a reinforcement. Eden, after all, was less interesting and so safer and less controversial. He had been the protégé of Stanley Baldwin, and remained a confidential friend. He represented the Baldwinian tradition of appealing to the high-minded, the middle ground: he stood for moderation and compromise. He had none of the combative, defiant quality of Churchill. Moreover, Churchill had, in the early 1930s, been the leading opponent of Baldwin's readiness to harmonize his policies with fashionably progressive opinions.

Neither Eden nor Churchill took up the notion of breaking from the Conservative Party and trying to form a detached anti-appeasement coalition. Both tried to change government policy by influencing Cabinet ministers, particularly Halifax; to some extent they succeeded, especially Churchill, in making ministers compel Chamberlain to disguise his policies. Greater success might come if a sufficient number of ministers resigned. Halifax was the potential ace of trumps. Resigning was not his style, but he kept friendly contact with a wide range of politicians including Eden and, more surprisingly, Churchill. Hoare and Simon were unlikely to detach themselves. The most significant of those who might was Oliver Stanley; Chamberlain took trouble to keep him acquiescent. The third way in which politicians could be forced into Cabinet was if their presence seemed essential to win the next general election, which would not be later than the autumn of 1940. Chamberlain expected that his policies would triumph and so bring almost automatic victory from a grateful electorate. Eden and Churchill assumed they would go wrong.

Eden and Churchill, mutually courteous and sympathetic, were rivals for supreme office. Churchill, perhaps, hardly considered Eden as a competitor, rather as someone to be patronized and encouraged. Eden, on the other hand, certainly did not see his political role as subordinate to that of the far more experienced Churchill, or see his function as that of helping Churchill's rise to supreme power. Two entries in Blanche Dugdale's diaries illustrate the fantasies and aspirations well-informed people attributed to Eden. She had Cabinet gossip from Walter Elliot and, as a niece of A. J. Balfour, had first-class social and political connections. Late in the evening of 22 May 1938 Boothby, possibly less than completely sober, telephoned her with a proposed government he and Anthony Eden had just worked out. Eden as Prime Minister would preside over a Cabinet, including Halifax, with the Liberal leader, Sinclair, at the Foreign Office, Churchill as Minister of Supply and Attlee, Dalton and Morrison from Labour. Later, in November 1938, when she had lunch with Robert Cecil, they discussed the 'lamentable failure of the opponents' of appeasement 'to cohere. Anthony has accepted to speak for LNU [League of Nations Union] but will not appear with Archie Sinclair and Attlee as co-speakers. This seems to show that his objective is to be PM of the Tory Party.' In practice, then, he refused to have anything to do with the Liberal and Labour leaders. Neither did he ever appear on the same platform with Churchill.[13]

In 1938 and early 1939, Churchill's prestige rose; Eden's remained static or declined. After Hitler's seizure of Prague in March 1939, Churchill clearly outshone Eden. They differed in appearance, in manner, in emphasis. Eden displayed a modish elegance which Churchill never attempted. Eden seemed glamorous, 'a matinee idol' in contemporary language. His suits were well cut, his waistcoats decorously daring. He combined good looks with political correctness. He had shown suspicion of Mussolini's violent conduct in Spain and Abyssinia; he supported, or was believed to support, the League of Nations. Above all, his resignation implied a broader range of difference from Chamberlain than actually existed. But, as he expressed opposition to Chamberlain's policies far less vividly than Churchill, his appeal tended to fade. He even began to shift away from foreign policy (defence he always neglected) to domestic issues. But foreign policy was what mattered in 1939. Churchill was more relevant and much more exciting. In a way Chamberlain summed it up in the Commons, when during the debate on defence at the end of February 1939 he spoke of Churchill as 'Bogy No 1 in some parts of Europe' – Chamberlain always avoided direct reference to Hitler and the Nazis. More and more the British people wanted a 'Bogy' to frighten aggressive foreigners.[14]

Early in 1939, even so, Churchill blunted his criticism of Chamberlain's foreign policy. In February he applauded the government's reinforcement of co-operation between France and Britain. The British military began to suggest serious staff talks to consider combined defence against Germany – the reason was the rumours that Hitler at the end of 1938 was thinking of an attack on the Netherlands (but not Belgium). British refusals to promise active support in France in 1938 might now lead to French refusal to help Britain to resist such a blow to its safety and prestige, which Chamberlain, his Cabinet and most of his supporters took for granted as essential objects of their policy. (Their differences with the anti-appeasers was always over how to ensure British security and prestige, not over its maintenance.) Churchill applauded too Chamberlain's declaration in the House of Commons on 6 February 'that any threat to the vital interests of France from whatever quarter it came must evoke the immediate co-operation of this country'. Hore-Belisha, the War Minister, explained on 8 March that a British field force of nineteen divisions would be equipped to intervene beside the French. All this, to Chamberlain's mind, did not mean a reversal of appeasement. On the contrary, these concessions to France would make it easier for him to press the French government to conciliate Mussolini and so encourage the Italian dictator to influence Hitler towards reason and disarmament.[15] However, it seemed to Churchill – as it seemed to other restless Conservatives – that Chamberlain was showing 'firmness'.

On 10 March, speaking at Chigwell in his constituency, Churchill thanked 'the Prime Minister personally for the firm and prudent declaration ... about the complete solidarity which exists between Great Britain and France'. He went on, 'I will cordially support the Government in the policy they have adopted.' Later in the speech he found 'much to approve in the Government's attitude. The Government have the whole nation behind them in their defensive alliance with France.' In these last days before Hitler's next act of aggression Chamberlain revealed his continued belief in appeasement and advertised his errors. Just before Churchill's speech he briefed lobby correspondents, predicting that disarmament negotiation would begin in the next few months. On the same day as Churchill's speech to his constituents, Samuel Hoare, then the Home Secretary, spoke to his, in Chelsea. Later he explained what happened.

As I wished to allude to foreign affairs, I consulted Chamberlain on the line I had better take. His comment was that I should discourage the view that war was inevitable, and insist upon the great possibilities of peace. When I spoke, I followed his advice, and claimed that if the four leading statesmen in Europe, Chamberlain, Daladier, Hitler and Stalin, found it possible to work together in peace and amity, the world could look forward to a golden age of prosperity.[16]

Hitler's armed seizure of Prague early on 15 March 1939 proclaimed the success of Churchill's prediction after Munich that Czechoslovakia would soon disappear and the total failure of the hopes of that more cautious and careful speaker, Neville Chamberlain. Churchill began, a little late in life, to seem the man who knew and the man who could be relied on to understand.

In Conservative Central Office the Research Department, headed by the furtive Joseph Ball, one of Chamberlain's closest associates, carefully watched and analysed by-elections after Munich. It concluded that Chamberlain would probably lose a general election, which 'would be fought largely on foreign policy'. Voting patterns after Munich showed little more than a normal drop in support for the government – 3, 4, or 5 per cent. Much more alarming were the high turnouts – 'a testimony to the strong emotions raised by current issues' – and the increase in votes for the opposition parties of 18, 19 or 20 per cent.

During these months, between Munich and Prague, Churchill's support from the high-minded friends to the League of Nations dramatically increased when the organ of the League of Nations Union, the monthly *Headway*, came with a new editorial slant. In October various respectable personages expressed their support for what now became a mouthpiece of Churchillian policies: it contained in that month two articles from Churchill himself. Of course, those who thought of the

League as an alternative to collective coercion of aggressors dropped out. Although the attempt to sell *Headway* on newstands was not a great success, Chamberlain was worried. Joseph Ball told him that League of Nations Union publications now 'popularise Mr Churchill and his policy'. Chamberlain proposed to encourage a rival 'British Association for International Understanding'.[17]

For Chamberlain in these months it became more and more difficult to keep Churchill – and Eden – out of his government. Yet to let in Eden and, much more clearly, to let in Churchill would make it impossible for him to continue what he thought he knew to be the correct policy towards Hitler. He had to persuade his existing Cabinet and Conservative MPs that his policy was sufficiently Churchillian to make it unnecessary for him to bring Churchill into the government. Sometimes he deceived Churchill himself into believing that he had abandoned appeasement. Chamberlain thought that at last Hitler would turn reasonable and pacific. Then he would be vindicated and could win the forthcoming general election without Churchill in the Cabinet. Alternatively, Hitler would go on threatening and ranting; then Labour might win the election, unless Churchill were added to the government; or Hitler might set off a war . . .

CHAPTER ELEVEN

A Call to Government?

ON 15 MARCH 1939 Hitler overturned the Munich agreement and contemptuously breached the series of assurances he had personally given to Chamberlain the year before. He did not consult the English governess before seizing Prague, nor warn nor threaten. The German army displayed all its dramatic prowess: columns of motorcycles made emotive photographs moving through Prague streets, sometimes in front of weeping Czechs interspersed with welcoming swastikas and Nazi salutes. Hitler, and Mussolini, it was claimed, liked to set off crises at the weekend when the machinery of British government was relaxed. This crisis, however, broke on Wednesday. The Cabinet met, as it did every Wednesday, this time bewildered and surprised. Parliament assembled as usual. Cadogan from the Foreign Office had barely time to work out for Halifax a statement justifying inaction for the Foreign Secretary to give to Chamberlain: the guarantee of Czechoslovakia against aggression had not yet come into effect and did not apply anyway – Czechoslovakia had, as it were, spontaneously dissolved itself.

At the end of question time, Chamberlain announced an immediate debate on Czechoslovakia, which he opened. Typically, he gave a dry narrative – 'The occupation of Bohemia by

German military forces began at 6 o'clock this morning' – followed by a defence of Munich. 'It is natural', he declared finally, 'that I should bitterly regret what has now occurred.' Then he added his own words to Cadogan's statement: we should not 'be deflected from our course ... the aim of this Government is now, as it has always been ... to substitute the method of discussion for the method of force in the settlement of differences'. John Simon, at the end of the debate, repeated the assertion that appeasement remained the Government's policy. The Prime Minister, he concluded, 'intends to pursue that policy and so do his colleagues'.[1]

Churchill took no part in the debate; if he had wished to speak he certainly could have done so. In the afternoon he was in the House of Lords listening to the debut there of Admiral Lord Chatfield, recently appointed Minister for Co-ordination of Defence in succession to a resentful Inskip – sacrificed, as he well knew, to Chamberlain's need to seem a serious rearmer. The day before, by coincidence, Churchill had arranged to speak again in his constituency. With the future existence of Czechoslovakia already under dire threat, he was able to expand 'I told you so' into a splendid rhetorical outburst, and so take another swipe at the local grasshoppers who squeaked their complaints of his denunciation of Munich. His first public appearance after Hitler's defiant display of force came the next day. As patron of the Early Closing Association he furthered its 'beneficent work' of limiting the hours of work of shop assistants. There was no reason why 'in massing the nation's forces to defend our freedom, we should be discouraged from pressing forward with other work in order to make sure that the people of this country will not lose any amenities already gained'. Here was no comment on the defence of continued appeasement made by Simon and Chamberlain. Nor did he make any comment on the collapse of Munich when he spoke that afternoon to the Commons on the navy estimates. On the contrary, he found it 'refreshing in times like these for us to take an afternoon off from black care and dwell upon the great and growing strength of our Navy'. And it was left to the combative Labour member Lieutenant-Commander Fletcher to point to the wreckage of Chamberlain's policy.[2]

However, Chamberlain had urgently to do more to keep the support of his party. There was even talk of persuading him to give up his position after the failure of the Munich policy with which he was so closely identified. On 17 March he recovered. He spoke at a long-arranged meeting of Birmingham Conservatives, in his own political territory, to his most devoted supporters. This audience acted as an audible opinion poll. The first part of his speech, a lengthy defence of Munich, evoked polite, restrained applause. The second part brought forth enthusiastic, noisy cheers. Now he called for the defence of liberty, for resistance to the domination of the world by malevolent, evil men. He did so in cautious, measured words but the effect was sensational. Appeasement seemed dead; confrontation had replaced conciliation. He spoke of a possible attempt to dominate the world by force:

> while I am not prepared to engage this country by new unspecified commitments operating under conditions which cannot now be foreseen, yet no greater mistake could be made than to suppose [a sudden stammer here, paradoxically, added emphasis] that because it believes war to be a senseless and cruel thing this nation has so lost its fibre that it will not take part to the utmost of its power [loud cheers] in resisting such a challenge if it ever were made [renewed cheers].[3]

There emerged Chamberlain's personally devised mouse of a plan to foil aggression. Britain, France, Poland and the Soviet Union would declare that they would 'consult together' about any threat of aggression. Chamberlain had to be pushed into agreeing that 'consultation' could lead to joint resistance. In the last two weeks of March, though frequently at Westminster, Churchill was silent except over the technicalities of defence. He did, however, contribute another of his articles, 'letters' as he called them, to the *Daily Telegraph*. On 24 March he applauded the 'veritable revolution in feeling and opinion' which he noted in Britain – 'indeed, a similar process has taken place spontaneously throughout the whole British Empire'. (The latter, implausible, assertion was characteristic of general British attitudes in those days. The 'Empire', whatever that was supposed to mean, could be relied on to follow London. Moreover, British observers, then, and later, imagined that opinion throughout the world would be influenced, even directed, by British beliefs.) In eastern Europe, he said,

> instead of being terrified by the fate of Czechoslovakia, Poland, Rumania, Turkey, Greece, Bulgaria, and by no means the least – Yugoslavia – have been roused to a lively sense of self-preservation . . . the loyal attitude of the Soviets to the cause of peace, and their obvious interest in resisting the Nazi advance to the Black Sea, imparts a feeling of encouragement to all the Eastern States now menaced by the maniacal dreams of Berlin.

All would be well in the end. Hitler might draw back, but it was difficult for a dictator to recede. In any event, 'the forces opposed to Nazidom are . . . still by far the stronger. A period of suffering resulting from the air-slaughter of non-combatants may lie before us; but this, if borne with fortitude, will only seal the comradeship of many nations, to save themselves and the future of mankind from a tyrant's grip.' Evidently, Churchill gravely underestimated the difficulties of co-operation between Stalin and Poland and Rumania.

Another critical misunderstanding emerged. Churchill had been correct; therefore Chamberlain now knew he had been wrong. Now Chamberlain would seek the Grand Alliance or, more decorously, a 'peace bloc'. He had renounced appeasement. The snag was that Chamberlain had not, and Churchill had misjudged him. Churchill collected these articles together and persuaded one of his publishers to bring them out as a book in June 1939. He added short linking commentaries. Before the reprint of this article of 24 March he wrote, 'Upon this', the German occupation of Prague, 'Mr Chamberlain decided to abandon the policy of appeasement.' It is a surprise that Churchill still believed this in May, when he wrote these words – if he did believe it. About the same time, Leo Amery correctly noted in his diary, 'The trouble with Neville is that he is being pushed all the time into a policy which he does not like, and hates abandoning the last bridges which might still enable him to renew his former policy.'[4]

At any rate, in public, Churchill praised the new Chamberlain. In the process he made more likely, it could seem, his entry into the Cabinet. Then he could cure any doubts or hesitations nourished by Chamberlain. However, he signed a Commons motion with more than thirty other Conservatives calling for a national government. It was one of those assertions of opinion never expected to be debated by the House. It occurred on the Order Paper for 28 March 1939 and declared that the menaces facing Britiain 'can only successfully be met by the vigorous prosecution of the foreign policy recently outlined by the Foreign Secretary'. That referred to Halifax's speech to the House of Lords on 20 March – a much less rousing and inspiring utterance than Chamberlain's Birmingham speech but one containing a hint of greater readiness to take on new commitments to defend the independence of foreign countries. The motion went on, in the manner of Eden, to urge that this vigorous foreign policy required a national government 'on the widest possible basis, and that such a Government should be entrusted with full powers over the nation's industry, wealth and man-power, to enable the country to put forward its maximum military effort in the shortest possible time'. It was devised by Eden and his associates; Churchill's signature came later.

This motion emphasized the ambiguous status of Lord Halifax, implying that he was less of an 'appeaser' than Chamberlain. It is true that he hesitated, but he was the indispensable foundation of Chamberlain's government. If he flamboyantly withdrew, Chamberlain would be crippled. He was the essential condition of Chamberlain's survival. He restrained Chamberlain from exaggerated displays of conciliatory appeasement. Yet in his speech he insisted that Munich was his work as well as that of Chamberlain, and that he and Chamberlain fully agreed – something not quite true. He was both Chamberlain's essential support and someone thought to diverge from him. He was everyone's friend. Conservative Whips quickly and very effectively squashed the divisive implications of this motion by collecting over 200 signatures to an amended motion. This affirmed 'complete confidence in the Prime Minister and deprecates any attempt at the present critical time to undermine the confidence of the House and the Country in the Prime Minister and the Government'. It was left to the Labour Opposition explicitly to press the question whether 'the Declaration which has been submitted to certain Powers is one merely for consultation'. And Chamberlain assured them that it 'goes a great deal further than consultation'.[5]

At the end of March, Chamberlain made a dramatic new commitment and pledged Britain to join in defending Poland if the Poles resisted a threat to their national independence. Once again, what he publicly seemed to be trying to do was different from what he hoped to do. He was encouraged to make this apparently dramatic gesture of support for Hitler's next potential victim by his discovery that Poland wished to avoid provoking Hitler by any Polish association with the Soviet Union. Then he sought to make the Germans understand that he was not ruling out negotiations over Polish frontiers, a proposition he had to explain away on 3 April after protests over a *Times* leader which he thought encapsulated his own view.[6]

These declarations and pledges posed for Churchill a familiar problem. Should he support Chamberlain or denounce his prevarications and shiftiness? His object had to be to enter the Cabinet. Only then could he ensure that British foreign policy devoted itself to the search for a Grand Alliance against Hitler. But should he hope that Chamberlain, at last converted to good sense, would welcome his support as a Cabinet minister or should he point out Chamberlain's defects in order to have himself forced on a reluctant Prime Minister? Of course, if Chamberlain were now a Churchillian, he would surely welcome Churchill's support in government. Chamberlain however was certainly not a genuine convert; he found it necessary to diguise his continued belief in the possibilities of appeasement. The process of disguise, which he found forced upon him by some of his Cabinet colleagues, by Conservative MPs and, more nebulously, by 'public opinion', had the consolation for him that it made it easier to keep Churchill out. If his policy was Churchillian there was no need of Churchill! On the other hand, it seemed even more peculiar to refuse the help of this highly articulate collaborator. Between 15 March and the outbreak of war on 3 September 1939 Chamberlain found the pressure on him hard to resist.

After the announcement of the Polish guarantee on 31 March, Churchill chose to support Chamberlain. It was on 3 April that the Prime Minister explained away what he called the 'misunderstanding' over the dramatic pledge to Poland: 'A declaration of that importance is not concerned with some minor little frontier incident.' This was on Monday when the Polish guarantee, which Chamberlain had announced on Friday afternoon, was debated by the House of Commons. Archibald

Sinclair, for the independent Liberal Party, as usual under-represented in the House and more influential outside, spoke next. He assumed that appeasement had been abandoned by Chamberlain, and called for the withdrawal from the government, not of Halifax, or even Chamberlain, but of Simon and Hoare and their replacement by Churchill and Eden. They would be more inclined, he seemed to suppose, to support the new model Chamberlain, a view which Chamberlain himself certainly did not share. 'It is vital', Sinclair argued, 'that government pronouncements should convey the impression of proceeding from a resolute and unanimous Cabinet.'

Churchill, understandably, praised the party which Sinclair led: 'I believe that at the moment they represent what is the heart and soul of the British nation.' Then, less opaquely, 'I find myself in the most complete agreement with the Prime Minister.' That was his theme: 'I find myself entirely in accord . . . being in agreement . . . I naturally am going to give him my support . . . I am going to give my full support.' He sensed 'a revival of the national spirit'. The Prime Minister has gone into a 'tremendous valiant adventure for the safety and the peace of the world'. Everything seemed good:

> the attitude of His Majesty's Government towards Russia appears to me also to be well conceived . . . no-one can say that there is not a solid identity of interest between the Western democracies and Soviet Russia, and we must do nothing to obstruct the natural play of the identity of interest. The Government have been wise in not forcing matters. Rumania, Poland, the Baltic States, all feel easier because this great mass of Russia is friendly behind them, and lies there in broad support. But we must be largely guided at this juncture by the feelings of those States . . . The worst folly, which no-one proposes we should commit, would be to chill and drive away any natural co-operation which Soviet Russia in her own deep interests feels it necessary to afford.

Did Churchill mean what he said? Did he believe it all? Almost certainly he did. That points to some misunderstandings. As happened to others, Chamberlain successfully presented himself to Churchill as someone who had changed his mind and changed his policies. In fact, the Prime Minister disguised his tenacious adherence to appeasement. Some of Churchill's remarks, too, were naive and even ignorant. Perhaps because of the enormous burden he imposed on himself as an author, he did not, it appears, comprehend the dread which the European neighbours of the Soviet Union felt towards its ominous power. He also showed symptoms of a general British assumption: Britain need only say that its policies had changed for long-standing enemies of Nazi Germany to welcome the now-to-be-trusted new associate in resistance to Hitler. Moreover, he came to believe, as most Britons did, that continued enmity between the USSR and Hitler's Germany could be taken for granted.

Lloyd George, who spoke after Churchill, showed fewer illusions about Soviet Russia. He recognized that Poland might be indefensible without Soviet support, but that support might be difficult to secure and Poland might not want it. This proved to be the central problem of the remaining months of peace. Lloyd George asked:

> the Government to take immediate steps to secure the adhesion of Russia in a fraternity, an alliance, an agreement, a pact, it does not matter what it is called so long as it is an understanding to stand together against the aggressor. Apart from that we have undertaken a frightful gamble ... If Russia has not been brought into this matter because of certain feelings the Poles have that they do not want the Russians there, it is for us to declare the conditions, and unless the Poles are prepared to accept the only conditions with which we can successfully help them, the responsibility must be theirs.

Advice from Lloyd George was the last thing Chamberlain would be likely to accept![7]

This debate was held on Monday 3 April; on Thursday the Commons adjourned for Easter. That day, Italian warships appeared off the coast of Albania and on Good Friday Italian troops occupied four coastal towns and entered Tirana, the capital. King Zog and Queen Geraldine fled to Greece. Geraldine's new-born child brought publicity and made even less plausible, to the British, Italian claims that the rulers of Albania had been threatening Italian interests. Mussolini, the Italian dictator, so it seemed, had determined to advertise his status as a man of power and violence, to rival his northern neighbour. Just as Hitler had betrayed the agreement Chamberlain and he had signed at Munich, so Mussolini now ignored the Anglo-Italian agreement, whose existence had been reaffirmed when Chamberlain and Halifax visited Rome in January 1939. Chamberlain, again let down by a flamboyant and noisy foreigner, in whose 'moderation' he had put special confidence, felt both angry and disheartened. Churchill was ready to help. He thought, no doubt, that the Prime Minister really must now renounce appeasement. Indeed any rational person would have done so. But Chamberlain, even more firmly than most distinguished politicians, always refused to admit that he had been completely wrong. Shortly before the Commons reassembled for yet another emergency debate, Churchill spoke to Margesson, the Conservative Chief Whip. He declared 'his strong desire to join the Government' and 'could do much to help the PM to bear his intolerable burden'. According to Margesson, Churchill thought Eden should come in too but believed that he could give much more help than Eden. Chamberlain told one of his sisters that he had evaded a clear answer: 'It caught me at a moment when I was certainly feeling the need of help', but he wondered whether 'Winston ... would help or hinder in

Cabinet or in Council'. On the day after the Italian invasion of Albania, he complained that Churchill 'was at the telephone all day' demanding the recall of Parliament and a preventive British seizure of Corfu. Churchill also wrote to the Prime Minister on Sunday: 'What is now at stake is nothing less than the whole of the Balkan peninsula' – which was perhaps an exaggeration.[8]

Churchill demanded, characteristically, firmness, strength and energy. On 12 April he addressed a meeting in his constituency: 'A year or so ago I went round the country making speeches in favour of a policy of collective security. So far as I can make out the Government has adopted that policy.' But, he observed, 'what the country is asking for is a vigorous and courageous lead'. When Parliament reassembled the next day, on Thursday 13 April, later than Churchill had asked for, he spoke in the debate after the Prime Minister, and after Attlee for Labour and Sinclair for the Liberals. This had become usual, as if Churchill, too, were a party leader. Another familiar feature was Sinclair's demand for the entry of Churchill and Eden into the government, this time to replace John Simon and Chamberlain himself.

In an ironical and slightly patronizing way, Churchill continued to support Chamberlain. 'We can readily imagine that it must have been a great disappointment and surprise to the Prime Minister to be treated in this way by a dictator in whom he placed particular trust . . . Everyone knows that his motives have been absolutely straightforward and sincere.' Even so, 'the great majority of the House, I believe, supports the Government in the policy which they are now adopting in building up a strong alliance of nations to resist further acts of aggression'. He complained, at length, about the dispersal of the powerful British Mediterranean fleet at the moment of the Italian invasion. 'Of the five great capital ships, one was at Gibraltar, another in the Eastern Mediterranean, and the remaining three were lolling about various widely separated Italian ports.' He also called for 'the full inclusion of Soviet Russia in our defensive peace bloc'. (Chamberlain had just announced guarantees of Greece and Rumania.) Churchill even, indirectly, suggested his own inclusion in the government: 'how can we continue – let me say it with particular frankness and sincerity – with less than the full force of the nation incorporated in the governing instrument?' Chamberlain did not enjoy Churchill's speech. He preferred the support given by Eden to the work of the government 'in doing what they can everywhere to build up what we may call a peace front'. Eden's speech, without Churchill's 'acid undertone', gave Chamberlain 'comfort' and he wrote to Eden a 'friendly note'.[9]

A theme of these depressing months before the war is the mounting pressure on Chamberlain to bring Churchill into the government. This campaign was more hopeless than everyone believed outside the tiny circle of those whom Chamberlain trusted, certainly more hopeless than Churchill himself imagined. On 20 April Chamberlain made one of his reluctant concessions to public demand when he announced the creation of a ministry of supply limited in function 'for the time being'. At the head of the new department would be Leslie Burgin, the notably unglamorous Minister of Transport. Oliver Harvey, Lord Halifax's Foreign Office private secretary, recorded: 'The effect can be imagined on a public which owing to rumours had been led to expect that it would be Winston. A ghastly selection which has gone very badly.' 'Serious' newspapers agreed. Even *The Times*, sycophantic in support of Chamberlain, noted that the Prime Minister 'has not accepted the advice pressed upon him in some quarters and looked outside his present team for a head of the new Department'. The *Manchester Guardian* and the *Daily Telegraph* were more emphatic. As the former stated, 'The House had been nursing the hope that Chamberlain "would go the whole distance, set up a full-blooded Ministry of Supply and give it to Mr Churchill".' After Burgin's appointment the *Telegraph* remarked that 'Mr Churchill's position was discussed on all sides. His name has been for many months prominently connected with advocacy of a Supply Ministry.' A more 'popular' newspaper, the *Sunday Pictorial*, added its voice on 23 April: 'Why isn't Winston Churchill in the Cabinet? . . . The injustice of his expulsion is outweighed only by the criminal disservice to Britain which allows this state of affairs to go on.'[10]

Victor Cazalet recorded his opinions at this time. He was a respectable and respected member of the more intelligent, though non-intellectual, section of Conservative MPs. His sister, Thelma Cazalet-Keir, was also a member of the House, and his brother was a top-quality steeplechase rider whom only bad luck (a broken rein) deprived of a Grand National victory. (After the war he trained the Queen Mother's horses.) Both brothers were from Eton and Christ Church, the very best provenance for well-bred English Conservatives. Though Victor Cazalet, with some of the extreme right, approved of Franco, his support of Zionism brought him into the company of more flexibly minded people and gave him the friendship of Baffy Dugdale, another Zionist well connected with influential Conservatives. Cazalet was on friendly terms with Baldwin, Chamberlain, Eden and Halifax; he is thus a sound representative of contemporary government supporters. In May, he reported to friends in America, 'there is a growing demand that Winston should be included in the Government. I spent five hours with him two days ago and there is no doubt that he could, and would, serve with Chamberlain and obviously has a "war" mind. He has been right about everything for the last five years and his inclusion in the Government would do more to show Germany that we mean business than anything else.'

To frighten Hitler: that was the great point, but to Chamberlain that was the big disadvantage. Similarly, Cazalet told Lord Tweedsmuir (John Buchan, now Governor-General of Canada), 'most people think that Winston will have to be included, as public demand for him grows every day'.[11] The

Gallup Polls of May 1939 give the impression that opinion wanted Churchill in the Chamberlain government – not, as yet, as the Prime Minister. This showed how far Chamberlain had managed to give the impression that he had renounced appeasement. One poll showed that 55 per cent were 'satisfied with Mr Neville Chamberlain as prime minister'; 56 per cent (or 68 per cent of those who expressed an opinion) were 'in favour of Mr Winston Churchill being invited to join the Cabinet'.

The month before, Gallup registered a decisive answer to a critical question. No fewer than 87 per cent of respondents wanted 'a military alliance between Great Britain, France and Russia'.[12] Chamberlain had to pretend to be determined to frighten Hitler and to struggle for a full Russian alliance. He wanted to do neither. Negotiations with the Soviet Union went on almost throughout the summer and a lot, though not everything, of what the government was doing became known. Chamberlain's contacts with Hitler were more spasmodic and furtive.

Firstly came the British suggestion to Moscow in March that the USSR should join in a declaration that Russia, Britain, France and Poland would consult together about what to do in the event of German agression. Poland objected to joining with the Soviet Union; the British guarantee to Poland alone soon followed. The Polish Foreign Minister thought that any association between Poland and Russia would make a German attack on Poland more likely. Chamberlain agreed with him and wanted to stop there. Reluctantly he was forced into instructing the British ambassador to propose that the Soviet government should declare 'on their own initiative' that Russia would give assistance, if desired by a victim of German aggression, against one of its European neighbours. The French went further, proposing mutual assistance between France and Russia. The British suggestion was sent out on 14 April. On the 18th Moscow replied with a proposed Triple Alliance. Britain, France and the

USSR would help each other if Germany attacked any of them. They would help any eastern European state bordering on the USSR which was attacked by Germany. A military agreement would determine what action would be taken. Britain, France and Russia, once at war, would agree not to make a separate peace.

The British government through its elaborate procedures of departmental advice, of committees, of Cabinet meetings, all excellently recorded, decided to suggest again that the Soviet government should make a unilateral, independent declaration of support for victims of German aggression. The British ambassador put this to the alarming new Soviet Foreign Minister, Vyacheslav Molotov, on 8 May. On the 15th Molotov insisted on an alliance. Halifax tried yet again to get an independent Russian declaration, this time offering military conversations. But the Soviet ambassador in London, Maisky, made it plain that Moscow would accept only a Triple Alliance. On 17 May Maisky had told Moscow that its proposals 'put the British government in a very difficult position'. The public, he explained, 'feels unquestionably in favour of "alliance with Russia"'. On the 19th there would be a debate in the Commons, with Lloyd George and Churchill due to speak. 'Both fully support our proposals,' Maisky stated.

Churchill telephoned to Maisky the day before. 'Tomorrow', Maisky reports him saying, 'there will be a foreign policy debate in Parliament. I intend to speak and to draw attention to the unsatisfactory way the negotiations with Russia are being carried on.' Churchill asked Maisky to brief him on what Moscow had proposed, and Churchill then commented, 'I don't understand what Chamberlain has found unsatisfactory with your proposals.' (Incidentally, it is reasonable to assume that this conversation was tapped by the British authorities.) Information from both sides had now enlightened Churchill. On 2 May he had discussed the Soviet proposals with Halifax. Churchill expressed himself, as Halifax reported to the Cabinet, 'entirely in favour of the proposed tripartite pact'. (Halifax, on the contrary, 'thought that a tri-partite pact on the lines proposed would make war inevitable'.)[13]

In the debate Lloyd George spoke first, then the Prime Minister, then Churchill. The Russian proposals, Churchill declared, 'contemplate a triple alliance between England, France and Russia, which alliance may extend its benefits to other countries, if and when those benefits are desired, against aggression'. His phrase 'if and when those benefits are desired' is arguably fundamentally misleading. The Soviet alliance proposal covered 'Eastern European States situated between the Baltic and Black Seas and bordering on USSR'. The only limitation that the USSR suggested on the giving of assistance to those states in the event of aggression was that 'England [foreigners then used this word even more often than today when they meant Britain], France and USSR were to discuss and to settle . . . extent and forms of military assistance to be rendered to each of those States.' The 'States' themselves would not be asked. Here lay a real problem, especially concerning Poland. None of these states wanted Soviet assistance. They felt Soviet help might be as dangerous as German attack.

Churchill had now seen this problem: Harold Nicolson recorded his haranguing Maisky in the Commons after the debate on the guarantee to Poland. 'Now I don't care for your system and I never have, but the Poles and the Rumanians like it even less. Although they might be prepared at a pinch to let you in, they would certainly want some assurances that you would eventually get out. Can you give us such assurances?' Perhaps Maisky had encouraged him to think that they might be forthcoming. The eastern European states felt, moreover, that association with the USSR might provoke rather than prevent a German attack on them. Much diplomatic ingenuity had to be deployed. It led on to the most awkward problem of all. Churchill put it in his speech: 'It is said "can you trust the Russian Soviet Government?" I suppose in Moscow they say "can we trust Chamberlain?" I hope that we may say that the answer to both questions is in the affirmative. I earnestly hope so.'[14]

Yet the answer to both questions was emphatically in the negative. Chamberlain thought that Stalin hoped to encourage a war between Germany and the Western powers, from which Russia could stand aside. Stalin, it seems, feared Chamberlain's proven inclination to seek bargains with Hitler and had cause to suspect that he had not renounced it in March 1939. If the USSR promised to help Britain and France against Germany, perhaps Chamberlain would find it easier to make a new bargain with Hitler, featuring, very likely, a free hand in the east for the Nazis. Churchill's entry into the government must have lessened mistrust: whether decisively we shall, perhaps, never know. More obstacles had to be overcome than he assumed to exist when they spoke: but someone who actually wanted to overcome them would be more likely to do so than a Cabinet still dominated by a Prime Minister who welcomed every obstacle he could discover.

One week later Churchill's closest associate in the House of Commons, Brendan Bracken, pressed the government about two Czechoslovakian issues. One was the formal recognition of German sovereignty implied in seeking German approval of a consul in Bratislava; the other that the Bank of International Settlements might transfer money held on Czech account in London to the German Central Bank. A back-bench member postponed, for a moment, his speech about safety in British coal mines to allow Churchill himself to intervene. He deployed one of his Parliamentary techniques: that of courteous, gently supercilious patronage of a senior minister, this time Sir John Simon, Chancellor of the Exchequer:

> We must all wish to compliment him on his fairness, his good temper and his readiness to answer questions ... I accept his statement that he will do all he can with all the resources of his legal brain, and with all the energy he possesses, to prevent what would be a public disaster, namely, the transference of this £6,000,000 of Czech money into the hands of those who have overthrown and destroyed the Czech Republic.

Thus Churchill took for himself a position of superior eminence, of sitting in judgement on ministers.[15]

Meanwhile, Chamberlain, in his own words, had had a 'very tiresome week'. He could not escape from the Triple Alliance with Russia, though it 'would make any negotiation or discussion with the totalitarians difficult if not impossible'. He found that 'refusal would create immense difficulties in the House even if I could persuade my Cabinet'. Opinions were turning against him in favour of the Alliance. In the Cabinet foreign policy committee, 'the only support I could get for my view was from Rab Butler and he was not a very influential ally'. Luckily for him, Chamberlain hit on a 'most ingenious' plan; he would make the Russian scheme seem less provocative than a military alliance by dressing it up as an application of the Covenant of the League of Nations. He did not grasp how great was the mistrust he aroused in Moscow and evidently thought the Soviet government would agree. On 24 May he told the Commons, 'I have now every reason to hope ... it will be found possible to reach full agreement at an early date. There still remain some further points to be cleared up, but I do not anticipate that these are likely to give rise to any serious difficulties.'

Vyvyan Adams, in his supplementary question to the Prime Minister, demonstrated how Chamberlain deluded even sceptical Conservative MPs: 'Is my Right Hon Friend aware that this step towards this massive deterrent against aggression will give throughout the country the most widespread relief, satisfaction and hope?' Churchill was silent in the Commons during June. Among restless Conservatives, it was Vyvyan Adams who kept up the pressure. He put questions to Chamberlain on 12, 14, 19, 21 and 26 June, all of them showing disquiet at renewed delay. Now the government began to encounter an objectively difficult issue. Molotov, with gathering clarity, demanded a free hand in the Baltic States to enable Soviet forces to move in if Moscow decided that 'indirect aggression' had taken place, irrespective of what the Baltic governments thought. Moreover, such 'indirect aggression' would require Britain and France to declare war on Germany. Molotov's argument was that Baltic governments might, like Czechoslovakia in March 1939, be driven into requesting German protection or, equally dangerously for the USSR, voluntarily do so.[16]

Churchill, in one of his newspaper articles early in June, showed more sympathy for the Soviet demands than the British Cabinet. On the Baltic States and Finland, he urged:

> if their independence or integrity is compromised by Nazidom, Poland must fight. Great Britain and France must fight. Russia must fight. Why not then concert in good time, publicly and courageously, the measures which may render such a fight unnecessary? It is too much to ask these small states at this stage, before the Triple Alliance has been signed, to commit themselves. It is quite sufficient for the three Great Powers to declare that the invasion or subversion of the Baltic States by the Nazis would be an unfriendly act in the full diplomatic sense of this term.

About this time, early in June, Chamberlain encountered yet another irritation. He wrote to his sister, Ida, 'You would hardly believe that anyone could be so foolish but Anthony [Eden] went to Halifax and suggested that we should send him as a special envoy to Moscow.' Chamberlain had to restrain Halifax and discover some reason for doing so. 'He [Eden] found a not unsympathetic hearer, but when I suggested that to send either a Minister or an ex-Minister would be the worst of tactics with a hard bargainer like Molotov, Halifax agreed and dropped the proposal. Nevertheless, Lloyd George repeated it to Butler and even suggested that if we did not approve of Anthony, Winston should go!' These were, of course, sensible ideas to reduce Muscovite mistrust – and no one has ever disputed that Eden was a first-class negotiator. However, Chamberlain regarded it as a dangerous plot.[17]

Churchill's oratory displayed itself outside Parliament. On 21 June he proposed a toast to Halifax at the 1900 Club, a right-wing Conservative group. Here was a special utterance, elegantly civil and warm in friendship. 'Naturally', Churchill remarked, 'I am a supporter of the foreign policy of His Majesty's Government,' which he interpreted as a search for the Grand Alliance he had called for more than a year before. His remarks contained no complaint about Chamberlain, but they contributed to the growing public belief that Halifax had renounced 'appeasement' more definitely and finally than Chamberlain. So, too, did Churchill's speech to the City Carlton Club a week later. The day after that, Halifax gave a famous speech to Chatham House, broadcast in full on the radio and fully reported in the press. The *Daily Telegraph* granted Churchill's speech second billing on the front page, and the next day Halifax became the main front-page news. Both speakers got from the paper leading articles of the most enthusiastic support. The support Halifax won got him wrong. He was unenthusiastic about the Russian alliance and more sympathetic to Chamberlain's conciliatory instincts than outsiders imagined. He was polite, pleasant, agreeable company and readily gave the impression, in contrast to Chamberlain, of fundamental agreement with any of his interlocutors. In fact, he agonized indecisively over all his speeches. His chief adviser, the permanent under-secretary at the Foreign Office, Sir Alexander Cadogan, found him 'very tiresome about his beastly speeches'. The Chatham House speech was the 'bane of our lives for days. At the last moment . . . I sat down and wrote two pages – a moving paraphrase of "We don't want to fight, but by Jingo if we do" etc.' These were the passages in the speech that won applause; they had been added, Cadogan noted, to 'put teeth into it'.[18]

June 1939 saw attention distracted by the disastrous loss of the submarine HMS *Thetis*, which failed to surface on a trial voyage, when only four survived of its ninety-nine crew, and by the provocative conduct of Japanese forces towards the British concession in Tientsin, though Japanese action in China never took up much of Churchill's time and attention. At the end of the month and in the first days of July, it was Churchill personally who dominated the news. Demands for his addition to Chamberlain's government reached a climax. From socialist left to reactionary right, voices were raised and newspaper headlines deployed. Sir Stafford Cripps, at this time, wavered between the conviction that capitalism had to be destroyed to save mankind and the notion that even the co-operation of capitalists might be sought to block Hitler and Nazi barbarism. Late in June, Cripps called on Churchill in London. Churchill, Cripps recorded, believed that Chamberlain kept Eden and himself out of government to retain the possibility of reviving appeasement. The outcome was a prominent essay in Cripps's left-wing organ, the *Tribune*, on 30 June. Its title 'Our Führer' was illustrated by a composite picture of Chamberlain as a Nazi stormtrooper. If Chamberlain had 'been determined to discontinue' appeasement,

> first he would have accepted the Russian offers for cooperation and second he would have accepted the reinforcements to his Cabinet . . . of Mr Winston Churchill, Mr Eden and others. He did not do this because to do so would have meant the closing of the door to all appeasement. Russia, as an ally, would not have approved of appeasement

> ... New elements in the Cabinet such as Mr Winston
> Churchill would equally have refused to take part in
> appeasement ... So we witness the interminable delays as
> to the Russian pact, and the appointment of such a person
> as Dr Burgin as Minister of Supply instead of the obvious
> Mr Churchill.

Cripps pressed his thoughts on Kingsley Wood, the Air Minister
in Chamberlain's government, who, according to Cripps, 'was
interested and sympathetic, but I felt he would not take any
initiative in the matter'.[19] It is probable that Cripps's efforts
derived from his worry about the Soviet alliance, supplemented
by the worries that week about German smuggling of arms and
ammunition into the 'free city' of Danzig (Gdansk), then (in theory)
controlled by the League and kept open for all commerce.

The most striking agitation of early July derived from a
different source. Late in June, Lieutenant-Colonel Count Ger-
hard von Schwerin visited London. An officer of the German
General Staff, he was then head of the section dealing with
'Foreign Armies West' in German military intelligence. He was
one of those German soldiers who believed Hitler to be leading
their country towards a disastrous war. To restrain him, or to
enable him to be restrained, Schwerin insisted that the steady
determination of the British government to resist any Hitlerian
use of force had to be proved. He presented various ideas to the
surprisingly large number of influential politicians and officers
whom he met. He was helped to make contacts in London by
David Astor, the son of Lord Astor, who was a close friend of
Adam von Trott, the aristocratic German anti-Nazi. Schwerin
suggested, for instance, the immediate dispatch of RAF units to
France, but his most emphatic demand was that Churchill
should be brought into the government. Only then would Hitler
believe that appeasement had finally ended.

On 29 June the group of supporters of Eden met, as they
often did, at Ronald Tree's house. Leo Amery, who was there,

recorded that 'Tree and others have in the last day or two had talks with a senior German Staff Officer, Schwerin, who . . . said that nothing could stop war except definite action, not merely speeches, on our part, making it clear that we were really prepared to fight over Danzig.' Harold Nicolson recorded, of this meeting, that Schwerin thought the easiest action would be to bring in Churchill, and other anti-appeasers, into the government. He went on to say that the meeting decided 'to mobilize the Astor family to put pressure on *The Times*' and that Harold Macmillan and Nicolson should see Lord Camrose, the owner and controller of the *Daily Telegraph*. Leo Amery was to speak to Margesson, the Conservative Chief Whip. It was probably one of this group, or another of Schwerin's contacts, who precipitated the letter one of Chamberlain's Cabinet ministers sent to the Prime Minister on 30 June. Oliver Stanley, the most amiable and charming of the ministers of 1939, had wide social and political contacts. Now he told Chamberlain 'that the only chance of averting war this autumn was to bring home to Hitler the certainty that we shall fulfil our obligations to Poland'. As this letter suggests, Stanley was not one of the convinced appeasers of 1938–39. He suggested the creation of a more broadly based government and said he would give up his own position as President of the Board of Trade to make it easier. Chamberlain replied non-committally. Only a threat from Stanley to resign could have disturbed the Prime Minister's self-confidence.

As for *The Times*, the Astors allowed Dawson, the docile Chamberlainite, complete freedom as editor. Astor influence had more effect on *The Observer*. Margesson, whatever his own opinions, had to evade Amery's pressure to support Churchill. The great catch was Camrose. Nicolson describes how, at 3 p.m. on Friday 30 June, he, Macmillan, Lord Astor and the lobby correspondent of the *Telegraph*, together with a highly respectable Tory MP, Lord Balneil, and a rather furtive Anthony Eden, met at the *Telegraph* offices. Astor led the discussion and explained that Schwerin had suggested that Churchill or Eden should join the government. Camrose imposed his priority: 'Winston is the vital figure.' Camrose had always openly proclaimed his control of the *Daily Telegraph* and asserted himself weightily. He now insisted, it seems, that his mighty outburst in support of Churchill should be his 'scoop' on Monday and not be anticipated on Sunday in the Astor-owned and -influenced (though not editorially controlled) *Observer*.[20]

In fact, *The Observer* on Sunday 2 July had a forceful leader by the editor, J. L. Garvin: 'Mr Chamberlain should reconstruct his Cabinet. He should do so without further delay ... This action would be better understood by the Germans than any words. It would exclude in their sight, no less than in our own, the delusions about British surrender. This decisive reconstruction of Government would expedite the Russian agreement.' Garvin did not name Churchill, but 'our special correspondent' did so on the opposite page: 'A movement for the inclusion of Mr Churchill in the administration has revived and is gathering strength.' Chamberlain was cross about Garvin. Certainly, he had a sound reason – Garvin was supposed to be writing a biography of Neville's father, Joseph Chamberlain, in several volumes, though it was never completed. The Prime Minister knew why. 'He can't concentrate any longer on a real job of work. He can write a Garvinian article about Winston's virtues and the propriety of taking him into the Cabinet because that requires no work and no concentration. And moreover he enjoys lecturing the world in general and the government in particular. But the thought of the book bores and frightens him.' *The Observer* mattered. Its circulation was about the same as that of the Chamberlainite *Sunday Times*, around a quarter of a million. In the politically influential and wealthy sections of society, these papers were widely read.

The *Daily Telegraph* was more important still. Its circulation equalled that of *The Times* among the richest members of British society, and greatly exceeded it among the middle class. It was a Conservative paper whose influence on right-wing Tories increased in 1937 when it took over the *Morning Post*. Its circulation had grown steadily in the 1930s, and by 1939 reached about three-quarters of a million, compared with less than a quarter of a million for *The Times*. On 3 July 1939 the *Telegraph* printed as its first leading article a passionate outburst of praise for Churchill. The government did not include all

> those counsellors who are best qualified to decide upon fateful issues and to plan strategic strokes. One name will leap at once to everyone's cognisance. It is that of Mr CHURCHILL – a statesman not only schooled in responsibility by long and intimate contact with affairs of state, but possessing an unrivalled practical knowledge of the crucial problems which war presents, especially in the higher strategy. With vision and energy he unites a conspicuous gift of exposition and popular appeal, and in this strait pass the nation cannot prudently dispense with the great services he is so capable of rendering. True, Mr Churchill has a strong and masterful personality which estranges and even antagonizes some persons; but strong and masterful personalities are just what the present situation demands.

Perhaps trying to make his acceptance easier for Chamberlain, the article claimed, wrongly, that 'there is no reason to suppose that the Prime Minister himself, conscious as he must be of Mr Churchill's pre-eminent qualities, would regard the great advantage of enlisting those qualities for the Government as being outweighed by any disadvantages ... The act of inviting Mr Churchill to join the Cabinet would be the most popular step which Mr Chamberlain could take.' The same paper consoled the Prime Minister by reporting the 'great ovation' accorded to him at Glyndebourne. After a Fritz Busch–Carl Ebert *Otello*, by Verdi, the audience gave Chamberlain a standing ovation.

The importance for Conservatives of the *Telegraph* caused Chamberlain to act at once. He asked Lord Camrose to see him at No. 10 that day, and insisted that 'steps were being taken all the time' to make Hitler aware of Britain's resolve. He 'appreciated Churchill's ability' but 'he did not feel that he would gain sufficiently from Winston's ideas and advice to counterbalance the irritation and disturbance which would necessarily be caused'. Chamberlain recalled what it was like to have Churchill as a colleague: 'Winston's ideas and memoranda tended to monopolize the time of the whole Ministry. If you did not agree with him he was liable to lose his temper in argument, and a number of his colleagues had found that the easiest way was not to oppose him.' He agreed, though, that 'Winston was Public Enemy No. 1 in Berlin, and Eden the same in Italy. Their inclusion in the Cabinet might strike both ways.' The two agreed 'that the question of Eden . . . was not of the same consequence as that of Winston'. As usual, Chamberlain complained of Churchill's 'lack of judgement'. He admitted, or boasted, that he himself 'was slow to make up his mind, and equally slow to change it'. He did not intend to bring Churchill in 'at the moment'. In the event of war, though, he would be in the Cabinet and in the War Cabinet. For Chamberlain, the central problem was that he thought Churchill, like the Russian alliance, would make war more likely, rather than, as most people believed, less likely. He had set out his opinion in a letter to his sister Hilda in April when he wrote of Churchill, 'the nearer we get to war the more his chances improve and vice versa. If there is any possibility of easing the tension and getting back to normal relations with the Dictators I wouldn't risk it by what would certainly be regarded by them as a challenge.'[21]

Other newspapers added their pleas: the *Sunday Pictorial* again, the *Yorkshire Post*, the *Star*, the *Sunday Graphic*, the *Daily Mirror*, while the *Daily Express* and even the *Daily Mail* expected Churchill to be brought back to government. The liberal papers,

the *Manchester Guardian* and the *News Chronicle*, continued as
before to call for Churchill and Eden. The *Evening Standard* noted
the 'terrific barrage from the newspaper artillery' but correctly
reported, as early as 4 July, that Chamberlain would resist. The
Monday of the *Telegraph* leader, which evidently took Chamberlain by surprise, seems to have been the peak of the agitation.
Next morning, Top Wolmer, on waking up, moved by his
conversations the day before, wrote, absurdly, to the Archbishop
of Canterbury. He explained the anguished concern of 'very
well informed' colleagues in the Commons who 'say (and this
comes straight from Germany) that in spite of all that is said by
the Prime Minister and the Foreign Secretary in Parliament and
elsewhere, Hitler will not believe that we are in earnest so long
as he has only the Munich Cabinet to deal with'. So a number
of MPs had suggested that he beg the Archbishop to write to
The Times to show that there is a public demand for a broadening
of the Cabinet 'from quarters which are above any suspicion,
either of hysteria or personal ambition', for otherwise Chamberlain 'might be indisposed to take such action on his own initiative
until it was too late'.[22] No such letter emerged – Cosmo Lang
never showed any signs of being a daringly controversial
Primate.

A counter-attack was quickly launched. Chamberlain could,
of course, count on *The Times*. Dawson, its editor, noted in his
diary for 3 July: 'The DT [*Daily Telegraph*] joined in the hue and
cry for the inclusion of Winston in the Cabinet in order to
impress the Germans. We continued the more effective process
of calling attention to the growing strength of the British Army.'
Dawson consistently acted as a comfortable conformist. He
embodied what later became known, and condemned, as the
'establishment', his diary recording suitable events of the Season:
Encaenia at Oxford, Hurlingham, an All Souls Gaudy, the
Fourth of June at Eton, Wimbledon, the Eton and Harrow
match. On 6 July he talked to Chamberlain at the House of

Commons, and found him 'full of vigour', with 'no intention of being bounced into taking back Winston'. Most important, the Conservative Party Whips now acted, explaining to the inarticulate government supporters among MPs that Churchill's appointment would not prevent war but provoke it.

Another, poisonous, response appeared in print. Chamberlain expressed pleasure at what he described as 'witty articles in *Truth*', which, he added for his sister, is 'secretly controlled by Sir J. Ball' – that is Chamberlain's confidant, and telephone-tapper, the head of the Conservative Research Department at Central Office. The first page on 7 June noted 'an intrigue, backed by a blatant press campaign, the purpose of which is to enable Mr Winston Churchill, with his satellites holding on to his apron-strings, to muscle into the Cabinet. MPs pay little or no attention to either. But as the public may be misled', the editor had to explain the folly of it all. The following week, more space was devoted to the question 'Is Winston Worth It?' 'The answer is, of course, a negative' – that is, 'from the point of view of the harm that this factitious, interested and altogether contemptible agitation . . . will do to the British cause in foreign countries'. The author's culminating witticism was peculiarly odious: 'Why not make a job of it, and have Vic Oliver in too?' – a reference to the new husband of one of Churchill's daughters, a stage comedian (it was a marriage which had caused distress and worry to both parents). In the next article another Chamberlainite point was made more clearly than the Prime Minister would dare publicly to do, that if the Russian negotiations failed 'this is no occasion for British lamentations'.[23]

The Times, in a further counter-attack, moved into pompous farce. On 10 July the most prominently printed letter was from J. A. Spender, a well-known Liberal. He denounced attacks on Chamberlain because now 'all parties had declared their agreement on the next steps in foreign policy' and unity should be displayed. The Liberal leader, Archibald Sinclair, should stop such attacks. Spender thus pointed out Chamberlain's new appeal – that he had renounced appeasement. Of course, the demand for Churchill represented a desire to make sure that this renunciation should be demonstrated as real and durable. A group of eminent Liberals, headed by Lady Violet Bonham Carter, wrote to *The Times*, disagreeing with Spender and calling for Churchill to be brought into the Cabinet. *The Times* refused to publish their letter. The writers promptly sent it to all the other national papers, and nearly all of them eagerly published it. *The Times*, heavily embarrassed, printed it after all the next day. But it cut out the closing sentences, with the demand for Churchill's return to government. The day after, it published a shifty leading article. It explained that the end of Lady Violet's letter joined 'in the now familiar clamour, which is not always inspired by the most ingenuous motives, for the instant inclusion of Mr Churchill in the Cabinet. From that particular clamour *The Times* has held aloof – not at all from any lack of appreciation of Mr Churchill's outstanding qualities but from the conviction that a newspaper agitation was both ridiculous and futile.' The *Times* editors wanted to defend Churchill's reputation since 'they feel intensely that Mr Churchill may well be needed in a Government again'. No doubt to re-establish their 'impartiality' they gave prominence two days later to a letter from Harold Macmillan, who, though not mentioning Churchill, urged a 'truly National Government including the most prominent and able figures in Parliament'.[24]

Chamberlain did not worry greatly. He told his sister on 8 July, 'this has been a comparatively quiet week only enlivened by the drive to put Winston into the Government'. Oddly, he misunderstood the cause. 'It has been a regular conspiracy in which Mr Maisky has been involved as he keeps in very close touch with Randolph [Churchill's son].' He did not worry that the *Daily Mail* and the *Daily Express* had reported that Churchill would get in; he was 'vexed' though about Camrose and the

Telegraph. The serious-minded weeklies (then more serious than they subsequently became) naturally gave their thoughts. The *Economist* continued to press for a broader and bolder government. The *New Statesman* recognized that nothing would happen to force Chamberlain's acquiescence. As the editor noted, 'The demand for the inclusion of Mr Churchill in the Cabinet has reached formidable proportions but I don't expect Mr Chamberlain to yield.' The *Spectator* reckoned that 'the political correspondents of the London dailies thought Churchill's prospects more hopeful than did MPs. 'If Mr Chamberlain were disposed to broaden the basis of his Cabinet there is no reason why he should not have done so several weeks ago. Yet it is almost platitudinous to say that nothing the Prime Minister could do would be received with more general approval than the inclusion of Mr Churchill and his fellow ex-Ministers.' This writer pointed out, however, that 'a very large body of Tories still distrust Mr Churchill and dislike his friends'.[25] The evidence suggests that in the summer of 1939 a majority of voters wished Churchill to be in the Cabinet but that Chamberlain felt able to refuse.

Chamberlain was a skilled twentieth-century politician who appeared to be doing enough of what potential Conservative voters wanted – especially resisting German aggression and trying for the Russian alliance – to enable him not to do some of the things they wanted, such as adding Churchill to the Cabinet. Voters wanted peace based on strength; this was what Neville Chamberlain seemed to offer, though many thought Churchill would add impressive emphasis to the 'strength' in British policy. What they wanted was not to turn Neville Chamberlain out, but to see a flourishing collaboration between him and Winston Churchill. Chamberlain believed that would destroy all hopes of peace, that Churchill would wreck his subtle manoeuvres, his furtive advances to Hitler, his cultivation of Mussolini's support. So far from helping the Prime Minister to succeed, Churchill would ensure his failure. Churchill was not a twentieth-century devotee of a political party: he never saw his role as that of helping his party's leader to win applause and acclaim and so to establish his own claim upon that party. On the contrary, he believed he should indicate what was correct, whether or not his party leader and his party agreed. His influence would rest on his being right, not on his value as a party fugleman.

Twentieth-century MPs with very few exceptions, mostly in the university seats which survived until after the Second World War, were in Parliament because they were the candidates approved by their party. It was their job, therefore, to back their party's leaders and to help them to win the next election, not to create dissension and unease. Winston Churchill was a politician who fitted the mid-eighteenth century more than the mid-twentieth. Then there were a small number of MPs, around 100, who struggled for a place, power and profit. Those among them who were out of power and place looked with hope to the intermittent descent on London of the independent members, the 'country gentlemen'. The independent members could, especially before George III's reign, readily be convinced that the administration contained corrupt, unpatriotic self-seekers. The difficulty, for those out of office, was that these independent members tended to dislike London and to absent themselves. If there were a great issue afoot, that of national safety for instance, they would come to Westminster. There they would listen to the debates (seldom, if ever, contributing to them) and decide how to vote on the arguments put before them. They were MPs because of their local rank and prestige, certainly not because of any attachment to a party.

William Pitt the Elder demonstrates the political power that a great orator could win in the eighteenth century. Like Churchill he never possessed a significant personal following in Parliament. He spurned political parties. In the eighteenth century political parties were small, unstable groups, not the portentous centralized mechanisms of the twentieth century. So a great Parliamentary orator could not merely secure an audience, he could win votes. It could be difficult, in times of crisis, when the country gentlemen were up and not leaving Westminster to the control of the routine political managers, for a government to survive without him. Few of the independent members harboured the resentment and envy which high talent can arouse among twentieth-century MPs whose party requires their continuous presence for mindless voting. It is an evocative coincidence that Winston Churchill's ancestor, the quarrelsome termagant Sarah, Duchess of Marlborough, bequeathed a substantial legacy to Pitt in 1744 to reward his independent critical spirit.

The editor of the *New Statesman*, comparing Baldwin and Churchill, described Baldwin as someone who 'acted like a Conservative, spoke like a Liberal and was always in words and actions a true representative of the Great British middle class': which certainly did not fit Churchill. He quoted Lloyd George, a man who was not in the least intimidated by Churchill:

> When Mr Churchill gets up, the House of Commons quickly fills; each quip is savoured and repeated, the eloquent passages form the subject of admiring discussion for days, the carefully prepared phrases stand out like jewels and are recorded by gossip writers and lobby correspondents. Every listener is conscious of the occasion, of being part of an audience, of being present at a great occasion. At the end of the speech they are applauding as when the curtain falls at the opera. They listen to Churchill but *they do not go along with him.*[26]

By the summer of 1939, though, many of the ablest Conservative MPs went along with Churchill, while outside Westminster most people did so.

Naturally, foreign embassies in London watched and reported on the attempt to get Churchill into government. The

German ambassador, Dr Herbert von Dirksen, in a long telegram to Berlin of 3 July, explained that 'an atmosphere of war in Europe' is being created by 'Roosevelt and his Jewish advisers' to help to make possible the sale of supplies to Britain and France in case of war, and by French 'circles ... who blame Britain for making too few concessions in the Soviet Pact negotiations' and by 'specially interested quarters here' who 'are desirous of thwarting any beginnings of a constructive policy towards Germany. In particular there are the Anglo-Jewish circles, and, in their wake, the Churchill group, which has been further strengthened by the Cliveden Set (Lord Astor). This tendency in domestic policy is evident from the demand voiced in various newspapers (e.g. *The Observer*) for Churchill to be brought into the Cabinet.' A week later, he sent a soothing report:

> Within the Cabinet, and in a small but influential group of politicians, efforts are being made to replace the negative policy of an encirclement front by a constructive policy towards Germany ... Though there are strong forces at work to stifle this very tender plant – among which may be numbered the press campaign of last weekend – nevertheless Chamberlain's personality gives a certain guarantee that British policy will not be delivered into the hands of unscrupulous adventurers.

Another piece of evidence confirms that the Führer himself thought Churchill dangerous. On 29 July Lord Kemsley, the Chamberlainite newspaper proprietor, spoke to Hitler; his visit had Chamberlain's approval. He explained that the Prime Minister would lead Britain into war 'if Germany had done something so serious as to affect the security of the world'. On the other hand, Chamberlain looked upon Munich 'as the forerunner of a different relationship with Germany in the future' and could count on support if he 'were to announce that he had come to an agreement with Germany which he could absolutely rely on'. Hitler, however, 'talked about the strength of the opposition to the Prime Minister and referred particularly to Mr Winston Churchill and his powers of expression. Lord Kemsley replied that in his opinion far more notice was taken abroad of the opposition than in England.'

The French government thought every means of deterring Hitler should be employed: they keenly desired both a Triple Alliance with the USSR and Churchill's presence in the British government. (Though, paradoxically, if Hitler attacked, the French government might be less determined on war than the British.) The French embassy in London saw it as possible that Schwerin's visit to London explained the renewed and emphatic demand for Churchill. The French ambassador, in a dispatch of 10 July – the last day of Schwerin's fortnight in England – reported that those Conservative MPs who had won the support of the *Telegraph* had justified their approach by 'suggestions' from the German General Staff. In a long, and subtle, dispatch the next day, the French embassy analysed the 'rather delicate position' of Mr Chamberlain. For the moment, they believed, Chamberlain commanded the confidence of the majority 'on condition that he put the accent sufficiently on the determination of Great Britain'. They divided the 'very strong current of opinion' behind Churchill into three categories. A small group of the general public wished Churchill to supersede Chamberlain; another small group feared that Churchill's entry into the government would prevent any renewed appeasement; most wanted Chamberlain and Churchill to work together, now that the Prime Minister had, as it seemed, renounced appeasement.

The French embassy saw that the stronger the desire for Churchill the more Chamberlain would fear a potential rival in Cabinet. And they saw that even those who wished for a united national policy might fear that a dominant Churchill could represent the end of all hopes of that peaceful solution which, after all, standing up to Hitler was meant to bring. So there were ambiguities; but Corbin concluded the dispatch with what turned out to be a prediction of 1940. 'If the situation gets worse it is Mr Churchill, more than anyone, who would embody the will of the British people not to permit Germany to dominate Europe and to compel the Reich to respect the principles to which the British people are above all attached.'

Friday of that week was the Fourteenth of July. The last, spectacular and, in retrospect, sad commemoration put on in Paris by the Third Republic was a glorious Franco-British display. The Royal Navy, the Marines, the Foot Guards in full-dress uniform and the fly-past by the RAF symbolized the belated Anglo-French alliance. Beside President Lebrun and M. Daladier stood on the saluting base the British Chiefs of Staff, the War Secretary, Hore-Belisha, and that unofficial but most celebrated opponent of the Nazi bullies, Winston Churchill.[27]

On 10 July, Ivan Maisky, the Soviet ambassador in London, had written to Molotov in Moscow to explain the outcome of the demand for new Cabinet ministers in London. Hitler was a terrible threat to the USSR. We do not know when Stalin and Molotov decided to do a deal with him rather than agree to fight him in 1939 or to help those who were pledged to resist Hitlerian aggression. It is obvious that they had to avoid giving assistance to Chamberlain in possible negotiations with Hitler, which a Soviet alliance might do, while too early a refusal to ally with Britain might help Hitler in getting Chamberlain to accept his terms. Rationally, the Soviet government had to spin out the negotiations to a date at which it would be too late for a German attack to penetrate deeply into Soviet territory. Only if Britain, and therefore France, could be relied on to stand up to Hitler would it then make sense to ally with Britain against Germany. Here is what Maisky wrote to Stalin's closest associate:

My scepticism concerning the imminence of a reconstruction of the British government . . . is being more and more confirmed. Despite the fact that the idea of including Churchill, Eden, and others in the cabinet is highly popular in the broadest spheres of British public opinion, despite the fact that the majority of the Conservative Party and a number of influential members of the government declare themselves in favour of a reconstruction, Chamberlain, supported by Simon, is so far successfully resisting such a step. Chamberlain's motives are both political and personal. The political motives boil down to the fact that including Churchill, Eden and others in the government would mean a final break with Germany and the final abandonment of any renewal of the policy of 'appeasement' in the future. For one cannot close one's eyes to the fact that at heart Chamberlain remains as ever an 'appeaser'. His concessions to the 'new course' have been and are being made unwillingly, from necessity, under intense pressure from the public mood. The personal motive, which functions in the same direction, is that Chamberlain greatly dislikes Churchill and fears him. Churchill is a much bigger man than Chamberlain, and, as well, strong-willed, energetic, and able to dominate his colleagues in the cabinet. Chamberlain considers – not without good grounds – that Churchill's coming into the government would be no more than the prelude to his own dismissal. Also objecting to Churchill's entering the cabinet is Baldwin, who still has strong influence behind the scenes in conservative circles.[28]

Churchill's entry into the government could justify Russian acceptance of an alliance with Britain; his continued exclusion pointed to a British deal with Hitler.

CHAPTER TWELVE

War

SOME SHREWD AND well-informed contemporaries believed that Churchill's continued exclusion from government would cause the collapse of the alliance with Russia and encourage Hitler to defy the 'peace front': indeed, within weeks of the failure of the newspaper campaign for Churchill's entry into the Cabinet, the negotiations with Moscow had collapsed and the second great war had begun. Perhaps it all would have happened anyway; we cannot tell. We shall never know if Churchill's presence in government and the pursuit of Churchillian policies would have restrained Hitler himself from risking a great European war or whether other Germans could have restrained him. We are not likely to find more evidence from Germany than we already possess. Certainly it is possible that by 1939 Hitler was ready to gamble on the outcome, for Germany and for himself, of a great war even if he had not been assured of Soviet co-operation, and even if he was certain of British determination, and perhaps no one could have stopped him. From Moscow we may hope to have more evidence on the chances of winning Soviet support against Hitler and of the more remote possibility of some degree of co-operation between Poland, the Baltic States and the USSR against the Third Reich. We may discover more evidence on whether or not Churchill and his policies might have helped.

We can be certain, however, that the policies pressed by Chamberlain, rational though they can be made out to be, encouraged rather than restrained Hitler's gambles. Britain, and the Empire, could hardly have been worse off under Churchillian direction. Acceptance of Nazi domination of Europe, which neither Churchill nor Chamberlain would agree to, still seems unattractive.

The campaign for Churchill continued. On Sunday 23 July 1939 Chamberlain wrote to his sister about the 'Churchill episode' that though 'Garvin in an insufferably dull and boring article tries to keep it alive, it has lost all life'. In the House of Commons, however, voices continued to be raised. One was that of the victor in the latest by-election, T. L. Horabin, in North Cornwall. His victory depressed Chamberlain: 'I get pretty sick of the perpetual personal attacks on me at home. I heard that in Cornwall the feeling in my favour was unmistakable, yet it hasn't shown itself in the by-election.' The local farmer standing for the Conservatives was defeated by a Liberal stranger, who replaced a Cornish landowner. Unusually, the poll was as large as it had been at the general election. 'Mr Chamberlain's policy', it was reported, 'is really the only issue before the electors. All other questions are subsidiary and, in fact, nobody is giving thought to them.' In the North Cornwall constituency there was an unusually high proportion of women and this, for some reason, was supposed to favour Chamberlain. Unexpectedly, the majority for the opposition Liberal against the government increased significantly, though not dramatically. Chamberlain wondered 'what would happen in a General Election'.[1]

The new member, daringly, gave his maiden speech immediately after the Prime Minister himself had spoken in a setpiece foreign affairs debate at the end of July. Horabin concluded by quoting Cromwell, inaccurately, but with forceful relevance. 'I beg the Prime Minister and his advisers . . . to ponder deeply the words that were used by Cromwell in this House when he said "I beseech you, by the bowels of Christ, to believe that you may sometimes be a little wrong."' He pleaded Churchill's cause. 'It is a national tragedy that . . . the nation is deprived of his strong moral purpose, his judgement and energy at this time, when we are perhaps putting up the last desperate fight for peace.' (He then made his remarks even less appetizing to Chamberlain by adding the name of Lloyd George.)

Horabin spoke in the first of the two portentous debates just before the House adjourned for the summer. From Labour, Liberals and Conservatives came support for Churchill. Frederick Bellenger, from the Labour benches, praised him: 'So many of the pictures he has given to the House have been very objective . . . So many of the events he has forecast have come true.' The Liberal expert on foreign affairs, Geoffrey Mander, asked

> that some of the Conservative leaders who have always proved to be absolutely right on questions of foreign policy should be in the Government. Why are they not in the Government? For two reasons: partly because the Prime Minister thinks that their presence there would upset and destroy his personal dictatorship and his domination in his own Cabinet, and partly because he thinks that Herr Hitler would not like it. I am sure that one of the reasons why the Prime Minister would not take the Right Hon Gentleman, the Member for Epping (Mr Churchill) into his Cabinet, is that he thinks it might antagonise Herr Hitler.

From the Conservative dissidents, Vyvyan Adams spoke out yet again. To convince Hitler 'of our will to resist his next aggression' there should be added to the government Churchill, Amery, Eden and Duff Cooper. Churchill 'has never wavered for the last five or six years in the very policy' which the Cabinet 'are now pursuing' (claiming to pursue would have been more accurate). Churchill 'has always stood on the side of the collective front in the cause of peace, and in resistance to aggression'. In the debate on the adjournment a few days later, Adams regretted that the 'reconstruction of the Government, which is widely desired throughout the country, without distinction of party, has not been carried out'. Adams declared, 'I should be less apprehensive about Hitler's state of mind if our Government . . . included some of those men whom Dr Goebbels and Herr Hitler described as "warmongers".' The Deputy Speaker intervened to prevent his saying more about the reconstruction of the government.[2]

Historians and biographers have neglected Vyvyan Adams, even when it was fashionable to single out for praise those politicians who are supposed to have supported Churchill. Boothby, a much more evasive and ambiguous figure, and the opaque and not particularly attractive Brendan Bracken, proclaimed their virtues or had them expounded. Adams, member for West Leeds, himself wrote that he showed 'tireless displays of individuality' and went to 'elaborate heights to convince his constituents that a Conservative can behave liberally'. He lost his seat in the Labour landslide of 1945, and six years later drowned swimming with his family near Helston in Cornwall. Churchill remembered. On the day of Adams's memorial service he was presiding over the Cabinet to discuss Mossadeq's seizure of BP's oilfields in Persia; he sent his son, Randolph, to represent him.[3]

The debate on the international situation on 31 July 1939 showed worried unease about the growing German threat to Poland and the continued delay in assuring the alliance with the Soviet Union. Churchill, though he was in the House, did not speak. The Prime Minister, before the debate began, announced that the British and French had agreed to begin talks at once between the military staffs of the three countries. This provided some reassurance; he did not explain that he intended the British and French military missions to go to Moscow by the slowest available means. On the contrary, he insisted that the government was showing a 'really strong intention to bring these negotiations to a successful issue'. The Prime Minister, and Rab Butler, who closed the debate for the government, both made it clear that 'indirect aggression', especially against the Baltic States, was the current political problem in the negotiations. As Chamberlain put it, 'we are extremely anxious not even to appear to be desirous of encroaching on the independence of those states'. Though the failure to win a definite promise of Russian assistance worried MPs, few grasped that if Soviet support for Britain and France against Germany was not secured, the alternative would be Soviet support for Germany against Britain and France.

The debate on Wednesday 2 August proved viciously bad-tempered. Chamberlain moved that from Friday the House of Commons should adjourn until 3 October, though the government could recommend earlier recalls if necessary. Churchill spoke after the party leaders, Greenwood and Sinclair. Like them, he urged a much sooner return, after about three weeks. It was obviously strange, considering the threats accumulating in that summer of 1939, to suggest any possibility of unbroken holidays lasting until October. Of course objections to Chamberlain's proposed adjournment implied lack of confidence in him. It suggested that he could not be relied on to give critics of government the chance to air their views in a crisis. Churchill, in his speech, remarked that members could disagree about 'the judgement which the Prime Minister might form upon the facts as they unfolded'. He asked, 'who can doubt that there is going to be a supreme trial of will-power, if not indeed a supreme trial of arms? At this moment in its long history, it would be disastrous, it would be pathetic, it would be shameful for the House of Commons to write itself off.' Chamberlain unusually spoke twice in the debate. His second speech asserted that this was a vote of confidence: 'do you trust the judgement and good faith of the Prime Minister and his colleagues?' His answer to Churchill's question whether his judgement alone should determine whether or not the House should sit was inept. Mr Churchill, Chamberlain said, 'was good enough to say that he did not distrust my good faith; it was rather my judgement that he mistrusted. I am rather inclinded to say *tu quoque.*' But no one had suggested that Churchill should decide when the Commons should reassemble.

One of the back-benchers on whom Chamberlain relied complained, correctly enough, that Churchill attended the House and voted less frequently than diligent party men such as himself. 'There are a good many back-bench Members', Victor Raikes complained, 'who stay on in the House all through the Session, and it does seem a little hard that those who are most anxious to bring the Session into operation again are those who, when the House is in Session, are so often absent.' Another Conservative back-bencher, H. G. Strauss, rebuked Raikes severely:

> Really this is a serious occasion, and to think that it is any answer to the Right Hon Member for Epping (Mr Churchill) to talk about his Division record seems to me quite fantastic. I have not been a follower, and I am not a follower, of the Right Hon Member for Epping, but he has certainly intervened in, I think, all the great Debates of this Parliament, and to talk about the Division record of so great a House of Commons man is quite unworthy.

Raikes was one of the most articulate of twentieth-century party men. He it was who told the House after Munich that Chamberlain 'will go down to history as the greatest European statesman of this or any other time'. This day was another of those increasingly numerous occasions when Churchill's appeal to the public outside Parliament grew. Roger Cambon, in temporary charge of the French embassy in London at that time, telegraphed a report to Paris on the two debates. He reported that newspapers that normally supported the government showed signs of dismay at Chamberlain's insistence on a long adjournment. Confidence in the government had declined.[4]

Another of Chamberlain's steadily voting supporters, Sir Patrick Hannon, earned discredit. Ronald Cartland, at thirty-two one of the youngest of the restless Conservatives, pleaded with Chamberlain to be less rigid. 'We are in the situation that within a month we may be going to fight and we may be going to die.' At this point, Hannon (aet. sixty-five) laughed. Angered, Cartland accused Chamberlain of giving 'jeering, pettyfogging party speeches which divide the nation'. Half an hour later Hannon rose to express 'profound devotion to the Prime Minister' and to denounce 'the poisonous quality' of Cartland's speech. Chamberlain did not like it either. He encouraged 'de-selection' of Cartland as a candidate for the next election. 'We may lose the seat as a result but I would rather do that . . . than have a traitor in the camp.' Cartland was killed on active service in the spring of 1940.[5]

At the beginning of August 1939 Churchill was working hard on his next book, *A History of the English-Speaking Peoples*. Then Kingsley Wood, Chamberlain's Air Minister, someone increasingly sympathetic to Churchill, invited him to watch RAF exercises. Shortly afterwards, on 14 August, Churchill returned to France and talked to Gamelin and Georges, the future commanders of French forces opposite Germany. They received him warmly. Georges personally escorted him for an extensive visit to the Maginot Line, that elaborate chain of fortifications on the French frontier with Germany. Spears went with him again: his subsequent post-1940 recollections reported much more unease from Churchill than he actually showed at the time. In fact, he was impressed and reassured by French power and determination. The British newspapers reported Churchill's inspection of French fortifications. The *Telegraph* had photographs. *The Times* explained that 'Mr Churchill has now seen the most secret parts of the line, and he is one of the few privileged visitors who have done so.' When he came back to Paris 'a big crowd had gathered at the Gare de L'Est to welcome him, and he was warmly cheered as he alighted from the train ... Mr Churchill declared that he had been profoundly impressed by what he had seen; "my confidence in your country", he added, "is more unshakeable than ever".' Churchill, it seems, was as popular in France as in Britain; Chamberlain need not worry about that. This took three days. Then Churchill allowed himself a brief holiday at his cousin's château, talking and painting. He returned on 23 August.[6]

When he got back, everything was changed; the international scene had been transformed. Late on 21 August Berlin announced that Ribbentrop, now Hitler's Foreign Minister, would fly to Moscow to sign a non-aggression pact. Stalin had decided that it was safer to help Germany destroy Poland than to help Britain and France to defend Poland and perhaps deter Hitler. It turned out later that Stalin would send Soviet supplies for the German war machine in return for German agreement that the Soviet Union could occupy the Baltic States, half of Poland and Bessarabia. For most people in Britain war seemed certain after the Nazi–Soviet pact. Curiously, Chamberlain and his closest advisers disagreed. They had never wanted the Russian alliance. Its failure meant that the deterrent to Hitler embodied in the British guarantee to Poland could be empha-sized with less risk of provoking the Führer and 'moderate' Germans. Hitler did indeed make last-minute efforts to persuade Britain to let him do as he wished in Poland. As a result, for a few days at the end of August, ministers believed that he was climbing down. As part of Chamberlain's attempt to deter him from violence and to display that British resolution which, the Prime Minister believed, would make possible another triumph for reason, Parliament was recalled on 24 August to pass emergency legislation, in case war should break out. Churchill was there but did not speak. Indeed, in late August he was silent, working hard, when he was at home, on his *History*. The House of Commons met again on the 29th for only fifty minutes. Chamberlain referred to the formal Anglo-Polish alliance signed the preceding Friday and stressed that British obligations to Poland 'will be carried out'. Now Churchill led the cheering that greeted this declaration.[7]

Hitler delayed the German attack on Poland while he tried to persuade the British government to leave him to it. He failed, and at dawn on 1 September the invasion of Poland began. Chamberlain, the Cabinet and Parliament prepared for war. That meant bringing Churchill into the government. The pretext for keeping him out so far, as circulated to Conservative MPs and sympathetic newspapers, was that his presence would make war more likely. Chamberlain could hardly resist Churchill now that war had come. Early in July 1939 when the clamour for Churchill had reached its climax, the political correspondent of the Chamberlainite *Sunday Times* set out the party line: 'If war came, or was seen to be inevitable, the Government would no doubt be reconstituted, and on the broadest possible basis; but, short of that, there is no reason to anticipate the appointment of new ministers in the near future.' Churchill had to be taken in to the War Cabinet, but in what role? Chamberlain found it difficult to decide. At first, soon after the German attack, Chamberlain invited Churchill to join the War Cabinet, not as head of a department, but as Minister without Portfolio. This was on the afternoon of 1 September. On Sunday 3 September, after he had announced that Britain was at war with Germany, Chamberlain asked Churchill instead to become, once again, First Lord of the Admiralty. He probably worried about how to prevent Churchill's grasping control of the whole government. He seems to have decided that Churchill, given direct control of an important section of British armed forces, would be less likely to interfere in everything else. The Conservative Chief Whip, Margesson, is recorded as explaining that Churchill had been sent to the Admiralty because 'he would be a most dangerous member of the Cabinet if he was left to roam over the whole field of policy, and it would be much safer to give him a job of work to get his teeth into'. Maurice Hankey, the long-serving Cabinet Secretary, had been included in the War Cabinet as 'a man whose experience and authority Mr Churchill would respect, and who would therefore be able to keep him in order'. Hankey believed it, too. He wrote to his wife, 'as far as I can make out, my main job is to keep an eye on Winston!'[8]

Germany invaded Poland on Friday; Britain honoured the guarantee to Poland and declared war on Sunday. In between, Saturday was a fraught and tumultuous day. The Cabinet met twice, the second time at midnight. Churchill was not brought in, though Chamberlain had invited him to become a Cabinet minister on Friday. Consequently, he felt inhibited from public pronouncements and no speech or statement came from him that day. At the afternoon Cabinet Halifax and Chamberlain suggested that Hitler should be given time to consider an Italian proposal for a conference to discuss differences between Germany and Poland. The Germans should cease their advance into Poland and agree to withdraw their forces from Polish territory before the conference could start. The majority of ministers, including Hoare and Simon, those dominant Chamberlainites, would not have it. Britain should be firm and declare war. It was Britain's duty and if Britain failed no one, including possible German opponents of Hitler, would ever take Britain seriously. The Cabinet wanted to go to war at midnight. Chamberlain had to agree, though he repeated that the French government had other reasons for delay and that he needed to consult them. Telephone calls to Paris showed that the French government wanted delay. He, and Halifax, agreed.

At a quarter to eight on Saturday evening Chamberlain rose

to report to the Commons. He explained that Hitler had not yet replied to the British warning. At that point, instead of the time limit for Hitler's response that ministers and the House expected Chamberlain to proclaim, he observed, 'it may be that the delay is caused by consideration of a proposal which, meanwhile, had been put forward by the Italian Government, that hostilities should cease and that there should then immediately be a conference between the Five Powers, Great Britain, France, Poland, Germany and Italy'. Munich again! The House reacted with fury. Arthur Greenwood rose to speak for Labour. 'Speak for the working class,' Greenwood was told, then 'Speak for England!' Ten minutes later Chamberlain, frightened by the hostility that any hint of a new Munich aroused, spoke again, this time insisting that the reason for British delay was to agree with France when to start the war.[9]

Duff Cooper and others, as so often, grumbled at the Savoy Grill. Thence, fortified by a plate of grouse, Duff Cooper repaired to Churchill's flat. He found Churchill complaining that he had heard nothing from Chamberlain all day, though he had agreed to join the Cabinet the day before, on Friday. According to Duff Cooper, 'he had wished to speak that night in the House, but feeling himself already almost a member of the Government had refrained from doing so'. That evening, though, his feelings found expression. The French ambassador was away at Downing Street when Churchill telephoned to the embassy. Guy de Girard de Charbonnières took the call. Churchill spoke with forceful passion, 'causing the telephone to vibrate'. He had been a friend to France but now he was indignant, 'disgusted by the attitude of your government. For two days Poland was under attack left to fight alone.' The British and French were neglecting their pledges to Poland. 'We are dealing with our government here,' but the French government was even more evasive. 'I, Winston Churchill, declare to you that if the French government does not declare war on Germany tomorrow, it is finished between France and me ... I shall publicly denounce the dishonour and cowardice of the France of today.' By the time the ambassador returned to the embassy, things had changed. After leaving the Commons, Chamberlain telephoned Halifax, who noted that 'I had never heard the Prime Minister so disturbed.' Halifax went over to No. 10, where Chamberlain told him 'that he did not believe, unless we have cleared the position, that the Government would be able to maintain itself when it met parliament the next day'. The Cabinet, hastily assembled at midnight, agreed that war should be declared before Parliament met.[10]

Thus began the second great war. Everyone assumed that Churchill would write its history – six volumes on *The Second World War* appeared after its end. At the start of the first volume, *The Gathering Storm*, Churchill composed a preface in March 1948. He wrote, 'One day President Roosevelt told me that he was asking publicly for suggestions about what the war should be called. I said at once "The Unnecessary War". There never was a war more easy to stop.'

That is the theme and the tentative conclusion of this book.

Conclusions

THE POST-WAR Churchillian interpretation of the history of the
1930s set out in the introduction to this book is, it seems, too
simple. Two reservations cast shadows on the picture. One is
international, the other at home.

More evidence is unlikely to emerge on what Hitler might
have done had he been faced in September 1938 or August 1939
with the threat of armed resistance from a Grand Alliance which
could guarantee a war against Germany on two fronts. In
September 1938 a few German generals discussed an attempt to
overthrow Hitler. Two of them mattered: Franz Halder, the
Chief of the General Staff, and Erwin von Witzleben, in control
of the Berlin region. Halder survived the war. Like some other
Germans who had been prominent under the Nazis, he blamed
the war on the British. All was ready, he claimed, when the
news of Chamberlain's flight to Munich showed that the essential condition for the plot had gone. They could only hope to
justify themselves if Hitler seemed to be setting off a great war,
at least against Britain and France and perhaps against the
Soviet Union. The British policy advocated by Churchill in the
second half of September 1938, so Halder claimed, would have
enabled the plotters to proceed. Whether they would have done
so or whether they would have restrained or removed Hitler we

cannot tell. Nor can we confidently say whether Hitler's conduct would have been different in 1939 had he been faced with the certainty of British and French action in the west and the certain hostility of Soviet Russia. What we can safely assert is that Churchill's policies gave the only chance of restraining Hitler in 1938 or 1939. Then, however, Hitler felt more and more that he had to win living space and 'solve the Jewish problem' soon. Potential enemies were growing stronger and Hitler worried about his own health. Only he could save Germany – so perhaps a British rejection of appeasement, with firm Anglo-French co-operation as the basis of a Grand Alliance, would not have prevented him from risking disaster to Germany and Europe.

In 1939 the Nazi–Soviet pact made it certain that Hitler would not be deterred. He showed some signs of dismay at threatened Anglo-French resistance, but that did not stop him. Whether an effective Grand Alliance would have done so we cannot know, but his prestige in Germany was certainly even greater than in September 1938 and mutterings of discontent among army officers even less likely. We do not know, yet, whether Churchill's direction of British policy might have caused Stalin to go for alliance against Germany rather than co-operation with Germany. Increasingly, information comes out at the levels in Moscow immediately subordinate to the Kremlin. It is possible that documents so far remaining closed may tell us something about discussions involving Stalin and Molotov in 1939. There is no doubt that Chamberlain tried to prevent the Anglo-Soviet alliance and that Moscow knew it. On the other hand, as Gabriel Gorodetsky has effectively shown, Stalin showed deep mistrust of Churchill even when in 1941 the German army was about to invade the USSR. However, we can be sure that for blocking Hitler, or encouraging Stalin, Churchill was better than Chamberlain.

Chamberlain's and Churchill's objectives were identical.

Both intended to preserve the independence of Britain and its Empire. Their methods were totally different. The difficulty about Chamberlain's plan to work with a Hitler rendered rational and moderate by concessions arranged by Britain to deal with justified German grievances was that it strengthened Hitler inside Germany, so making easier his pursuit of the irrational, and moreover it alienated potential allies against Germany. Chamberlain did not accept German domination in Europe, or the free hand in the east for Hitler. He sought Anglo-German co-operation in rational discussion to prevent Hitler securing the mastery of Europe: in the end, Churchill's ideas were taken up only when Chamberlain's had failed. There are authors, most brilliantly John Charmley, who suggest that Chamberlain might have done better to accept the free hand in the east for Germany and that Churchill should have accepted it in the summer of 1940 or in 1941. The assumption is of a protracted German–Soviet war of which Britain could dictate the outcome. One problem is that the British military, like those in the United States, assumed the quick defeat of the Soviet Union, which would have made Hitler irresistible. Moreover, it is not certain how far British help and American help, which depended on Britain's remaining in the war, were essential to prolong Soviet resistance. These problems take us even further into the uncertainties of what might have been.

British internal politics need less conjecture and speculation. One thing is sure: throughout the 1930s Churchill urgently preached the need for British military strength, especially for a formidable air force. Like many, but not all, of his demands, that for British armaments won more support as threats from Europe grew. To begin with, though, Churchill wanted a strong isolated Britain which could ignore the League of Nations, oppose disarmament and rely on French power to keep Europe quiet. The United Kingdom had to keep out of Europe and its quarrels: these were right-wing opinions. They harmonized with

Churchill's challenge to Baldwin's leadership of the Conservative Party in his sustained opposition to government policy towards India. Churchill's concern for the European balance increased as German power increased. By 1935 he had begun to detach himself from those who thought first of the Empire and cared little or nothing about increased German power, especially in eastern and south-eastern Europe. By 1935, however, he stood with the right-wing diehards in the Conservative Party. Challenging Baldwin's leadership of the party had made political sense when Baldwin had presided over a party defeat. It made less sense when Baldwin went into coalition in 1931; then the Conservative Party became the basis of what was in theory, Ramsay MacDonald's government. In 1935 Baldwin won a general election. Conservative dominance became open when he became Prime Minister. Churchill found himself a victim of the party system that he complained of in Queen Anne's reign in *Marlborough*.

Neither Baldwin nor Chamberlain wished to bring Churchill into the governments they dominated between 1931 and 1939. Churchill had insulted and denounced Baldwin; though Churchill felt this was normal in parliamentary politics and was no barrier to friendly co-operation, it is less certain that Baldwin felt the same. Chamberlain intended to lead his government; Churchill's presence would make that impossible. Churchill would have been better off when political parties were less powerful than they became in the twentieth century. Someone of his oratorical force would have been difficult to keep out of government in the mid-eighteenth century. He would have appealed to independent members, even when he opposed the government, perhaps especially then. Independent MPs did not attend regularly, but if crisis loomed they would more often be in Westminster, and politics would become more fluid. In the 1930s Churchill could only free himself by winning the Conservative leadership or, if the existing leaders were well established, by ingratiating himself with them. As for opposition parties, they would be interested only if Churchill could detach significant numbers of Conservatives to join some sort of centre-left coalition. Baldwin himself was adept at the politics of the centre and Chamberlain inherited Baldwin's majority after the election of 1935. Moreover, Chamberlain proved skilful in political manoeuvre, often successfully deceiving Churchill himself.

After seeking British isolation from the European continent Churchill, alarmed by German rearmament, came to believe that an Anglo-French alliance should be the basis of a wider anti-German grouping which could justify itself by sheltering under League of Nations principles. Earlier in the 1930s, Churchill had dismissed with contempt British supporters of the League and denounced League action against Japan. Then in 1935 he showed indifference towards Mussolini's invasion of Abyssinia, which evoked the fullest hostility of British enthusiasts for the League. In the summer of 1936 Churchill chose the wrong side of the Spanish Civil War, diverging from most of those who cared about it in Britain and certainly from an overwhelming majority of League of Nations supporters. (It may have suggested to Stalin that you could not trust even the most anti-German of capitalists.) Later in 1936, over the love-life of Edward VIII, Churchill dramatically demonstrated his inability, in contrast to Baldwin, to assess British opinion. In 1937 he began to weaken his reactionary position over the Spanish Civil War by insisting pointlessly that Britain, or the great powers, should somehow intervene to settle the Spanish conflict.

Before the war broke out Hitler militarily occupied some territory – in western Germany – and set off the Rhineland crisis. This crisis largely consisted of British explanations to the French government, easily convinced, that they should do nothing. Churchill fell into line, taken in by the 'staff talks' between the British and French and by Eden's assertion that he did not intend to dishonour a British signature – that is, of the Locarno Treaty. In 1937, after Chamberlain became Prime Minister and, with the Halifax visit to Hitler, embarked on his clearly defined policy of appeasement, Churchill thought all was well because French ministers had been called to London to discuss the visit. In 1938, after the Anschluss, Churchill was partly reassured when Chamberlain made a glowing reference to France in his speech rejecting any promise to support France over Czechoslovakia. Of course, Neville Chamberlain, effectively controlling the Conservative Party, controlled Churchill's access to power. The most striking, and unfortunate, example of Churchill's conformity with Chamberlain came when Henlein came to England in the spring of 1938. Henlein tricked Churchill into the belief that all that was needed to make Czechoslovakia safe were some concessions to the demands of the German population in the Sudetenland. Until September 1938 Churchill sometimes supported Chamberlain in thinking that Prague was the problem, not Berlin.

Chamberlain's visits to Hitler in September 1938 changed everything, especially after Godesberg, when Hitler tried to dictate his wishes. Now Churchill categorically differed. In the debate on Munich in the House of Commons, he made it plain. Chamberlain survived the ensuing months only by appearing to carry out the policies advocated by Churchill, especially in the acceleration of rearmament. After the German occupation of Prague, Churchill's dramatic prophecy that Czechoslovakia might not survive much longer raised his prestige and the desire for his policies to unprecedented heights. After 15 March 1939 Chamberlain was reduced to pursuing his policies by stealth. When, on 2 September, that became known, he came close to being turned out.

After 1940 and especially after victory in the Second World War Churchill was sometimes credited with infallibility. This book shows that he was often wrong. But, as Hitler elevated Germany into a terrifying force, so Churchill came to be easily the most effective expression of British opinion. But it was too late to prevent the horrors of the Second World War.

Notes

Abbreviations used for MSS and printed sources and location of unpublished sources.

Unpublished
Balliol College, Oxford
    Harold Nicolson diary
Birmingham University Library
    NC: Neville Chamberlain
Bodleian Library, Oxford
    CRD: Conservative Research Department
    Dawson Papers
    Selborne Papers
Cambridge University Library
    Baldwin Papers
    Templewood (Samuel Hoare) papers
Churchill College, Cambridge
    CHAR: Chartwell (Churchill)
    DUFC: Duff Cooper
    Inskip Diary
    Microfilm: Halifax
    MRGN: Margesson
Nuffield College, Oxford
    Lindemann (Lord Cherwell) papers

Public Record Office, Kew
  CAB: Cabinet
  FO: Foreign Office
  PREM: Prime Minister
  T: Treasury

Printed
  DBFP: Documents on British Foreign Policy
  DDF: Documents Diplomatiques Français
  DGFP: Documents on German Foreign Policy
  EHR: English Historical Review
  HC Deb: House of Commons Debates
  HL Deb: House of Lords Debates

CHAPTER ONE

1 Mary Soames, *Winston Churchill. His Life as a Painter* (London, 1990), pp. 21, 37, 48; John Lavery, *The Life of a Painter* (London, 1940), p. 177; David Coombs in *Painting as a Pastime* (Sotheby's, London, 1998), p. 18; John Rothenstein, *Time's Thievish Progress, Autobiography III* (London, 1970), pp. 130, 138, 144.
2 Paul Maze, *A Frenchman in Khaki* (London, 1934), Introduction; Mary Soames (ed.), *Speaking for Themselves. The Personal Letters of Winston and Clementine Churchill* (London, 1998), pp. 309, 657, 659; David Coombs in *Painting as a Pastime*, pp. 21–2 and *Churchill His Painting* (London, 1967), p. 11; Eric Newton in *Dictionary of National Biography* 1941–50 (Oxford, 1959), p. 632.
3 Churchill College, Cambridge, CHAR 2/357A, fol. 104.
4 Soames (ed.), *Speaking for Themselves*, p. 657; Coombs in *Painting as a Pastime*, pp. 43–9; Christopher Hassall in *Dictionary of National Biography* 1951–60 (Oxford, 1971), pp. 694–6.
5 Soames (ed.), *Speaking for Themselves*, pp. xix, 358, 426, 650, 658–9; Gilbert, *Companion*, V. 2 pp. 382, 390, 394; *Life*, V p. 920. R. W. Thompson, *Churchill and Morton* (London, 1976), pp. 198–9.
6 Soames, *Winston Churchill. His Life as a Painter*, p. 97; Gilbert, *Life*, V p. 835 n. 1.
7 *EHR*, Jan 1939 p. 32; W. S. Churchill, *Marlborough. His Life and Times*, 4 vols (London, 1933, 1934, 1936, 1938), vol.IV p. 168; Gilbert, *Companion*, V.3 p. 860, V.2 pp. 489, 491.

8 Gilbert, *Life*, V p. 364; *Companion*, V.2 pp. 473, 520, 940–6, 955, V.3 pp. 955, 979–81.

9 Soames (ed.), *Speaking for Themselves*, pp. 422–3, 427; Gilbert, *Companion*, V.3 pp. 1456–7; Maurice Ashley, *Churchill as Historian* (London, 1968), pp. 7–10, 22–37, 138–58.

10 Gilbert, *Companion*, V.2 p. 515, V.3 p. 746.

11 Gilbert, *Companion*, V.2 pp. 515, 625, V.3 p. 746; Churchill, *Marlborough*, vol.I p. 146.

12 Churchill, *Marlborough*, vol.I pp. 397, 441, vol.III pp. 357, 538.

13 Ibid., vol.I pp. 346, 510, vol.IV p. 372; R. A. C. Parker, *EHR*, April 1956 pp. 247–8.

14 *EHR*, Oct 1934 pp. 716–18, April 1935 pp. 338–41; *History*, June 1935, p. 36; *American Historical Review*, vol.41, pp. 376–7; vol.44 July 1939 pp. 86–7.

Chapter Two

1 Robert Rhodes James, *Speeches*, p. 4668.

2 Philip Williamson, *National Crisis and National Government, British Politics, the Economy and Empire* (Cambridge, 1992), pp. 124–5, 171–91; Phillips O'Brien, 'Churchill and the US Navy 1919–29', in R. A. C. Parker (ed.), *Churchill. Studies in Statesmanship* (London, 1995), pp. 32–40.

3 James, *Speeches*, pp. 4710–11.

4 John Charmley, *Lord Lloyd and the Decline of the British Empire* (New York, 1987), pp. 158–67; 230 HC Deb 5s, cols 1658,1656.

5 247 HC Deb 5s, cols 692, 702, 744–6; James, *Speeches*, p. 4985; Stuart Ball, *Baldwin and the Conservative Party. The Crisis of 1929–31* (New Haven and London, 1988), pp. 108–29.

6 249 HC Deb 5s, cols 1422–6, 1454, 1467.

7 Williamson, *National Crisis and National Government*, pp. 222, 267–9, 273, 284; Gilbert, *Life*, V p. 411; Keith Feiling, *Life of Neville Chamberlain* (London, 1946), p. 190.

8 Peter Clarke, *Hope and Glory. Britain 1900–1990* (London, 1996), p. 158; Williamson, *National Crisis and National Government*, pp. 274, 336–43; Gilbert, *Life*, V p. 412; *Companion*, V.2 pp. 348, 352; 256 HC Deb 5s, cols 40–50.

9 James, *Speeches*, p. 5085.

10 Clarke, *Hope and Glory*, p. 175.

CHAPTER THREE

1 James, *Speeches*, pp. 5089–104.

2 265 HC Deb 5s, cols 2346–53.

3 272 HC Deb 5s, cols 81–92.

4 James, *Speeches*, pp. 5225; 276 HC Deb 5s, cols 542–9; 275 HC Deb 5s, col. 1820.

5 275 HC Deb 5s, cols 2745, 2759, 2762, 2770.

6 281 HC Deb 5s, cols 137–43, 675–7; Henry Page Croft, *My Life of Strife* (London, 1948), pp. 288–9.

7 281 HC Deb 5s, cols 649–51, 659, 146, 686, 607–8.

8 Ibid., col. 613.

9 Ibid., cols 63, 600, 701, 161; DBFP 2, 6 no. 322 pp. 488–9.

10 281 HC Deb 5s, col. 158; 276 HC Deb 5s, col. 562; Winston L. Spencer Churchill, *Romanes Lecture* (Oxford, 1930).

11 285 HC Deb 5s, cols 1020, 1025, 1193–1208.

12 James, *Speeches*, pp. 5319–464; 286 HC Deb 5s, cols 2064, 2070, 2074, 2077–8.

13 Ibid., cols 2085, 2119, 2121–2, 2141–4, 2046–7, 2155–66.

14 James, *Speeches*, pp. 5376–7; 292 HC Deb 5s, cols 675, 2365, 2376–7; CAB 16/123 fols 97, 103; Peter Bell, *Chamberlain, Germany and Japan 1933–4* (Basingstoke and New York, 1996), p. 23.

15 292 HC Deb 5s, cols 2336–7, 2431; 270 HC Deb 5s, col. 632.

16 CHAR 2/216 fol. 45; Cambridge Univ. Library, Baldwin MSS vol.1 Defence Papers fol. 378; CAB 23/80, 41(34)2, 42(34)2, 43(34)1; DBFP 2, 12 nos 211, 215–16, 221, 223–5; DDF 1, 8 no. 148; Gilbert, *Companion*, V.2 p. 947.

17 295 HC Deb 5s, cols 857–71; *The Times*, 8 Aug. 1934, p. 11.

18 295 HC Deb 5s, cols 871–85; 980; 292 HC Deb 5s, col. 1279; DBFP 2, 12 no. 219; CAB 23/80, 41(34)2, fol. 214.

19 James, *Speeches*, p. 5434.

CHAPTER FOUR

1 CHAR 2/199, esp. fols 21, 31; James, *Speeches*, p. 5272.

2 *The Times*, 7 Nov. 1934, p. 8; 293 HC Deb 5s, cols 992–4, 1550–5, 1832–41; Gilbert, *Companion*, V.2 pp. 915–16.

3 James, *Speeches*, p. 5220.

4 Ibid., pp. 4936, 4912, 4926–7, 5007, 4934–5; 249 HC Deb 5s, col. 1467.

5 Leonard Barnes, *Empire or Democracy* (London, Left Book Club, 1939), pp. 84–5, 94–5, 99; James, *Speeches*, pp. 4917, 4937, 5276; 302 HC Deb 5s, col. 1921.

6 Carl Bridge, *Holding India to the Empire. The British Conservative Party and the 1935 Constitution* (London, 1986), pp. 101, 92, 94, 97, 115, 118, 133–6; 276 HC Deb 5s, col. 2192; Gillian Peele and Chris Cook (eds), *The Politics of Reappraisal 1918–39* (Basingstoke, 1975), pp. 133–5.

7 Carl Bridge, 'Churchill, Hoare, Derby and the Committee of Privileges, April to June 1934', *Historical Journal*, 1979, pp. 215–27.

8 John Barnes and David Nicholson (eds), *The Empire at Bay. The Leo Amery Diaries*, vol.2: *1929–45* (London, 1988), pp. 382–3; 290 HC Deb 5s, cols 1742–75.

9 Gilbert, *Companion*, V.2 pp. 1096–7; 'Watchman' [Vyvyan Adams], *Right Honourable Gentlemen* (London, 1940), p. 285.

10 297 HC Deb 5s, cols 1187, 1722–6; 276 HC Deb 5s, cols 794, 1099, 1069.

11 *Economist*, no. 4772, 9 Feb. 1935, p. 299; no. 4725, 17 March 1934, p. 561.

12 302 HC Deb 5s, cols 1922–3.

CHAPTER FIVE

1 Gilbert, *Life*, V pp. 591–601, 607–11.

2 Gilbert, *Companion*, V.2 p. 1119; 299 HC Deb 5s, cols 1204, 1049–50, 1063.

3 *The Times*, 8 Aug. 1934, p. 11, 15 Aug., p. 11, 28 Aug., p. 6; Frederick Smith, Earl of Birkenhead, *The Prof in Two Worlds* (London, 1961), pp. 175–6; H. Montgomery Hyde, *British Air Policy between the Wars 1918–39* (London, 1976), pp. 319, 325–6, 328.

4 Cherwell MSS F7/1/3, 11, 12; F10/4–5; CAB 23/85, CAB 50(36)1 fols 47–8; 299 HC Deb 5s, col. 1003; Cambridge Univ. Library, Baldwin MSS vol.47 fol. 85.

5 Thomas Wilson, *Churchill and the Prof* (London, 1995), pp. 6–7; R. F. Harrod, *The Prof. A Personal Memoir of Lord Cherwell* (London 1959); Cherwell MSS F8/1/7; Gilbert, *Companion*, V.2 pp. 1215–25.

6 CAB 16/133 fols 286–8, 295–8; Cherwell MSS F8/6/5–6.

7 CAB 23/85 fols 44–50; Gilbert, *Companion*, V.3 pp. 230–6.

8 CAB 16/132 fols 49, 50; CAB 21/426 fols 105–7, 120; Cherwell MSS F7/1/2, F8/5/11; Gilbert, *Companion*, V.3 pp. 419–20; Ronald W. Clark, *Tizard* (London, 1965), pp. 140–6.

9 302 HC Deb 5s, cols 361, 416–17, 1490; 304 HC Deb 5s, cols 544–5; 303 HC Deb 5s, col. 706.

10 304 HC Deb 5s, cols 550, 545–6; James, *Speeches*, p. 5673; 305 HC Deb 5s, cols 363, 365–6, 358.

11 Parker, *Chamberlain and Appeasement*, pp. 46, 50; Gilbert, *Companion*, V.2 pp. 1239–40.

12 *The Times*, 4 October 1935, p. 14; 305 HC Deb 5s, col. 361.

13 Gilbert, *Life*, V pp. 696–7, 702–3; *Companion*, V.3 pp. 5–7, 12, 17–18, 24–6, 35, 41.

14 Parker, *Chamberlain and Appeasement*, pp. 52–5; 309 HC Deb 5s, cols 192–3.

15 E.g. *The Times*, 7 Jan. 1936, p. 13, 10 Jan., p. 13, 13 Jan., p. 13, 18 Feb., p. 15, 19 Feb., p. 8, 20 Feb., p. 10, 22 Feb., p. 13, 24 Feb., p. 13, 6 Mar., p. 15; 308 HC Deb 5s, cols 1370, 501, 1295.

16 309 HC Deb 5s, col. 2003–4; NC 2/23A, 8 and 11 Mar. 1936.

17 309 HC Deb 5s, col. 1873, 2008–19; NC 2/23A, 11 Mar. 1936; *The Times*, 14 Mar. 1936, pp. 13, 19.

18 PREM 1/194 fols 58–60, 39–42; Gilbert, *Companion*, V.3 p. 71.

19 Gilbert, *Companion*, V.3 pp. 68–9; W. S. Churchill, *The Second World War*, vol.I: *The Gathering Storm* (London, 1948), p. 153; James, *Speeches*, pp. 5704–5; *The Times*, 17 March 1936, p. 16; 310 HC Deb 5s, col. 1115.

20 310 HC Deb 5s, cols 1439, 1446, 1523–4, 1530, 1445, 1545, 1449, 1548; CHAR 2/282/2.

Chapter Six

1 James, *Speeches*, p. 5747.

2 Ibid., pp. 5772–3; 313 HC Deb 5s, cols 1729–30, 1221–33, 1197–1211.

3 314 HC Deb 5s, cols 119–25; 313 HC Deb 5s, col. 1728; CAB 21/437 fol. 71.

4 315 HC Deb 5s, cols 1272, 115–19, 1294, 138–9.

5 Gilbert, *Companion*, V.3 pp. 171, 369.

6 311 HC Deb 5s, cols. 335, 428–35; CAB 16/123 fols 102–4.

7 CAB 23/85 fols 45–9; 315 HC Deb 5s, col. 122; Gilbert, *Companion*, V.3 pp. 257–9, 265; CAB 21/437 fol. 204.

8 CAB 64/22, Parliamentary Deputation, July 1936, p. 26; NC 7/11/32/294; CAB 16/123 fol. 90; CAB 4/24 fols 206–7.

9 CAB 23/83, 8 Apr. 1936, concl. 8; R. A. C. Parker, 'British Rearmament 1936–9: Treasury, Trade Unions and Skilled Labour', *EHR* (Apr. 1981) 308; CAB 64/22, Parliamentary Deputation, p. 31.

10 CAB 21/437 fols 11, 43, 124; T 161/720/S49175.

11 CAB 21/437 fols 52–4.

12 T 161/720/S41975, paper by RGH 23–10–36, copy Hopkins-Hamilton 28–10–36, Bridges memo 24–10–36, note for defence debate 10–11–36; CAB 24/265, CP 297(36); CAB 24/273, CP 316(37).

13 Tom Buchanan, *Britain and the Spanish Civil War* (Cambridge, 1997); Paul Preston, *The Spanish Civil War* (London, 1986); Raymond Carr, *The Spanish Tragedy* (London, 1977); Tom Buchanan, 'The Politics of Internationalism: The AEU and the Spanish Civil War', *Bulletin of Society for Labour History* 53.3 (1988) 47–55.

14 W. S. Churchill, *Step by Step* (London, 1942), p. 52; Gilbert, *Companion*, V.3 pp. 396–8; 317 HC Deb 5s, cols 318–19.

15 317 HC Deb 5s, cols 1098–1118, 1144; Churchill, *The Gathering Storm*, pp. 169–70 and index p. 615.

16 Gilbert, *Companion*, V.3 pp. 362–4, 357, 401; Buchanan, 'The Politics of Internationalism', p. 48; Parker, 'British Rearmament', p. 339.

17 *Manchester Guardian*, 4 Dec. 1936, p. 16, 8 Dec. 1936, p. 14; *The Times*, 4 Dec. 1936, p. 18; *Evening Standard*, 4 Dec. 1936.

18 Lord (Walter) Citrine, *Men and Work* (London, 1964), pp. 356–7; *Manchester Guardian*, 7 Dec. 1936, pp. 13, 15, 8 Dec. 1936, pp. 11, 14; 318 HC Deb 5s, cols 1641–4; *The Times*, 8 Dec. 1936, p. 16; R. R. James, *Memoirs of a Conservative: J. C. C. Davidson's Memoirs*

and Papers 1910–37 (London, 1969), p. 415; DDF 2, 4 no. 113 pp. 175–6.
19 Gilbert, *Companion*, V.3 pp. 466–72.
20 318 HC Deb 5s, cols 2175–91; *The Times*, 11 Dec. 1936, pp. 8, 16.

CHAPTER SEVEN

1 *Leeds Chamber of Commerce Journal*, vol.13, no. 8 pp. 131–6 [thanks to Mark White, Chamber Management Services, Bradford]; Soames (ed.) *Speaking for Themselves* pp. 424–5.
2 Gilbert, *Companion*, V.3, p. 340; Churchill, *Step by Step*, pp. 58–61, 98–9, 135–8.
3 Churchill, *Step by Step*, p. 112; CAB 24/267, CP 6(37) pp. 1, 7; CAB 23/87 fol. 4.
4 Parker, 'British Rearmament', pp. 335–43.
5 319 HC Deb 5s, cols 963–1017.
6 Soames (ed.), *Speaking for Themselves*, p. 426.
7 James, *Speeches*, pp. 5855–7, 5895; DDF 2, 5 no. 461 pp. 791–2.
8 CAB 23/88 fols 73–4; 322 HC Deb 5s, cols 598–9.
9 322 HC Deb 5s, cols 1063, 1070–3, 1141–6.
10 DDF 2, 6 no. 297 p. 525; 326 HC Deb 5s, cols 1828–36, 2922–30, 2961–3.
11 Parker, *Chamberlain and Appeasement*, p. 111; Gilbert, *Companion*, V.3 p. 766.
12 DGFP, D, 1 no. 29 p. 53; Parker, *Chamberlain and Appeasement*, pp. 92, 96–7; PREM 1/330 fols 176–90; CAB 27/626 fol. 248; DBFP 2, 19 no. 349, pp. 580–1.
13 DBFP 2, 19 nos 346, 354 pp. 572–3, 592, 599; DDF 2, 7 nos 287, 299 pp. 531, 576–9.
14 330 HC Deb 5s, cols 1829–39.
15 302 HC Deb 5s, col. 367; Gilbert, *Life*, V preface pp. XX–XXI; R. J. Overy, *The Air War* (London, 1987), Table 1 p. 21; Wilhelm Deist, *The Wehrmacht and German Rearmament* (London, 1986), p. 61.
16 Uri Bialer, *The Shadow of the Bomber. The Fear of Air Attack in British Politics 1932–1939* (London, 1976), p. 79; Hyde, *British Air*

Policy between the Wars, p. 430; Malcolm Smith, *British Air Strategy between the Wars* (Oxford, 1984), pp. 256–7.

17 Gilbert, *Companion*, V.3 pp. 164, 561, 793–5, 798–9, 802–8; Sebastian Ritchie, *Industry and Air Power. The Expansion of British Aircraft Production 1936–41* (London, 1997), pp. 147–68; Parker, 'British Rearmament' EHR (Apr. 1981) pp. 335–43.

18 David Irving, *Rise and Fall of the Luftwaffe. The Life of Erhard Milch* (London, 1973), pp. 76, 171; R. J. Overy, *Goering the 'Iron Man'* (London, 1984), pp. 167–8.

CHAPTER EIGHT

 1 Gilbert, *Companion*, V.3 pp. 877–8, 882, 884; Parker, *Chamberlain and Appeasement*, pp. 115–18, 102–3; Churchill, *The Gathering Storm*, p. 201.

 2 332 HC Deb 5s, cols 45–50, 242, 246.

 3 Eden, speech at Leamington, *The Times*, 7 May 1938, p. 7d; DDF 2, 7 p. 470; 332 HC Deb 5s, col. 255.

 4 332 HC Deb 5s, col. 252; Robert Rhodes James, *Victor Cazalet* (London, 1976), p. 200.

 5 Barnes and Nicholson (eds), *The Empire at Bay*, vol.2 pp. 456–8.

 6 R. A. C. Parker, *Europe 1919–45* (London, 1969), pp. 303–6; 333 HC Deb 5s, col. 52.

 7 333 HC Deb 5s, cols 55–6, 62, 99–100; CHAR 2/328, fol. II.

 8 333 HC Deb 5s, col. 100; *The Times*, 15 March 1938, p. 14b; R. A. Butler, *The Art of the Possible* (London, 1971), p. 64; *Punch*, 23 March 1938, p. 325; *Economist*, 19 March 1938, p. 616.

 9 *Tribune*, 18 March 1938, p. 3; G. D. H. Cole, *The People's Front* (London, 1937), pp. 183, 160, 19.

10 David Blaazer, *The Popular Front and the Progressive Tradition* (Cambridge, 1992), pp. 179–80; *Tribune*, 18 March 1938, p. 8, 22 April, 1938, p. 6.

11 *The Times*, 16 March 1938, p. 106; NC 7/11/31/30; CHAR 2/237 fols 129–31; 335 HC Deb 5s, col. 1166.

12 Gilbert, *Companion*, V.3 pp. 880–1; CHAR 2/343A fols 14–15, 19. Colin Crooke, *The Life of Richard Stafford Cripps* (London, 1957), pp. 196–7.

13 333 HC Deb 5s, cols 144–5; James, *Speeches*, p. 5917.

14 CHAR 2/345, 13 June 1938.

15 Gilbert, *Companion*, V.3 p. 961; CHAR 2/328 fol. 123.

16 Gilbert, *Companion*, V.3 pp. 1037–9; CHAR 2/329 fol. 116; *The Times*, 14 May 1938, p. 7e.

17 NC 18/1/1041.

18 CAB 27/623 fols 139, 164–9, 211–12; Bodleian Library, Oxford, Dawson MS 42 fol. 48, Diary 23 Mar. 1938; CAB 23/93 fols. 32–44.

19 NC 18/1/1043.

20 NC 18/2/1065, 18/1/1043; *The Times*, 19 March 1938, p. 14d, e.

21 333 HC Deb 5s, cols 1399–1413; CAB 23/93 fols 39, 42; NC 7/11/31/26; DDF 2, 9 p. 82.

22 333 HC Deb 5s, cols 1444–55.

23 Ibid., cols 1455–1510; M. R. D. Foot in Lord Blake and C. S. Nicholls (eds), *Dictionary of National Biography* 1971–80 (Oxford, 1986), p. 653.

24 CHAR 2/329 fol. 28; Ronald Tree, *When the Moon was High. Memoirs 1897–1962* (London, 1975), p. 76; Richard Cockett, *Twilight of Truth* (London, 1989), pp. 9–12.

25 Churchill College, Cambridge, Phipps Papers PHPP 2/1 fol. 2; 1/20 fols 22–3; FO 800/311 fols 16–17; Gilbert, *Companion*, V.3 pp. 959–64.

26 Gilbert, *Companion*, V.3 p. 997; 335 HC Deb 5s, cols 1094–1106, 1163; *The Times*, 6 May 1938, p. 17d.

27 *Manchester Guardian*, 10 May 1938, p. 14.

28 CHAR 2/343A fol. 107; Gilbert, *Companion*, V.3 pp. 1023–4; G. E. R. Gedye, *Fallen Bastions* (London, 1939), pp. 392–4, 405; James, *Speeches*, pp. 5963, 5976, 5978.

29 Gilbert, *Campanion*, V.3 pp. 1112–14, 1119–22, 1147.

30 *The Times*, 26 April 1938, p. 13d, 4 May 1938, p. 10d; James, *Speeches*, p. 5946.

CHAPTER NINE

1 *Daily Telegraph*, 23 June 1938, p. 16.

2 337 HC Deb 5s, cols 923–36, 1343–51, 1381–90; 338 HC Deb 5s, col. 2953.

3 337 HC Deb 5s, cols 1534–9, 1915–29, 2155–222 Accounts &

Papers. House of Commons Reports from Committees (3) vols VII, 1937–8, VIII, 1938–9.

4 337 HC Deb 5s, col. 2215; 342 HC Deb 5s, cols 935–6.

5 *Tribune*, 8 July 1938, p. 5; 338 HC Deb 5s, cols 2034–5, 2040–2, 2957–8, 2963, 3020.

6 *The Times*, 13 Aug. 1938, p. 10, 16 Aug., p. 12, 26 Aug., p. 10.

7 Gilbert, *Companion*, V.3 pp. 1117–20; James, *Speeches*, pp. 6001–2; PREM 1/266A.

8 CAB 23/92, fol. 294; Gilbert, *Companion*, V.3 pp. 1130–1, 1137–8.

9 Churchill College, Cambridge, Inskip Diary Pt 1, fols 4–7; DBFP 3, 2 pp. 277–8, 280, 283–4; Cambridge Univ. Library, Templewood MSS X:5 Crisis Sept. 1938, pp. 2–3; CAB 23/95 fols 8, 14–15.

10 CAB 23/95 fols 9, 15; *The Times*, 12 Sept. 1938, p. 12.

11 DBFP 3, 2 p. 316; Parker, *Chamberlain and Appeasement*, pp. 160–1; *Daily Telegraph*, 15 Sept. 1938, pp. 12, 13.

12 *The Times*, 12 Sept. 1938, p. 12; CAB 24/278, CP200/38.

13 Winston S. Churchill jun. *His Father's Son. The Life of Randolph Churchill* (London, 1996), p. 160; Lord Birkenhead, *Halifax* (London, 1965); Andrew Roberts, *The Holy Fox. A Biography of Lord Halifax* (London, 1991).

14 Parker, *Chamberlain and Appeasement*, pp. 164–5; David Dilks (ed.), *The Diaries of Sir Alexander Cadogan* (London, 1971), p. 101; Max Egremont, *Under Two Flags. The Life of Major-General Sir Edward Spears* (London, 1997); Churchill, *The Gathering Storm*, p. 237; DBFP 3, 2 p. 444; John Harvey (ed.), *The Diplomatic Diaries of Oliver Harvey* (London, 1970), p. 190; Gilbert, *Companion*, V.3 pp. 1171–2.

15 Parker, *Chamberlain and Appeasement*, pp. 168–73; *The Times*, 27 Sept. 1938, pp. 12, 14; *Daily Telegraph*, 27 Sept. 1938, pp. 10, 14.

16 Parker, *Chamberlain and Appeasement*, p. 173; Churchill College, Cambridge, Microfilm A-410, 19, 2, 3; DBFP 3, 2 pp. 550, 559.

17 Parker, *Chamberlain and Appeasement*, pp. 177–8; 339 HC Deb 5s, cols 5–28; *The Times*, 29 Sept. 1938, p. 7.

18 Gilbert, *Companion*, V.3 pp. 1187–9.

19 DBFP, 3, 2 p. 640.

20 Feiling, *Life of Neville Chamberlain*; David Dilks in *Proceedings of the*

British Academy 1987; Alec Douglas-Home, Lord Home, *The Way the Wind Blows* (London, 1976), pp. 66–7; Parker, *Chamberlain and Appeasement*, pp. 182–5.

21 339 HC Deb 5s, col. 96; NC 18/1/1071; Vaclav Kral (ed.) *Das Abkommen von München 1938* (Prague, 1968), no. 251 p. 276.

22 Churchill College, Cambridge, DUFC 2/14; 339 HC Deb 5s, cols 34, 88, 361, 371.

23 Alistair Horne, *Macmillan*, vol.I: *1894–1956* (London, 1990), pp. 117–18; Charles E. Lysaght, *Brendan Bracken* (London, 1979), pp. 157–8; Hugh Dalton, *The Fateful Years 1931–45* (London, 1957), pp. 198–201.

24 339 HC Deb 5s, cols 360, 367, 372, 551; *The Times*, 6 Oct. 1938, p. 13.

25 339 HC Deb 5s, cols 370, 365–6, 547.

CHAPTER TEN

1 *The Times*, 10 Oct. 1938, p. 14, 7 Nov. p. 12, 9 Nov. pp. 13, 14, 11 Nov. pp. 14, 15; Gilbert, *Companion*, V.3 pp. 1259–60.

2 Bodleian Library, Oxford, MS Eng Hist c. 1014 fols 59–63; NC 18/2/1096; NC 18/1/1071.

3 *The Times*, 17 Oct. 1938, p. 16, 13 Oct., P. 16, 14 Oct., p. 9, 12 Oct., p. 14.

4 Gilbert, *Companion*, V.3 pp. 1213–15, 1239.

5 Colin Thornton-Kemsley, *Through Winds and Tides* (Montrose, 1974), p. 94; David A. Thomas, *Churchill. The Member for Woodford* (London, 1995), p. 98.

6 341 HC Deb 5s, cols 1195–6; James, *Speeches*, pp. 6047–8.

7 Thomas, *Churchill*, pp. 103–5; Thornton-Kemsley, *Through Winds and Tides*, pp. 96–7, 104–5; Gilbert, *Companion*, V.3 pp. 1394–6.

8 Iain McLean, 'Oxford and Bridgwater', in C. Cook and J. Ramsden (eds), *By-elections in British Politics* (London, 1997), pp. 112–29, 140–63; CHAR 2/332 fols 25, 37, 117, 128, 157, 171; Gilbert, *Companion*, V.3 pp. 1197–8; Harold Macmillan, *Winds of Change 1914–39* (London, 1966), pp. 583–4.

9 Gilbert, *Companion*, V.3 pp. 1038–9; CHAR 2/239 fols 116–19; McLean, 'Oxford and Bridgwater' in Cook and Ramsden (eds) *By-elections*.

10 Sheila Hetherington, *Katherine Atholl 1874–1960. Against the Tide* (Aberdeen, 1991), pp. 183–4, 194, 197, 206, 209–13; E. T. Williams and H. M. Palmer (eds), *Dictionary of National Biography 1951–60* (Oxford, 1971), pp. 926–7; Gilbert, *Companion*, V.3 pp. 1308–9; Churchill College, Cambridge, Archives MRGN 1/3, 23 Dec. 38; Churchill, *Step by Step*, p. 312.

11 Gilbert, *Companion*, V.3 pp. 1308–9, 1256; 340 HC Deb 5s, cols 115–16.

12 Tree, *When the Moon was High* p. 78; 341 HC Deb 5s, cols 1128–9, 1099, 1145–6, 1177, 1209–14.

13 N. A. Rose (ed.), *Baffy. The Diaries of Blanche Dugdale 1936–47* (London, 1973), pp. 91, 115.

14 Tree, *When the Moon was High*, p. 76; Hugh Dalton, *The Fateful Years. Memoirs 1931–45* (London, 1957), pp. 202–3; Nigel Nicolson (ed.), *Harold Nicolson Diaries and Letters 1930–39* (London, 1969), pp. 354, 366, 371–2, 374, 390, 395, 399; 344 HC Deb 5s, col. 234.

15 343 HC Deb 5s, col. 623; 344 HC Deb 5s, col. 2173; Parker, *Chamberlain and Appeasement*, pp. 192–5.

16 James, *Speeches*, pp. 6071–2; Parker, *Chamberlain and Appeasement*, p. 197; Viscount Templewood, *Nine Troubled Years* (London, 1954), p. 328.

17 Bodleian Library, Oxford, MSS CRD 1/7/35 esp. doc. no. 15; D. S. Birn, *The League of Nations Union 1918–45* (Oxford, 1981), p. 190; Cambridge Univ. Library, Baldwin MSS 174 fols 19–27.

CHAPTER ELEVEN

1 CAB 23/98 fol. 17; Dilks (ed.), *Cadogan Diaries*, p. 157, 15 Mar. 1939; 345 HC Deb 5s, cols 437, 440, 559.

2 *Daily Telegraph*, 16 Mar. 1939, p. 16; Gilbert, *Companion*, V.3 p. 1390; James, *Speeches*, p. 6090; 345 HC Deb 5s, cols 684, 730.

3 *Manchester Guardian*, 18 Mar. 1939, p. 13; BBC Sound Archives, Chamberlain, 17 Mar. 1939.

4 NC 18/1/1090; Dilks (ed.) *Cadogan Diaries*, p. 161; Churchill, *Step by Step*, pp. 340–5; Barnes and Nicholson (eds), *The Empire at Bay*, p. 553.

5 *Votes and Proceedings, House of Commons, Session 1938–9*, pp. 1876, 1900–3, 1927; 112 HL Deb 5s esp. cols 316–18; 345 HC Deb 5s, col. 1884.

6 Parker, *Chamberlain and Appeasement*, pp. 206, 216–17, 219.

7 345 HC Deb 5s, cols 2483, 2490, 2497, 2505, 2501–2, 2510.

8 Gilbert, *Companion*, V.3 pp. 1455–6, 1461, n. 2, 1438.

9 James, *Speeches*, pp. 6097–9; 346 HC Deb 5s, cols 28, 30–8, 46; Gilbert, *Companion*, V.3 p. 1456.

10 346 HC Deb 5s, cols 494–7; Harvey (ed.), *Diplomatic Diaries of Oliver Harvey*, p. 282, 20 Apr. 1939; *The Times*, 21 Apr. 1939, p. 17; *Manchester Guardian*, 21 Apr. 1939, p. 11; *Daily Telegraph*, 21 Apr. 1939, p. 14; Gilbert, *Companion*, V.3 p. 1473.

11 James, *Victor Cazalet*, pp. 211–13.

12 Gallup Poll pp. 16, 18, April–May 1939, G. H. Gallup (ed.), *Gallup International Public Opinion Polls. Great Britain 1937–75*, vol.I (New York, 1976).

13 Parker, *Chamberlain and Appeasement*, 206–7, 214, 223–9; *Dokumenty vneshnei politiki: 1939 god* (Moscow, 1992), no. 316 pp. 379–80; Ivan Maisky, *Who Helped Hitler?* (trans. from Russian, London, 1964), p. 125; CAB 23/99 fols 128–9.

14 347 HC Deb 5s, col. 1841; DBFP 3, 5 no. 201 p. 228; Nicolson (ed.), *Harold Nicolson Diaries and Letters 1930–9*, p. 387, 3 Apr. 1939.

15 347 HC Deb 5s, cols 2729–37, 2759–60.

16 NC 18/1/1100; 1101; 347 HC Deb 5s, cols 2267–8; 348 HC Deb 5s, cols 881–2, 1282, 1789–90, 2204; 349 HC Deb 5s, col. 4; DBFP 3, 5 pp. 722, 725–7, 753–4.

17 *Daily Telegraph*, 8 June 1939, p. 16; NC 18/1/1102.

18 Gilbert, *Companion*, V.3 pp. 1527–31; *Daily Telegraph*, 29 June 1939, pp. 1, 14, 15, 30 June 1939, pp. 1, 14.

19 *The Independent*, 3 December 1999, p. 12, 6 December 1999, p. 21; Gilbert, *Companion*, V.3 p. 1531; *Tribune*, 30 June 1939, p. 1.

20 Klemens von Klemperer, *German Resistance against Hitler. The Search for Allies Abroad* (Oxford, 1992), pp. 119–20; David Astor, letter in *New York Review of Books*, 27 Mar. 1997; Barnes and Nicholson (eds), *The Empire at Bay*, p. 554; Harold Nicolson, Diary, Balliol College Archives, 29–30 June 1939; NC 7/11/32/243.

21 *Observer*, 2 July 1939, pp. 14, 15; Political and Economic Planning, *Report on the British Press* (London, 1938), pp. 49, 232–3; *Daily Telegraph*, 3 July 1939, pp. 3, 12, 84; Gilbert, *Companion*, V.3 pp. 1544–6; NC 18/1/1095, 1106, 1107.

22 Stephen Koss, *The Rise and Fall of the Political Press in Britain*, vol.2: *The Twentieth Century* (London, 1984), pp. 587–9; Bodleian Library, MS Eng Hist c. 1014, Selborne MSS fols 136–8.

23 Bodleian Library, Oxford, Dawson MS 43, 3 July 1939, 6 July; *Spectator*, 14 July 1939, p. 39; NC 18/1/1108; *Truth*, 7 July 1939, front page, 14 July, pp. 40–1.

24 *The Times*, 10 July 1939, p. 13, 12 July, p. 5, 13 July, p. 17, 15 July, p. 2; *New Statesman*, 15 July 1939, pp. 75–6.

25 Gilbert, *Companion*, V.3 pp. 1556–7; *Economist*, 8 July 1939, p. 59, 15 July, pp. 101–2; *New Statesman*, 8 July 1939, p. 43; *Spectator*, 7 July 1939, p. 3, 14 July, p. 39.

26 Kingsley Martin, *Editor* (Harmondsworth, 1938), p. 200.

27 DGFP, D, 6 pp. 833, 892–3; FO 800/316 fols 155–6; DDF 2, 17 pp. 284, 303–7; *The Times*, 15 July 1939, p. 12.

28 *Dokumenty vneshnei politiki: 1939 god*, no. 422.

CHAPTER TWELVE

1 Gilbert, *Companion*, V.3 p. 1574; NC 18/1/1107; *The Times*, 11 July 1939, p. 8.

2 350 HC Deb 5s, cols 2031, 2472, 2490, 2065.

3 'Watchman' (Adams), *Right Honourable Gentlemen*, p. 248; *The Times*, 14 Aug. 1951, p. 6, 28 Sept., p. 6.

4 350 HC Deb 5s, cols 1991–2100, esp. 2023, 2022, 2099, cols 2440–1, 2485, 2459, 2475–6; DDF 2, 17 no. 404 pp. 677–8.

5 350 HC Deb 5s, cols 2495, 2503–5; Nicolson (ed.) *Harold Nicolson Diaires and Letters 1930–9*, p. 401; NC 18/1/1111; NC 7/11/32/38.

6 Gilbert, *Life*, V pp. 1100–4, *Companion*, V.3 pp. 1588–97; *Daily Telegraph*, 16 Aug. 1939, p. 13; *The Times*, 16 Aug. 1939, p. 10, 18 Aug. p. 9.

7 351 HC Deb 5s, cols 63, 113; *Daily Telegraph*, 30 Aug. 1939, p. 1.

8 *Sunday Times*, 9 July 1939, p. 17; Gilbert, *Life*, V pp. 1106–7,

1113–14; John Vincent, 'Chamberlain, the Liberals and the Outbreak of War 1939', EHR (Apr. 1998), pp. 381–2; Gilbert, *Companion*, V.3 p. 1611.

9 Parker, *Chamberlain and Appeasement*, pp. 338–40; 351 HC Deb 5s, cols 280–5; *Sunday Times*, 3 Sept. 1939, p. 12.

10 Duff Cooper, Viscount Norwich, *Old Men Forget* (London, 1953), p. 259; Girard de Charbonnières, *La Plus Evitable de toutes les guerres* (Paris, 1985), pp. 206–7; FO 800/317 fol. 84; CAB 23/100 fols 474–83.

Index